TEARS FOR TEARS

MINORITARIAN AESTHETICS

General Editors: Uri McMillan, Sandra Ruiz, Shane Vogel

Minoritarian Aesthetics promotes scholarship that develops a minor position toward aesthetics and an aesthetic stance toward minoritarian experience. The aesthetic—the domain of sensation, beauty, value, taste, (dis)pleasure, and the sublime—instructs not only representations and judgments of the social, but the relational bonds that form between objects, subjects, and entities across spatial-temporal domains.

Tears for Tears

Aesthetics in Grief Minor

Sandra Ruiz

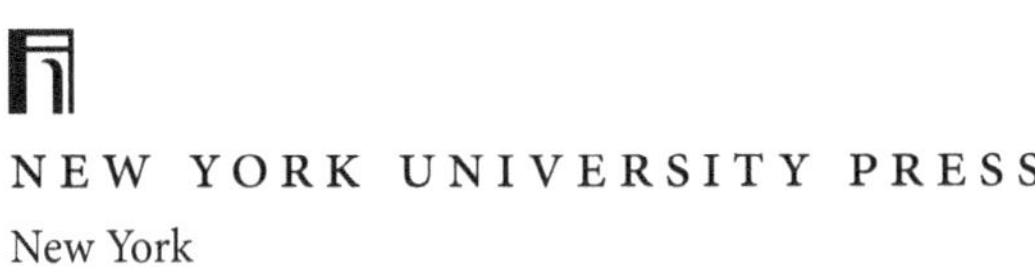

NEW YORK UNIVERSITY PRESS

New York

NEW YORK UNIVERSITY PRESS
New York
www.nyupress.org

© 2025 by New York University
All rights reserved

Please contact the Library of Congress for Cataloging-in-Publication data.

ISBN: 9781479826650 (hardback)
ISBN: 9781479826667 (paperback)
ISBN: 9781479826704 (library ebook)
ISBN: 9781479826681 (consumer ebook)

This book is printed on acid-free paper, and its binding materials are chosen for strength and durability. We strive to use environmentally responsible suppliers and materials to the greatest extent possible in publishing our books.

The manufacturer's authorized representative in the EU for product safety is Mare Nostrum Group B.V., Mauritskade 21D, 1091 GC Amsterdam, The Netherlands. Email: gpsr@mare-nostrum.co.uk.

Manufactured in the United States of America

10 9 8 7 6 5 4 3 2 1

Also available as an ebook

CONTENTS

A Prefatory Message

(Entrances)

In *Tears for Tears*, grief is at once theme, theory, and method. It is the object of analysis and its means. Breaking discursive logic, it requires no permission for its impossible praxis. It carries, beholds, releases, shutters, and shatters. Rarely a solo composition, it requests ensemblic surrender, splitting force to shapeshift across forms. Like an unshrinking cascade across the personal and communal, it is often disobedient, running over categories to silence and syllabize, honor and hail. But it runs through us, too, in tender assaults, at other times in sharp hums, and often through careful devastation by virtue of immaterial directive. A chameleon, *duende*, tiny hysterical child, vengeful sky, nostalgic object, conjured demon, an unhurried teacher, or a river to wade into, grief is regularly a referential character. To feel its tremors is to identify its analogy. It is always something else. It is always now in everything soon to come.

Grief is anything but linear, static, transparent, or generous. It requires motion in place of any narrative dialectic as it courses through space and time's clemency ambushing the living. Ever possessing, vital and alive, grief obliges one to shelter with the oncoming loss imposed by colonial/imperial/capital/racial hegemony through both vulnerability and force. Felt where the dead remap the provisional essences of the living, and the living retrace their outlines, grief is allusive and circumstantial, as-sociational, and painfully intimate. Like particles gracing ether, it is a persistent undertaking, exceeding discretion, matter, and its very own communicability. Thrown into suffering without distance and address, we, the most minor of subjects, are its stabled instabilities crossing thresholds to meet the portal's center.

Yet these conditions are anything but unparalleled conditionings. In conscious and unconscious time, grief is contingent labor—an ongo-ing rehearsal in bargaining, searching, letting in, letting go, anticipating, counter-transporting, and falling into uncoordinated vulnerability across social, affective, and political terrain. In routinely reencountering loss, it may advance as a violent introjection, a radical incommensurability, a targeted projection, and an evolving countertransference. Never little and hardly direct, grief rarely extends its unwieldy schedule and expiration date. Its deadline: multidimensional, formless, an infinite entrance. Inexhaustibly communicative, grief rings like a ripple into transformative strategies for being together.

As grief is all these things, *Tears for Tears* attempts to track down its landscapes, geometries, and choreographies as vibrating archives, rather than immobile sensibilities. In tracing over place and time, we locate not only dynamic scenes and their things—animating specters, new versions of the self—but each other's shared desires. If to have found these interlaced entities in grief is to have been assumed missing, how might the search, ongoingly consistent, yield the simultaneous transport and release of one another beyond deadening extremity? From here, the space between longing and despair, individual crisis and global disaster, we hold on so un/intentionally to let go so tightly.

In this spirit of shared contagion, *Tears for Tears* is an anti-treatise across anti-stages, an invitation to grieve collectively, across nonlinear dimensional planes, with and for another's sorrow. Embodying grief's shifting content/form/process, the book performatively travels across the pages as the subjects and objects determine; and, propelled by multiple protagonists and performances, the text encircles, entangles, and evolves. Side by side with grief's inherent force, *Tears for Tears* incorporates the deep-seated grief of artists-theorists Eva Margarita, Erica Gressman, Pedro Lopez, and Blair Ebony Smith along with their evocative objects and mounting spectral and historical reappearances. The nature of grief, across circumstance and consequence, pushes writing and method outside its limits. And it is at these very limits that possibility materializes and transforms everything in grief's orbits and edges.

Tears for Tears makes no claim to objectivity, standardized teaching, singular construction, or interpretative labor outside of mourning. While written across various theoretical, poetic, political, and aesthetic notions of grief, the chapters are rather shaped by multiple and intersecting dialogic and disorderly narrations—all impersonal, personal, known, unknown, material, and affectively spiritual. Driven by the voices of contemporary minoritarian cultural workers, the book crosses performance and video art, photography, sculpture, and music to demonstrate how hegemonic structures for gathering are reformulated through alternative archives and movements in motion. From plural and singular to impending and consecutive loss due to state-sanctioned violence, colonial racial capitalism, unnatural disaster, global crisis, and social and personal circumstance, *Tears for Tears* theorizes the minoritarian grief-act as a psychic, cultural, and political practice that creates openings for social transformation. These openings, while not without heartache, are apertures for interwoven sorrows, or collective ways forward into ways past through the actuation of portals. Given and taken outside of any spatial-temporal propriety, *a tear for a tear* is an omniversal gateway awaiting animation.

In rattling the domains of life, death, and spectral vision, every chapter is *a tear for a tear*, overlying everyday life with staged events to defend the dead and reanimate graveyards. Rather than chapters that synthesize and pull from traditional archives, every section in this book explores how loss tears holes across worlds to initiate new collective social orders. Rarely transparent and centered, these tiny holes still bear light over the encircling film, illuminating the anharmonic sparks flowing, deforming, cruising, consuming, cleansing, foretelling, and looping across space and time. To chart these movements in motion, one must sift and shift with and through the aesthetic productions of living artists very much still living in grief. Each *chapter-as-tear* advances a composition scored with the assistance of *unfettered archives*. Deliberately loose and unrestrained, these archives are generated by uniquely known and not-yet-widely-written-about artists-theorists who collect, engineer, and constantly remodify given repositories by crossing over designated topographies.

By homing in on a singular artist and performance per chapter, *Tears for Tears* allows for extensions, interruptions, notations, emergent details, tangents, digressions to explode into narratological (in)determinacy so that every piece tells the story of aesthetic production as inseparable from its form. Drawing from intimate artifacts, spiritual summons, extended interviews, virtual and in-person correspondences by way of shared meals, walks, and texts, along with social media and email exchanges, including readings, playlists, and personal anecdotes, the text deploys a mimetic methodology. This mimetic methodology, as form-as-content, enables shared grief with the artist, artist's objects and its specters, and the lingering residues across elemental forms. As an emulative and perhaps even empathetic method, energy counter transfers and grants the communal entrance of tears upon more tears.

If *unfettered archives* are living entities, ever evolving depositories, dead-not-dead matter, bodies and energies in signifying motion, these cultural workers not only build their own formless sites over already marked stations but place pressure on the tensions rising between life, death, and immateriality. Even though no two grieving processes are ever the same, they mobilize similar sentiments and symptoms to re-shape the landscapes of grief. These shared losses reorient conventional world-making practices to produce new social orders in which grief-work is not contained singularly, but a process enacted in feminist, Black, Brown, and queer ensembles, or a process completed to lift the dead and not merely contain them. A vessel for each cultural maker, their objects and specters, the entire book is a compilation of tears drying too slowly and ever quickly.

Tears for Tears communally wonders past the ache driven by and re-routed in grief. It is committed to material and immaterial entrances, the desire to touch and the dread of no longer touching, the anticipation of death and the imposition of finitude, the burden of difference alongside fragmentations of language. Under global peril and aggressive governmental sanction, ongoing catastrophe and impending social doom, grief's roads are paved with both shattering foreclosures and glistening introductions for minor entities. As moments of negotiation, incommensurability, and profound suffering between individual and mass death charge the pages, trails of depredation and unknowing resettle and rectify singular mappings. Moved into grief's unknowing, *Tears for Tears* is composed of one another's imminent sorrows as intersecting channels for collectively pushing forward and honoring our loss(es) by animating our portals.

1

Deathless Fire

Ghostly Choreographies and Spirited Companions

To explore conjure, ritual, and "cere-mourning" is to inves-
tigate diasporic sociological haunting with the intention of
unsettling colonial forms of gathering.
—Eva Margarita, in conversation with the author

A Flame for a Flame

Driven by unbearable grief, Eva Margarita carries the weight of death on
her fingertips in *Light of Ours* (2020–2021),[1] an endurance piece staged in
her Los Angeles home on New Year's Eve. Broadcast live to catch the turn-
ing of the calendar year, the performance appropriates personal space to
restore collective time in honoring Black lives brutally lost to state violence.
For nearly two hours, this Afro-Latinx interdisciplinary performance
artist, poet, scholar, and playwright keeps vigil within and across her fam-
ily residence as online viewers witness the slow gesture of lighting 750
candles. In deep "cere-mourning," or what the artist articulates as an alter-
native to colonial gatherings concerning death, Eva Margarita carefully
curls these candles into closely conjoined floor lamps. Defying normative
ceremonial rituals experienced across wakes, vigils, and funerals through a
feat durational in its nature and undertaken at incredible risk,[2] she initiates
new rites of passage across service, liturgy, and celebration.

Beginning within the home but eventually moving outward, the
artist forms spiral-like flammable enclosures across the living room,
kitchen, and office floors, before light spills into the yard. Fractal in
aesthetic composition, the spirals generate a series of still-developing
helical forms that add continuity to impermanence's contours. Met-
aphorically endless in design, the installation breaches finitude as

flames flow in and out of space, overlying categories of inside and outside, and private and public. For seventy-two hours, the performance pours over and out of space and time: a gentle warning that this light of ours is delicate, dangerous, but persevering. Fire may burn, but it also generates growth to sustain numerous ecological systems: it is both end and invitation, abundance, and flux amid orthographic spillages subverting colonial forms of assembly.

To remind viewers of life's precarity, impending risk directs every motion made by Eva Margarita in *Light of Ours*.[3] Adorned in a long white linen gown, the artist slowly swirls across space, intensifying the exposure to being burned while holding calculated concern for those already extinguished. These unhurried movements, formed in premediated time, build a gentle but perilous waiting place for Black life. With each lit flame, *Light of Ours* resembles a winding vigil led by Eva Margarita as the visitation officiant, conjurer, and mourner. As fire glints, swaying back and forth, Black life is held alive to illuminate existence's playground as always already belonging to the dead. Every candle recalls a Black life taken by state violence and terror, intentional oversight, police brutality, resource disparity, and unmitigated hate, all social matters constituted by and constitutive of a global anti-Blackness.

Yet every lit candle is also incapable of capturing the immeasurable magnitude of Eva Margarita's installation and its implications for oncoming violence. In generating a constellation of loss, the ephemeral confines of living in provision are enacted with simultaneous attention for the dead while co-commitment, danger, and intentional care for those gone too soon evolve in accompaniment, never through opposing force. This circumspect inter-articulation, embodied by Eva Margarita, exposes how she, too, as Black feminist scholar Christina Sharpe contends, becomes part of "the *carriers* of terror, terror's embodiment . . . the ground of terror's possibility globally."[4] Battling the impossible possibility of terror's undoing, Eva Margarita bears the quotidian horrors forced upon Black lives and pays tribute to already endangered ones. In eulogizing, she instantiates herself within a deathly paradigm to summon our communal obligation to each candle. Flickering across a scene of responsibility and memorialization, each flame, regardless of intensity, denies the option of ever looking away.

Inviting spectators to witness the agony of death and its anticipated grief, Eva Margarita transforms the home into an atmosphere of peril, eulogy, and scene of subjection by producing the conditions of the viewer's liability.[5] Unable to separate everyday life from staged performances for minoritarian subjects, she invites death to cameo as communal accountability wavering in temporal capacity and spatializing logic. As a direct response to political unrest and social protest, Eva Margarita confronts and enacts these events of death through repetitive gestures that implicate the live-video viewer. This move to broaden social accountability is understood as indivisible from what Black and African studies scholar Hugo Canham proposes as Black bodies as "the site of devastation for centuries" producing ongoing mourning in the name of anti-Blackness as an "unending pandemic."[6] With every motion formed, Eva Margarita coils us within a vortex of conjoined light, fire, suffering, and amenability, and in so doing, redesigns collective being toward one end. Offering homage to ongoing existence, the artist wraps us in social obligation, and, in cherishing Black life on her family's land, discharges the deliberate co-commitments loosening the neoliberal categories of private and public that assist in both capitalist individuation and fragmentation across dispossession as historical precedent.[7] Eva Margarita's material demands never supersede immaterial engagement; in fact, every ritualized shift is a committed undertaking to experience the possibility of death: hers, theirs, those gone too soon, and those to come as markers of communally implicated spillages beaming across deathless light.

This extinguishable (spiritually inextinguishable) fire has everything to do with the material and political components of the candles themselves. The 750 donated candles were collected over many months through community sites from mailed-in deliveries across the United States to online funded sources.[8] Varying in color and design but adhering to similar texture, structure, and durability, the candles contribute to the overall experience of the piece and call forth those slender devotional glass jars purchased at city corner stores. Seemingly minor in matter, these characteristics, pre-recorded by the artist, help manage the temporality of the performance. Each flame of every candle, then, is not merely fire flickering in unintentional memory, but fire that works to survive its own durational ephemerality. By tightly curling these tall candles throughout space, the artist assembles a particular "cere-mourning" that unites personal and communal grief, a collective enterprise across injury, death, and impending loss. These candles belong to a plural affliction and mark the warmth of unbearable heat—a heat known to both blaze across subjects and connect communities.

For Eva Margarita, death and grief materialize and burn particularly, with vulnerable communities suffering the consequences of crises at a disproportionately higher rate. *Light of Ours* acknowledges this social reality and paves the space for the reauthorization of anticolonial gatherings often requiring cultural and political redirection during social disaster. Global catastrophe, failing national infrastructures, and systemic racism, while seemingly unique disparities, are inseparable from gov-

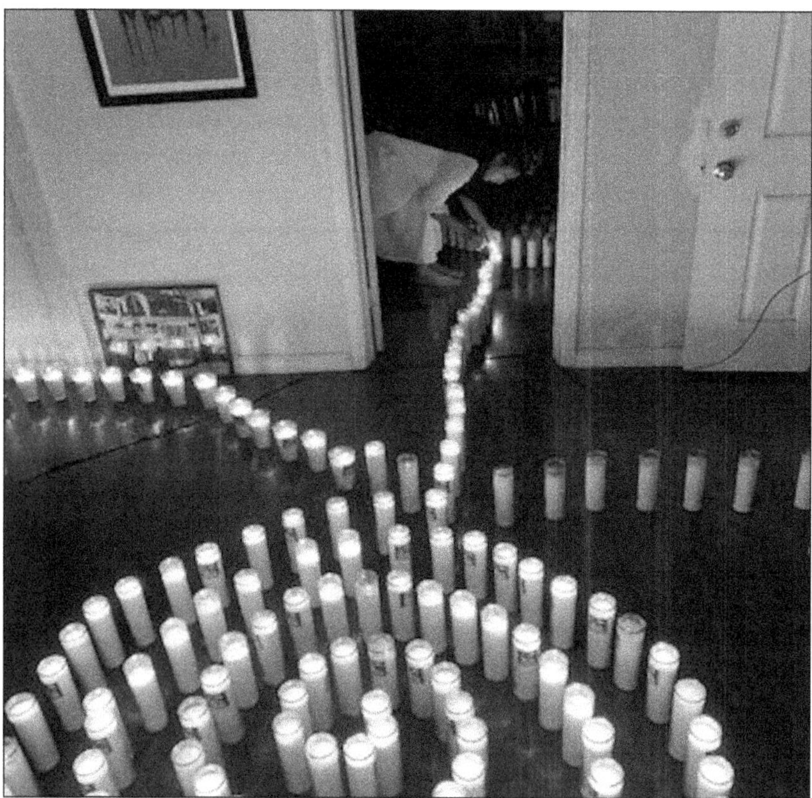

Figure 1.1. A photographic still from Eva Margarita's *Light of Ours* (2020–2021). Photo courtesy of Eva Margarita.

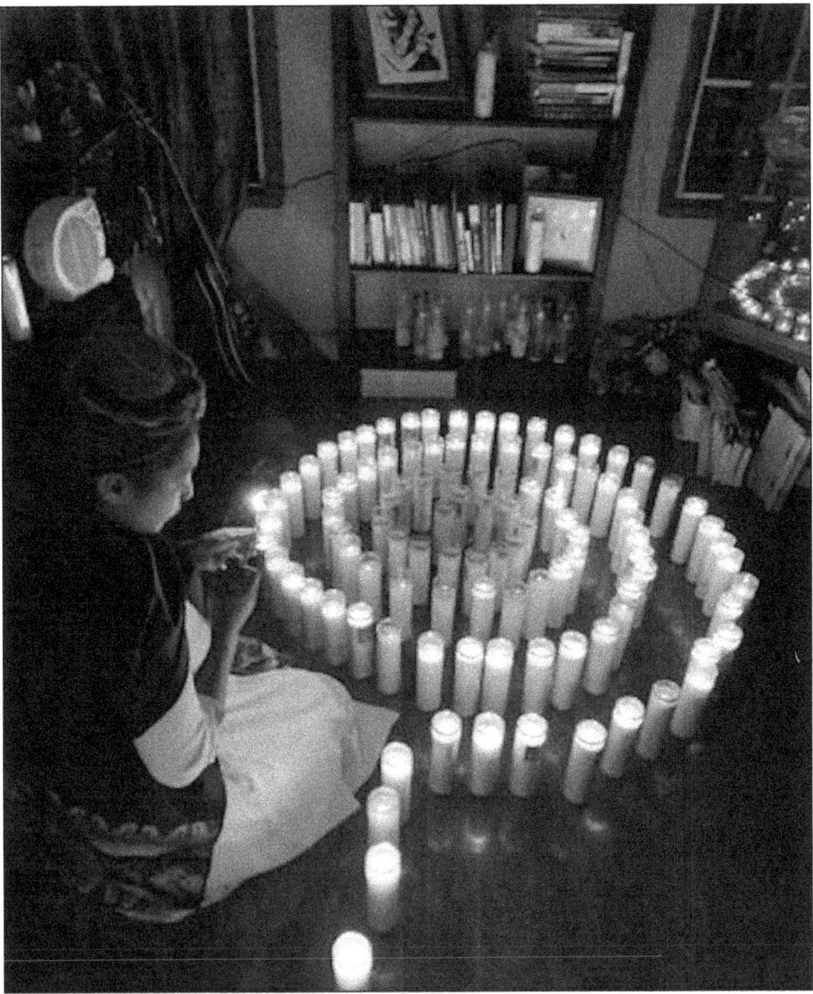

Figure 1.2. A photographic still from Eva Margarita's *Light of Ours* (2020–2021). Photo courtesy of Eva Margarita.

erning social mechanisms. According to Eva Margarita, "2020 was the deadliest year in US history, in which about 3.3 million deaths occurred as we witnessed people being taken by COVID and saw a larger number of Black lives being lost to racial violence."[9] She adds that "in the face of a public health catastrophe, Black loss and the ongoing risk of death was heightened, proving to affect Black people on a larger scale than other cultural groups."[10] Each lit candle, neatly assembled, one between others, visually dwells in this tension: with the candles susceptible to being blown out by motion, resistance to ephemeral passage is enacted to reorient the labor of remembrance joined to racial injustice. But to remember is to set a scene of both endangerment and subjectification, one Eva Margarita takes seriously as she slips in and out of time and space by risking self-harm. As she becomes a spiraling entity herself, the entire milieu sheds coiled light from the ground up. While fire burns, it also produces its own gravitational sustainability: it is its own renewed recollection and energy. Compromising corporeal safety for social accountability, the artist embraces the warmth of fire to be touched by death-in-life, revealing how, as cultural theorist and poet Fred Moten declares, certain "death was already haunted."[11]

Eva Margarita's aesthetic oeuvre underlines how grief-work breeds an ensemble of resonances and invitations for reckoning with the residue of persevering historical violence across sites and subjects under siege. For this artist, grief-work is a conscious deliberation, even when it may feel like an unconscious happening prompted by personal affliction. Across terms and conditions, grief-work is also communal labor committed in acts of historical admission, intimate meditation, suffering, temporal spillage, co-committal risk, and durational transformation. Obscuring the tenuous lines between life and death, Eva Margarita's grief-works shift one's attention toward the immaterial energies summoning all material gatherings. Every movement, fluttering light, blurred edge, and discriminate outline pulls the viewer into overflow, flux, and abundance. To follow Eva Margarita's tracks is to attempt to mirror these spilling and spiraling motions of sorrow, and to demonstrate how writing, like her winding choreography, chases sentiment and social consequence to embody the affective circumstances of movement itself.

By rechoreographing Eva Margarita's aesthetic shifts throughout a series of minoritarian grief-acts, one reignites the possible plural compositions across minor keys. Every ideological move abides by the movements of flow and overflow by traveling across Black and Brown feminist thought and queer-of-color critique, and between social, cultural, political, and psychical notions of grief. From Sharpe's "orthography of the wake" to José Esteban Muñoz's conjoined racialized suffering and "being-in-common" to Leticia Alvarado's haunted communions as relationality to Jennifer C. Nash's "slow loss" and Judith Butler's precarity of vulnerable life, to name a few theoretical co-contemplations,[12] I consider the co-presence of "a choreography of singularities" that "should not dissolve incommensurability and difference into equivalence" when navigating communal grief amid ongoing colonial violence.[13] This kind of labor, across and between every motion by Eva Margarita, is a temporal admission to tend, as Sharpe shares, to "a past that is not a past" in a present that moves swiftly into a futural recurrence, and inevitably resurfaces as "that past not yet past" in eternal continuance.[14]

Vortexes of Communal Loss: Wake-Labor

What is required to participate in a non-past past or what Eva Margarita deploys as "cere-mourning," an anticolonial gathering for grieving that equally cherishes vulnerable life and death? What does it mean to disturb imperial forms of coming together by tending to the immaterial-material energies encircling existence? It means, in large part, to defend the dead. Or, as Sharpe contends, it requires one "to tend to the Black dead and dying: to tend to the Black person, to Black people, always living" into death.[15] To protect the dead, then, one must commit to the intentional drive of wake work. In arriving at such consciousness, Sharpe concludes that it necessitates "work: hard emotional, physical, intellectual work that demands vigilant attendance to the needs of the dying, to ease their way, but also to the needs of the living."[16] By analyzing both aesthetic and everyday accounts of Black life assembled into "the orthography of the wake," Sharpe demonstrates how Black life weathers beyond the afterlives of slavery, even in spaces of impending death, terror, and erasure.[17]

In this interplay between life and death, one might also ask, what are the intimate gestures, senses, sounds, affects, and elements involved in tending to both the living and the dead at the same time? Are these conjoined elements driven by a "ghostly matter" inevitably reorganizing the politics of social tenderness, materiality, and labor all at once?[18] These inquiries call for labor to be seen as a material and an immaterial ethics of care, a working "in the wake" that exceeds the normative ways one has been trained to respond to and organize for loss. To weather on, then, is to always return to tending to the dead and the living simultaneously, and to consider how loss consciously rechoreographs a collective new social order in which grief-work is not contained singularly but is rather movement prepared in ensemble.

Since 2018, Eva Margarita has simultaneously tended to the dead and living by generating ritualistic work focused on grief across form and media. From poetry to dramatic scripts and scholarly essays to serving as a board director on The Vortex (an organization dedicated to implementing strategies for performance events across venues) to performance pieces such as *Entierro* (2022), *Viajes* (2021), and *Obituary* (2021), her oeuvre translates the inarticulate into dialogic encounters across dimensions, terrain, and spirits.[19] While those 750 candles are specific to the political logics of *Light of Ours*, they contribute to a series of aesthetic projects by Eva Margarita devoted to grief in which the artist fades the edges of existence to catch those audible glimmers spilling over finite lines, even when formidably unheard. So, to honor those taken too soon by state violence, Eva Margarita lifts the dead into new existences, listening deftly to muted narratives. Or, as Sharon Patricia Holland notes of "raising the dead," "the task [is] both to hear the dead speak in fiction and to discover in culture and its intellectual property opportunities for not only uncovering silences but also translating inarticulate places into conversational territories."[20] Conceding to these inaudible sounds and the full sensorial landscapes of unearthly energy, Eva Margarita's aesthetic projects are inextricable from brutal quotidian social scenes—every candle is an extension of biting sound, a phonic score for multi-presences joining the living and the dead-not-dead in an endless orchestration of resurrection.

In staging a series of ghostly communions, Eva Margarita serves as the social channel and ancestral vessel for communication across energies and entities. The artist openly discloses that she studies "conjure, ritual, and 'cere-mourning' to investigate diasporic sociological haunting with the intention of unsettling colonial forms of gathering."[21] To rattle these forms, then, obliges a dedication to bodily exposure and the courage to risk one's flesh for and with another's. Take for instance *Pan de Coco* (2018), a ten-minute self-produced play in which Eva Margarita becomes an Afro-Latinx *bruja* who summons the dead through familial culinary recipes to combat racism. Turning to everyday activities, she deliberately communes with those gone too soon to reunite through unconventional assembly. In *Conjuring Stains*

(2020), an endurance piece completed over nine days, the artist collects and scrutinizes government documents such as census forms as "sites of haunting."[22] In this piece, "the submission to and of the form" leaves "the subject with the residue of caste painting, an ink made of ghostly matter."[23] Understanding residue as infinite accompaniment, Eva Margarita conveys that the antithetical determination between life and death is rather an entwined circuit of various stains, never a neat and final destination.[24] Between duration and exhaustion as sites of endurance for more capacious communal anticolonial assemblies, she lingers between fire, ash, and light to reveal something about what their interconnectedness *does* and *co-enables* rather than what they singularly *are* for the world's consumption.

Likewise, wearing a long white dress in *Conjuring Stains*, Eva Margarita reproduces the outpouring of mourning as an act of spillage yet again. This piece, according to the artist, was conceived while caring for her terminally ill father, who lamentably passed away during the process. Because of this occurrence, the performance required immediate alterations across meaning, scope, sentiment, territory, and shape. Of *Conjuring Stains*, the progenitor of *Light of Ours* and *Salt, Fat, Ashes, Heat* (2020), Eva Margarita confirms that the goal was "not only to subvert the documentation process but to allow flesh to spill outside of the boxes" one is destined to inhabit.[25] As witnessed in *Light of Ours*, the artist's conception of flesh stretches beyond the strict dualism of material–immaterial to include singular bodies across communal forces in unearthly embodiment. In this piece, like many others, she manipulates the notion of embodiment through choreographic shifts building across entity and energy to enact projective identifications and subtle introjections, and yet, no process fully elaborates or nullifies sorrow. Eva Margarita notes that overflow often just happens in accordance with everyday life matters: "I was faced with having to fill out forms about my father's cause of death and his race. The boxes were filled with mourning. They spilled over."[26] Expected to fill in for her father, she drops into and over designated matters, all racially and relationally coded. As she carries out living-for and dying-with, her performances cultivate vortexes of grief—at times fractural in composition but always extending outward to reanimate the immaterial-material within. These implicating flows move across cosmic energy to reactivate space across alternative time.[27] And in spilling over and filling in, Eva Margarita circumvents the death–life dialectic threatening to colonially suffocate us all.

If death is a consecutive event and grief-work is a mechanism by which to demand renewed existence from said event, to "insist Black being into the wake," as Sharpe declares, how do we attend to its geographic choreographies?[28] What is this operative site of suffering and how is it communally galvanized? The place of grief, while particular to the bereft, often expresses universal feelings and liabilities that do not, in doing so, sacrifice singular contextualization. For as unruly as grief appears and performs, it both shelters and marks territory. According to feminist geographers Kathryn Gillespie and Patricia J. Lopez, grief "travels geographically, creating a topography of emotion, at once providing a site of connection and distance."[29] That is to say, as the authors add, that "the spaces, places, and scales in which grief occurs shape the manifestation, processing, and understanding" of its character and circumstance.[30] Or, grief is textured context, territory's burden; it is both everlasting and calculating—a spatial-temporal dynamic reordering existence to meet the longevity of feeling. While Eva Margarita's candles retain a fire both inside and outside her family home for almost half a week to symbolize those often unnamed, unseen, unheard, their reanimation does not dissolve our responsibility to one another, or our individual neglect toward public reproach and social complicity. Grief is geographically local in all its politically global authority—neither destination nor social position is ever antithetical to the other.

In ongoing correspondences with Eva Margarita, she stresses how *Light of Ours* is at once wake work for the people and at the same time deeply personal. For this artist, appropriating space into new and emancipatory forms of assembly must include gratitude and service to family, land, and community. As such, to perform this piece on kinship's compound is central to the politics of subverting conventional colonial gatherings in the name of ongoing loss. Eva Margarita reveals that three different structures sit on one plot of land—one for her, one for her brother, and another for her mother. "Lined up horizontally like dominos," she lives in front, her brother in the middle home, while their mother takes up the main house in the back.[31] The yard sits in between her mother's and brother's houses, with the spillage between sites producing communal environments and engagements.[32] In creating such

an atmosphere, Eva Margarita counters the deadweight of racial capital-
ism's historical insistence on individualization whereby even grieving is
commodified as a private event for sale; instead, she invests in spillage as
a necessary strategy for anticolonial gathering.[33] As a conscious reaction
to the encroaching reaches of neoliberal and fascist agendas against all
kinds of commons, she splinters the singular into alternative forms of
communions and productive hauntings—spaces for world-making that
rupture the tidy binds and binaries that constrain dynamic life forces
into individuated constructions.

Invited into Eva Margarita's personal space, then, one cautiously waits
for and with her as the candles exhaust and burn through their entirety.
The waiting occurs alongside the figurative mediation to remap corpo-
real exhaustion, to pause to witness yet again the unbearable horrors
saturating the commons with imposing agency. Or there is always more
waiting in the wait of waiting to wait to be seen. Cradling incredible
patience, danger, and skill, Eva Margarita's endurance act reflects the
delicate sinews of life, death, and alternative temporalities instantiated
to survive an ongoing brutal present. As the candle's fire sways, it also
gradually disappears—a slow fade coursing over and into a new set
of unearthly circumstances and blurred material edges. To light these
candles is to allegorically lift the dead—and, in consequence, to defend
those who have passed on without regard for their very lived lives. For-
warded by great exposure, *Light of Ours* is one example of the intentional
grief-work Eva Margarita assumes to let go and let in through a tangled
web of shared sentiment, risk, and unpredictable encounter. In all her
ability to not burn the house and herself down, she rides the temporal
wake of slavery to unsettle colonial erasure in the proceeding present.

To add to the fracturing temporalities of Black death, Jennifer C.
Nash theorizes "slow loss" in countermeasure to the binary of life and
its afterlives.[34] Following the trails of Black feminist archives, Nash sug-
gests that loss be rethought along nonlinear time frames so that grief
and mourning are seen not as the aftereffects of death or the remnants of
lost subjects, but as an always present condition coursing through time's
endurance. For Nash, loss is never not around; "its felt manifestations
are not a longing for life where what was lost was present, but rather an
attention to its constitutive presence."[35] What "remains" in persistent
loss from ongoing "slow death" is the durational phases of endurance

itself—perpetual, distinctive, and always oncoming.[36] Endurance is the remainder that remains looping in magnitude, reorienting one's connection to space, time, subjectivity, and death.[37] Refusing to romanticize mourning, resilience, suffering, or endurance, Nash contends that the domain of slow loss "might be constitutive of Black female subjectivity, that the labor of Black feminist theory might be to understand the ecology of this space."[38] By forming new spaces against "the colonization of time,"[39] Nash shifts loss away from undocumented temporal repertoires into the terrain of Black feminist archives—a form of rearranging loss into the depths of epistemological and genealogical immutability. For, as Nash sharply notes, what remains might not be clearly demarcated, and perhaps "there never was a coherent 'before and after'" but rather conditional provisions for the still living.[40]

To weather on, to endure, to embrace slow loss is to also return to the question of tending to the dead and the living at the same time. This entails considering how loss produces a hole within normative world-making practices to generate new social orders in which grief-work is an ongoing praxis in feminist, Black, Brown, and queer ensemble; or a process done to "raise the dead," not merely contain them.[41] In consequence, this ritualized process shifts the temporal grounds of grieving into conscious quotidian life strategies; or, fashioned this way, to intentionally grieve is to develop a set of political and social arrangements that enforce our conjoined terrors and transformations without reducing difference to a set of universal and conflating protocols. It also signifies, as Nash affirms, to account for grief's life as unending, ever-present, as a protagonist of existence and a means and measure for ongoing study, communicability, and recognition.

Behind these various conclusions sit the plural conditions that target the most vulnerable of populations for and into death; and if not immediate death, a "slow loss" that often mitigates grieving channels.[42] Those lost to state violence, unnatural disasters, deadly viral strains, police brutality, and an enveloping anti-Black violence are rendered not only *grievable* throughout this book, but *livable* within other forms of energy flowing beyond the physical body. If we tend (not only defend) to both the dead and the living simultaneously, we might begin to sense how grieving not only powerfully undoes us but reshapes the communal into revitalizing forms of multi-dimensional embodiment—always in "co-presence with other modes of difference" as a counterstep to colonial precedent and state violence.[43] To attend to the shifting materialities of all life forces involves an intentional co-laboring to grieve not just bodies, but the residual sparks that linger and sound of spirit.

Eva Margarita lives and breathes in this space of grief-work by "finding comfort in recognizing the entanglements of social, personal, and artistic practices."[44] In grief, she "best theorizes and works beyond archives to embrace our living repertoires."[45] And to expose how this mutually constitutive dynamic is rather an unsettled and ongoing experience, she provides new meaning to the archive's permanence in *Light of Ours*. As air hits against each flame, for example, sparks of light enliven bodies controlled by quotidian violence and often excluded from canonical archives. American studies scholar Lisa Cacho cautions one to actively rethink the universal and personal accounts of "the devalued dead" when configuring the language of mourning, for one must always decipher "value into language."[46] Under colonial-racial-capitalist logics, minoritarian life is not valuable, but rather assessed according to systematically violent and biased categories such as "deviant" or "criminal," terms that falsely approximate worth and the grieving processes necessary to survive such myopic grammars. As only certain lives qualify as grievable and archivable—a cyclical narrative of forced exclusion (and discriminate inclusion)—the notion of filtering worth extends the colonial enterprise whereby certain lives evolve as the only representational model for viable documentation. How do we, against this colonizing logic, thoughtfully defend, tend, and value the dead, and in the process, remain curiously connected to them, ourselves, and one another as we re-record experience to reorder existence? How do we recirculate life's currency amid death's veil via our shared responsibilities to one another? And where do we communally land, and collectively deposit worth, as we foster new accountabilities for social value?

Where There's Smoke There's Fire: This Little Fight of Ours

Designed during the heights of the pandemic and social protests across the globe in 2020, *Light of Ours* recognizes how loss submerges daily life, leaving one to renavigate and reshape communal grieving spaces. In counterpose to racist and fascist deadly impulses, Eva Margarita conceptualizes loss as a ramification of institutionalized violence against the most vulnerable of constituents. Even though the artist may not personally know those who have passed on, all Black death and life is inevitably personal for her. As she vehemently expresses, "Each time we lost a Black life, a sense of time, a sense of normalcy, it hit home."[47] George Floyd, Sandra Bland, Breonna Taylor, Elijah McClain, and David McAtee are among the names that mobilized people to take to the streets in protest of the state's violent conditions shortening the durations of Black lives. These lives are frequently made the subject of police violence, spectacle, and incarceration such that in the midst of a deadly pandemic, Black subjectivities become entangled with and even bound by perpetual death—death by inaccessible medical care, death by infrastructural aggression, and death that, as Canham contends, "always latches onto existing social fissures of inequality."[48] While these names marshaled people to march in the name of Black Lives Matter and Say Their Names, they can never index the totality of lives lost. Nor do they fold the long histories of resistance to violent anti-Black racism or the individual lost lives that these movements name.[49] Yet grief oscillates between the personal, private, public, communicating the knotted ensembles that inform their co-production, even when facile separations persist between states, subjects, scenarios. As Eva Margarita herself reveals, death is our communal responsibility to one another; in loss, violence implicates everyone, even when we remain divided by institutional markers of difference and the agendas formed by difference's markings.

Shaken into oppressive grief, *Light of Ours* was designed by the artist to express shared agony, to provide room for memorial and ritual, and to re-enliven life (or the dead?) by cherishing the silences still breathing across unearthly energies. Through mutual respiration, Eva Margarita's work attempts to renew our commitment to being and living together, to sharing our collective cultivations without fear of state-managed claims about resource scarcity and individualization. If living is done, as Sharpe argues, "in the wake of slavery, in spaces where we were never meant to survive, or have been punished for surviving and for daring to claim or make spaces of something like freedom," Eva Margarita dares to fill in voids, to reconstitute a common space for grief. The artist envisages this transformation for being together into what Sharpe calls "practices of an ethics of care (as in repair, maintenance, attention), an ethics of seeing, and of *being* in the wake as consciousness."[50] This requires an ethics of care as explicit attention to evolve stale epistemologies and genealogies that fail to embrace Black feminist labor and archives, archives that, contrary to conventional beliefs, have always made possible the tracing of unexpired remains, even when presented as valueless or disappeared.

Seeing scant ideological separation between live performance, everyday life, and documentation, Eva Margarita assembles an ethics of care as explicit attention by offering the private as public via a blaringly beautiful but incredibly dangerous chapel. Driving one well beyond a cemetery of light filled with neat chasms for buried corpses, one rather arrives to church to recall the ritualistic practice of standing in line to light candles before or after sermons. Uninterested in normative cultural and religious protocols, Eva Margarita instead repeatedly bends and kneels to generate light from the ground up. No devotion is lent to standing candle altars as the artist bows before these objects in attention, gratitude, and collective care to inevitably command and summon the spectator's participation through flaming lights.[51] To capture the precision of such movement, the camera follows every gesture, frequently changing angle and frame. At times, the artist stares right into the lens, sustaining gazes as she re-illuminates those negligently gone too soon one narrow candle at a time. At other times, with a tender ambush toward the frame, her peering eyes request closure in asking, do you *see me, us, now?* In *seeing her now*, do we recall our own capacities and responsibilities to them, her, us, all?

In an anticolonial move that models the crawling effects of living while minor, Eva Margarita's camera hits the ground and remains there throughout the entire performance.[52] Of the very placement of the camera, she comments on how such a decision is meant to counter the colonial lens's spatial preference. A periscope that rarely touches land, the camera rather captures frames and scenes aerially, and in so doing, breeds a superior position to subjects lying beneath its shot. Forced to engage seeing in this way, how do we socially adjust and transform in the narrowing frames? In staring back, might we instantiate what Moten calls the "polyphonic affectivity of the ghost, the agency of the fixed but multiply apparent shade, an improvisation of spectrality, another development of the negative" or an aural looking that demands haptic seeing across kinesthetic immaterialities?[53]

Seeing is only one sensory instruction in action throughout this performance. Without a candle holder to navigate the dripping wax, Eva Margarita's body toils within flammable tight space, careful not to entangle the long white dress with the fire. With only a sliver of space between each movement, she travels from candle to candle by bending toward the earth—a choreographically political move executed so slowly that motion carries the heaviness of endurance, and the very exhaustion felt in the everydayness of being Black. It is here that Eva Margarita matches the shifts of calculated movements by minor subjects, coursing through space and time in countermeasure to the vertical colonial precedent. If colonial logics demand the ground as a Black dwelling, Eva Margarita recharges death's stillness by animating life forces once again. The suspense of each move, albeit taxing, is willfully meant to tire, as the viewer's exhaustion is deliberately moderated by the ground's leading role in this performance. For close to two hours, the viewer also hits the ground and remains there in weariness, fatigue, frustration, and sadness, mirroring the living effects of debased subjugation. On top of everything else, the time shared between the camera, artist, viewer, and floor objects is tempered by the very temperament of fire, for at any moment a candle could be extinguished, or the artist could go up in flames as she encircles herself in wheeling currents traveling between seconds for hours.[54]

The spectator's exhaustion from being engrossed for hours records another quotidian occurrence: the certainty that authorizes Black life to the ground and the ready conclusions of watching/letting it happen repeatedly. Between the friction of knowing and unknowing, the limits of living and possibility of dying, the spectator is planted within the resolute conviction that not even individual flames can redeem collective complicity. Here, time and its impending fatigue, along with space and its ongoing horizontal limitations, become instigator, gatekeeper, and protagonist as hours quickly feel like minutes nearing finitude. These spatiotemporal tensions turn Eva Margarita into the animator, facilitator, litigator, timekeeper, and conduit of an illuminating vortex for mourning, obligatory witnessing, and collective conjuring. Through terrifying recall, she both lives and restages quotidian terrors, compelling motion into urgent but slow movement—exhaustingly, dangerously, and regularly through fire and always against mediated time.

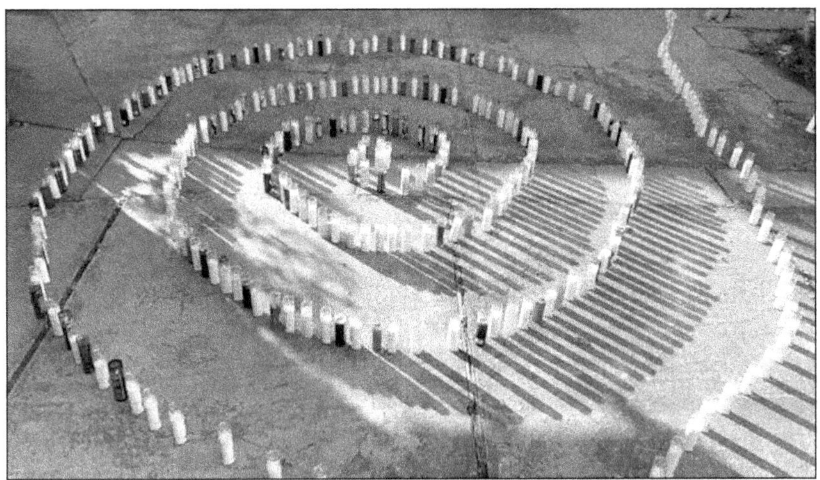

Figure 1.3. A photographic still from Eva Margarita's *Light of Ours* (2022–2021). Photo courtesy of Eva Margarita.

Near the end of the performance, the anticipated consequence of risk eventually occurs as a section of her long, white dress catches fire and Eva Margarita must negotiate continuing with the performance despite the fire's threat to mobility. As she puts out the unexpected but anticipated fire, she makes the dress both a site of danger and evidence, lifting and sheltering extended historical stains as a black-brown hole lingers across the garment. That is to express that the front portion of this dress carries the "murky brown fingerprints from having picked up the dress so many times so as not to be set on fire once again."[55] For Eva Margarita, this particular fabric and color are deliberate aesthetic choices, as they "function as a blank canvas for spillage," in accordance with "the residual stains of life and performance" that inevitably manifest between both.[56] The white material helps highlight what the artist signals as "the particular ways *lo sucio* cultivates a lingering presence in the production of labor" in the name of Brownness within scenes of overwhelming whiteness as property.[57] Or how Brownness, even if it appears as historical residue, shares out into the world, creating new forms of attachment that undo the concealing racialization of whiteness.[58] By participating in interdisciplinary scholar Deborah R. Vargas's notion of *lo sucio* as affirmative disidentification, Eva Margarita, via her dress, collects historical dirt and debris, along with the elements of an earthly and present Brownness refusing erasure through the abundance of excess.[59]

While sliding on delicate knees to light every candle, Eva Margarita's brown hands also pound the pavement, generating yet another type of overflow and accompaniment between flesh and concrete, fire and dirt, ash and body. If the artist's white garment is a canvas to be painted over, we must critically account for the flesh's role, underneath this dress, throughout this scenario. To rethink the visceral conditions of her material existence is to revisit her brown skin against the death-trapping ground.[60] That is to say, if Blackness moves in slow loss, a weathering on that porously evolves across life and death, and Brownness is a sharing out, a flowing into of swerving matter and swarming singularities, then how do we tend to Eva Margarita's negotiations between both, with those gone but embroiled within these ontological emancipations as she hits the ground repeatedly?[61] Might the artist be returning from the dead as a reproducible artifact of slow loss? While we witness her entity as flesh and bone joining the dead in all her performances, *where* do we put our finger on Eva Margarita's distinct essence across this material–immaterial dialectic?

This Black and Brown feminist practice of tending to the dead while still living within perpetual death is no easy task under colonial logics but one that proves an enduring facet of subjugated lives. Of this reality, Eva Margarita reveals, "I am fascinated by how we are stained by history, by performance and its process, and if I am wearing white throughout the entire process, one can see what duration does to a material object."[62] This material object is an implication of historical precedent demanding that one think of the human body in relation to the subject as object in durational motion. Articulating this sentiment otherwise, Eva Margarita directly indicates that "often the performances are longer in duration because I am in conversation with something else in accompaniment with time."[63] While time remeasures the object–subject dialectic, color—or lack thereof—produces a different set of determinations. The artist advises one to notice color and fabric details and how they inevitably re-shift racializing significance when donned by women of color. In addition to being a blank canvas, she insists that the dress is also "a white palette, a celebration of life, rather than an ominous darkness worn to a funeral."[64] In this way, Eva Margarita marks the liberating angles of "cere-mourning" in which colonial forms of assembly for grieving become reinvented sites of communion and commemoration, and accompaniment. The stylistic decisions of the performance, from time to fabric and color, are spiritually and politically motivated as she also divulges that while accompaniment is done in the present, it is integrally historical, for "in many Afro-Latinx cultural practices the spiritual leaders often wear white."[65] As Eva Margarita affirms, one must be thoughtful with historical and ancestral data and detail, even if practicing such evidence presents personal danger in recurring (p)reconjured form within the present's past.

Conjuring is never a solo choreography. In fact, conjuring is hardly ever merely corporeal; often it strikes in the unseeable-seeable of ether taking shape and making sounds, all built from centuries of silence, invisibility, and social immutability. While grief-work is a type of choreographic process mobilized "to think about the dead and about our relations to them" also expressing the "rituals through which to enact grief and memory," as Sharpe formulates, it does not necessarily adhere to the strict confines of embodiment as anything bodily engaged.[66] Grief-work, like all conjuring, is precarious, unstable, often incorporeal, a series of shaken deliberations that place Eva Margarita against the screen, near the ground, in a space that no longer singularly belongs to her, but rather to a communal sense of responsibility across ghostly companions.

If *Light of Ours* is a piece devoted to communal grief, the title of the performance hints at such an orchestration as Eva Margarita riffs on the popular gospel song and freedom anthem "This Little Light of Mine."[67] In this artist's aesthetic rendition, however, the plural leads the lyrical score for further social mobilization. From "mine" to "ours," she recollects the sweeping ways mutual grief cracks open the boundaries of attachment by creating what she calls "swirling patterns of exhaustion that design a future that flows" within and across social change.[68] But how do we literally contend with a suffering *ours* that does not conflate the delicate contours of what is *mine*? Perhaps the flow and spillage across both resemble the adjacent cultural formations that recall the labor of creating, as Muñoz notes, "a cosmology that responds cogently to precarious histories of singular and multiple dispossessions."[69] A type of vitalism that travels, without superficial fusion, through multiple cultural registers and pasts while also understanding the mysteries of both "life and death-in-life as something like mystical force"—a force not always known to ourselves and to each other but experienced as a "sharing out of the shareable" into the world amid a series of overlapping vulnerabilities.[70]

But how are these overlying vulnerabilities given simultaneous singular and plural attention, not only in everyday life but via performances emanating from the everyday? To contemplate the quotidian afterburns engendered by performance artist Ana Mendieta's body of work (often in conversation with ritual, death, and mourning) as a "node of attachment" that is Brownness, Muñoz travels through Jean-Luc Nancy's notion of the shareable-incalculable.[71] The incalculable that flows in accompaniment is never quantifiable but is rather "the inoperative, the invaluable . . . art, friendship, love, thought, knowledge . . . emotion"; and, importantly for Eva Margarita, death's transformative undertaking via grief.[72] Like Mendieta's commitment to the elements of the earth that store bodies, spirits, and histories needing to be re-enacted to be remembered, Eva Margarita participates in the complex ontological choreographies of Black and Brown life and death that manifest a multitude of singularities.

If Brownness swarms in liberation and conjoined uprising, Eva Margarita's 750 candles muster beams of light to illuminate shared histories of colonial violence while also flickering in personal subjectification.[73] In line with the minoritarian aesthetic tradition to see difference as uniquely inseparable due to overlapping modes of dispossession, Eva Margarita, like Ana Mendieta, follows the ephemeral patterns of the earth to mark, realign, trace, archive, and share out worlds that counter territorialization and extraction. The artist tracks and traces not only lines of reference, but the affective elaborations that maintain "the urgencies and intensities we experience as both freedom and difference" across a motley crew of energies, forces, and vulnerabilities.[74] These are, as Muñoz notes, the intricate and wavering ontological choreographies of Brownness that labor to disidentify as a strategy against the rapid colonial practices unmarking the lines of connection between sites under attack and siege.[75] Or lights, that are in danger of dying out in Eva Margarita's case, counter the chasms of death's fire in locating "difference without separability."[76]

Deathly Communions: Imprints across Entangling Grief

As Eva Margarita performs, fire entangles. Fire releases. Fire blazes. It reignites and, when lit repeatedly, rebounds in the spaces of abundance, flux, spillage, and communal incandescence. Fire is display and representation; it is spectacle, "fury and rage," delicate, dangerous, wavering, "cleansing, requiring, expecting, demanding devout surrender."[77] That is to also communicate that fire is a radically "ultra-living element"—a permanent-ephemeral offering of presence, transformation across exquisite remains.[78] Its enduring residue shimmers of ghostly companions and material-immaterial commons requesting modification to accelerate the conduits of time and "the life of a log to the life of a world," for "it is renewal."[79] Fire is the light that hardly goes out by traveling ongoingly across time and space as it marks the earth and leaves a series of imprints that congregate and collect in the communal trails of archives, always ephemerally and permanently shifting.

These communal trails are theorized, enacted, and differently followed movements that sketch ideological, ontological, aesthetic, and political lines of convergence and flight. In following these tracks by writing about avant-garde contemporary minoritarian performance artist Nao Bustamante, American studies scholar Leticia Alvarado suggests that we think of "haunted communion as a site of relation," a way to catch glimmering avenues of life and thought across archives and energy.[80] But she also asks us to think of this communion as a way to re-coordinate time, space, subjectivity, history, and bodily interconnections and approaches to "queer sociality."[81] Pursuing the tracks of communal mourning, Alvarado pieces together genealogical and epistemological loss through Bustamante's aesthetic work—intellectual labor that speaks with Muñoz's trajectory of Brownness through Mendieta's art and through so many other Brown artists creating in a similar vein. Alvarado contributes to sites of archival abundance by returning to what has already been documented, shaping memory into memorialization.

For instance, she discloses how in pieces such as *Given Over to Want* and *Somewhere, My Love*, Bustamante grieves the loss of a loved one (José Esteban Muñoz himself) by conjuring his essence and body of thought to afford the public an opportunity to relive his spirit—one never removed from this material plane. Alvarado locates Bustamante's art as a "melancholic conjuring of brownness" that elaborates a Muñozian sense of brown in which to feel the pangs of sorrow together is to survive "the hostile present" as a form of co-sharing into the world.[82] In asking one to enter such communion, Alvarado, like Bustamante, welcomes "to the stage a panoply of ghosts" and a monopoly of feelings.[83] And like Eva Margarita, Alvarado remembers that to conjure is not only to hold close the lost one via sentence, but to actively reanimate existence into every syllable, sounding out movements from traced over motions.

These haunted communions carry ghostly consumptions that emerge as past and futural affective production—contagious feelings that reconstitute genealogy as embroiled within systems of ontology and epistemology. A student of Muñoz's, Alvarado disintegrates the haunting, and unveils her own mourning tethered to Brownness, to Bustamante, her late teacher, and to the energies subsisting beyond ready understanding and consumption. In remembering, connecting, theorizing, and feeling, Alvarado summons as an extension of previous citational conjuring. To extend this minoritarian aesthetic practice as a kind of Brownness that swarms, repeats, and flows into the world, Alvarado retraces Muñoz's relational encounters between Mendieta and Bustamante; and in the spirit of kinship as performativity, and Brownness as citation,[84] ghostly choreographies ensue between worlds, remains, before and after parties—sustaining and returning the source across tracks and traces.[85]

In re-following these tracks, I locate Eva Margarita's footprints to find the methodological and aesthetic practices listed above prevailing within all her grief-acts. In form and content, she contributes to the genealogical and epistemological ambition to raise the dead by laboring with spirits to move beyond the earthly given. By gathering space for the living and the dead-in-life, she undertakes Sharpe's contemplation that "wakes allow those among the living to mourn the passing of the dead through ritual."[86] To carve out space for the dead, then, requires the implementation of certain methods, patterns, material, and cumulative gestures.[87] These memorials, often born from "the absence, lack of immediacy, or inadequacy of officially sponsored memorials to convey reverence, grief, and loss," develop in fugitive terrain whereby what is readily available for some is unreadily mobilized to pay homage.[88] From Eva Margarita's reiterative candles to Mendieta's and Bustamante's earthly offerings, similar compositional components echo across decades of minoritarian aesthetics: visual, sonic, textual, kinesthetic, discursive, symbolic, and elemental repetitions across cultural, political, and aesthetic assemblies. This trail of art by minoritarian subjects supports the deceased by advancing expansive openings through which to listen to them. In so doing, these cultural workers and makers allow "the living to petition for the dead, for interventions on behalf" of those still present.[89]

Of Spillage and Responsibility: In Vulnerability We Remain

Even when death presents itself singularly, grief is still politically and socially inseparable from public loss. In mutual grief, we rebuild and cultivate alternative communions. This is not to clumsily conjoin deaths across cultural difference and histories of dispossession, or across artists and aesthetic praxis, but to ride their overlying experiences "not in spite of but because of their difference."[90] Thinking through the singular-pluralities of death, Judith Butler reminds us that "loss has made a tenuous 'we' of us all."[91] In this conjoined proposition, the singular folds into the plural, not as a negation of unique suffering, but as a consequence of state violence rendering certain lives unworthy of being lived and consequently mourned. From casualties due to pandemics, epidemics, global war, genocide, and governmental sanctions against vulnerable populations, loss is imbricated in the contours of the world because bodies, albeit unique, are constitutive of one another. Butler attenuates on the matter by adding that "each of us is constituted politically in part by virtue of the social vulnerability of our bodies—as a site of desire and physical vulnerability, as a site of publicity at once assertive and exposed."[92] Our equivocal connections to one another also adhere to other forms of relation, for "loss and vulnerability seem to follow from our being socially constituted bodies, attached to others, at risk of losing those attachments, exposed to others, at risk of violence by virtue of that exposure."[93] Via our social constitutions and ghostly constellations, shared grief restores some quality to life; or differently elaborated, grief extends across, spills into and over, and as a result, shatters normative social cues to rebuild us in sorrow's transforming domain across plural ensembles.

Nonetheless, grief is not prescriptive, linear, formulaic, mono-political, or impartial. To mourn is to commit to asking oneself "Whose lives count as lives?" and "What makes for a grievable life?"[94] These questions lead to larger inquiries about the limits of the individual as a category of singular identification. If not all lives are worthy of being bereaved, then, as Butler argues, we must reimagine how loss comprises singularity, and how prior to any formulation of the individual, we are "given over to the Other" and "undone by each other" in a nuanced matrix of vulnerabilities reproducing the very constrictions of the human as category—a constricted construction imbibed with the possibility of dying all the time.[95]

So, how do we reconstitute the "we" that binds us in grief? How do we move past the idea that grief is exclusive and without an arsenal of social politics? Could loss, as Butler advises, provide "a sense of political community of a complex order . . . by bringing to the fore the relational ties that have implications for theorizing fundamental dependency and ethical responsibility?"[96] Knowing that we all experience loss, and that in this process we are embroiled in systems of desire and accountability, Butler proposes a practice of collective responsibility—not to conflate the singular within the plural but to advance a commons by way of mining through the particularities of collective mourning. To do so, one must insist "on a 'common' corporeal vulnerability" that disappears neither the matter of everyday violence, nor the dehumanization of certain humans, nor the unrecognizability of some vulnerabilities.[97] Understanding that the *we* is as tenuous as the *I* in this schema, Butler provides no easy claim for how to encounter one another but instead commits to being confounded, even if such confusion courses throughout the already shaky politics of language.

Like Butler, Eva Margarita acknowledges social entanglement by locating lines of connection across language, and translation, and the inevitable fracturing and fragmenting logics of discourse. That is signifiers, like flames, ephemerally evade and permanently mark. Butler approaches the apprehensions of language by sharing the following: "I cannot muster the 'we' except by finding the way in which I am tied to 'you,' by trying to translate but finding the way my own language must break up and yield if I am to know you."[98] This investment in communicative yielding is what allows Eva Margarita to reorganize the Freudian constructions of mourning and melancholia whereby loss is either successfully replaced by another object, toxically introjected forever, or felt without interchanging companions through language itself. For Eva Margarita, mourning is always more than Freud's apolitical assertion. It is a site of relational transformation, not only of introjection. It is also a way of becoming momentarily split open and subsequently remade by ongoing dialogic encounter, especially as a minor subject in an ongoing hostile present. To engage mourning in this way enacts an outward mobility for organizing internal motility, for grief is an errant reminder "that we are not singular insular beings despite capitalism's insistence."[99] As Butler empathetically puts it for all grievers across worlds: "You are what I gain through this disorientation and loss. This is how the human comes into being, again and again and again, as that which we have yet to know."[100] Being, loss, and unknowingness are inextricably linked and evolving, for even time and energy can be lost and reconstituted, leaving grief open to not just human concern, but making it a planetary matter for imagining our compounded frequencies and sorrows.

Another way of imagining this connection is to push against the strict categories of life and death that organize and limit the potential of coexistence.[101] Spilling over these narrow parameters, Eva Margarita's body of work (a)wake(n)s the dead to labor in life as communal agents of existence. This action involves making room for the inarticulate sounds across ghostly matters that re-enliven finitude along endlessly audible latitudes and longitudes. That is to also communicate that living in this way is an expansive constellation that does not merely begin and end in flesh, or via one sense, but rather evolves through a series of energizing encounters. These transmutations provide new ways of occupying the restraints of the human as positioned under the opposing realms and categories of the living and not still alive. Expressed slightly differently, embodiment does not take on only human form but deforms the body into formless formations of possibility that linger, thrive, and speak amid swirling choreographies hardly ever seen or known.[102]

Grief-work is political labor executed in the service of existence not because of its ostensible absence, but because it is embroiled in a system of a "tenuous we" that generates something other than *being gone*. In endeavors to mend collective suffering, Eva Margarita fuses sentiments, social orders and customs, energies, differences, and the communal from singular possession.[103] Or as Butler positions it, "to grieve, and to make grief itself into a resource for politics, is to not be resigned to inaction, but it may be understood as the slow process by which we develop a point of identification with suffering itself."[104] For throughout "this disorientation of grief—'Who have I become?' or, indeed, 'What is left of me?' 'What is it in the Other that I have lost?'—posits the 'I' in the mode of unknowingness."[105] But both the "I" and "we" are more than finalities of being, for losing, like returning, necessitates an ensemble of forces that blend these categories in ways we may never logically understand or know. Unknowingness might be all "we" know in our efforts to unfurl a common way through intelligibility and communicability, and Eva Margarita comfortably rides this line to labor from unknowingness, running over and into various feelings, worlds, social anguishes, and pluralizing forms.

To attend and tend to the dead and living simultaneously is to also draw connections across sites and stories formed in dispossession. For example, minoritarian aesthetics scholar Iván Ramos recreates a death scene and a public funeral for collective mourning by calling attention to those murdered and harmed through state-sanctioned violence, in particular via the governing parties that facilitate the Mexican drug wars. Enacting a version of Eva Margarita's "cere-mourning," Ramos reads the performance art of Mexican artist Teresa Margolles, who reframes spectacles of death by reproducing a drug-war crime scene for the Venice Biennale. Ramos suggests that the artist's installation reorients conventional constructions of loss, grief-work, and violence to upend state control over ways of living, gathering, and remembering the disappeared.[106] Writing specifically about the viscosity of public mourning through the textured consequences of blood, he refashions our communions with the dead—"particularly with the deaths of anonymous victims of drug-war violence whose names and lives we have never known."[107] In doing so, Ramos attempts to redefine the corporeal and linguistic entity that is death by activating revolutionary ways of mourning those we may not know and those who continue to remain unknown. He carefully wonders, "what if in encountering corpses, blood stains, outlines, and the debris of a murder there can also be figured a new relationship to loss and death . . . ?"[108] Given governmental negligence with both minor lives and deaths, Ramos articulates a way forward through loss that honors all death, even when those casually lost to injustice remain infinitely unnamed. Thoughtfully, he places pressure on typical forms of embodiment by reconstituting the body via traces along nuanced lines between life and death, knowing and unknowing, seeing and touching, marked legibility and invisible subjectivity. That is, to share, and, as Eva Margarita also employs, to conjure the dead is to re-remember the non-linear facticity of death, those named and never known across a series of residual tracks.

In such acts of intimate entanglement, the aesthetic is the stable link between the social, political, and psychic, where, in unique and common suffering, we grieve the state's *ungrievable*. The minoritarian aesthetic often operates as a refuge for the living and those always already marked for death. It leaves ample room for not only memory and memorialization to be ignited but "More Life."[109] That is to also communicate that laboring intentionally to respect the dead cultivates extended life in our quotidian strategies to rebuild existences through renewed meanings and repositories. In our doing so, the minoritarian aesthetic is not what happens after or before the revolution but is everything that informs and incites the revolt by actively deforming fundamental and inherited terms, forms, and conditions for being together. In shaping the revolt, the minoritarian aesthetic becomes the revolt's ongoing uprising, revealing the entanglement of performance and everyday politics and the inseparable contours of material precedence and unearthly evidence. Even when it appears that this term itself (*minoritarian*) may negatively situate agency, as the minor in subject demarcation is now the global majority, its historical and social power courses through individuation to reveal how difference differs in flocking assembly and attunement— here, there, above, and always underneath our shared grounds.

Consuming Grief: Desperately Injurious Rituals

But how far can the minoritarian aesthetic be stretched to reorganize our commitment to one another, to life and death as equals, in partnership, across everyday life and staged events? To lead us toward an answer, I turn to another grief-act performed by Eva Margarita, *Salt, Fat, Ashes, Heat*, a continuation of *Conjuring Stains*. With a live-stream on September 23, 2020, from 8:00 a.m. to 8:00 p.m. EDT over her YouTube channel, the artist reperforms how aesthetic spillage is a consistent method for politically imploring the dead. Directed by Breanna Taylor, produced by Mateo Rodriguez-Hurtado and The Brown Theatre Collective, stage-managed by Yarie Vazquez, and presented at The Tank NYC,[110] *Salt, Fat, Ashes, Heat* highlights Eva Margarita grieving her father's death by cooking, conjuring, and consuming his remains.[111] Occurring over twelve hours in her family home once again, this piece is an invitation to join the artist in her personal loss and to also commemorate all Black lives lost in 2020. As both a grieving daughter and performing artist, Eva Margarita confesses that "given that I was experiencing my own personal grief at a time when it felt that the world was also mourning, I simply knew I wanted to cook with my father's ashes."[112] Desiring to be with her father "one last time," the artist redefines the spectacular and ordinary milieu of one last meal together in the name of closure formed ever so carefully by reiterative consumption.[113] Of this wish Eva Margarita adds the following sentiment about eating and cooking as an anticolonial gathering: "My entry point to gathering has almost always involved food, and when I thought about putting together this piece, my immediate thought was I must cook the last meals my father asked me to make for him: Guatemalan *tamales*, rice and beans, and *fritas*."[114] She importantly adds, "My dad's ashes were the main ingredient, allowing me to quite literally cook with him."[115] As in *Light of Ours*, this cultural worker relies on repetition, exhaustion, meticulous and methodical care as a methodological apparatus to set the scene of a sorrowful desire for more life, affirming and also challenging the cyclical nature of conventional existence in this piece.

The artist swallows the dead—a desirous consumption that transmutes father and daughter to eventually become, at a future time, excrement in and for the ground. This choreographic action of ingestion is not metaphorical; soil harbors the dead like fertilizer to our entwined consumptions. There is death in Eva Margarita's act of eating as there is death in our inseverable earthly lands, enveloping communities in overlying circles of soil, toxicity, afterlives, waste, and their consequent sustenance of life. And there is, without being too dismal, another kind of consumption that warrants notice. In consuming her father's ashes, Eva Margarita also swallows pieces of herself. From the site of deepest despair, their dissimilar existences become further embroiled through intake and digestion, through settlement and excrement, and reproduction's very own reproducibility.

Eva Margarita's feast is not without further terms, conditions, forms, and cultural politics, however. Each dish incorporates the manual labor of generating a complex dish like tamales, for the long hours it takes to produce them is never done for one person. Traditionally, this type of dish is made by many for many to enjoy together over extended periods of time. As viewers remain for over ten hours, they participate in this cultural practice by watching the methodical mixing of ingredients, the gathering of pans and utensils, the creation of the *masa*—the everyday detailed actions performed when preparing large meals. Experiencing the condensation of time, they witness Eva Margarita fill two large pots with thirty-five tamales in each to then add them into a smaller pot of twelve—these twelve items become what she calls *papá's tamales*—made of him, for him, and only for her to eat. While the remaining tamales are for friends and family to join in the ceremony of eating and grieving together, these twelve specially marked tamales contain a portion of her father's ashes. Throughout this communal act of mourning with food, the flow between singular and plural grief-work manifests, not as antagonistic discharge, but as a circulation of care for one another that does not simplify singular loss. To demonstrate this communal aspect of grieving, she lightly dusts her father's ashes, "like a blessing," across the lard incorporated into every dish. In this way, "everyone is able to experience her father's essence."[116]

Although the community of gatherers feast together, they do not suffer the same aggrieved entity. The intensity of grieving may inevitably produce similar emotional conditions within this gathering, but only Eva Margarita wears personal loss to this last supper. At once formless, the father evolves through others into a new material agency through the very act of shared endurance, all through cooking and eating together.[117] A seemingly pleasant encounter over a heavy meal, her father's remains animate an archival production formed by ephemeral longevity. In other words, Eva Margarita generates an internal cultural storehouse of swallowed ashes that develop across infinite entities, remains, and lives.[118] As she performs these sets of haunted relations across durational documentation, the tamales themselves become "an appropriate representation of the accompaniment work that runs throughout this piece."[119] Accompaniment is not the conflation of experience or loss through bodily form, but a series of entwined relations that defy material and visceral logic across grievable domains.

And accompaniment is also not merely a type of understood social advocacy, but rather "a critical sitting, which allows one to acknowledge the affective forces that bring us to endure time together."[120] Deploying an endo-cannibalistic approach in *Salt, Fat, Ashes, Heat,* the artist makes and consumes three different meals that enclose her father's remains, so that while loss is surely particular, it also travels plurally.[121] To expose how communities pass on knowledge through a practice of eating and conjuring with one another, Eva Margarita attempts to transfigure normative and natural ideas about flesh, labor, and consumption. With no recognizable physical body of the deceased present, this cultural worker celebrates and mourns beyond form. In doing so, she complicates and challenges our commitment to minor bodies and flesh, asking one to re-evaluate mourning to include what cannot be seen or known in corporeal conclusion.

Put slightly differently, Eva Margarita contemplates how the politics of flesh is tied to remembering how humans were morphed and mobilized into living and working property and reduced to what Hortense Spillers calls "that zero degree of social conceptualization" but simultaneously persisted as critical sites for social, civic, and cultural re-conditioning.[122] Or, as queer-of-color critique scholar Amber Jamilla Musser sharply contends, flesh is never an immobile construction without social politics; rather, it often moves between categories according to circumstance and consequence, "between being a symptom of abjection and objectification and a territory ripe for reclamation."[123] Musser makes clear that the flesh, even when ignored or intentionally overlooked or overworked, is a site for difference's ongoing details and movements.

Specifically for Eva Margarita, flesh is not merely a body, but a vessel, a forceful container for immaterial entanglements, evolving within the methodological approach to conjure through the endo-cannibalistic design for compassionate consumption.[124] This cultural worker extends an intricate explanation about consumption that dissolves a capitalist undertaking of the term as she generously notes: "to consume the flesh of the other is to commit to their history and its reinvention through sharing, and this endo-cannibalistic (re)activation necessitates accompaniment."[125] In other words, as she also emotionally communicates, "it takes two, at minimum: someone to create the entry point, and someone else to journey through it. Almost as if to say, where you go, I go. I will break bread and bone with you, for you. For our love, we create a collective mourning."[126] Situated at "the crossroads of morgue, stage, and spiritual practice," Eva Margarita's grief-work indexes how we tend to the dead, the living, and all life energies appearing across co-presences by deliberately remaking stable notions of the marked body.[127] These sets of connections compel one to understand Blackness and Brownness beyond legible body forms, two-way relationalities, and comparative transactions, and toward the domain of knotted sensorial ensembles. Or, as Eva Margarita conveys of all her performances in relation to these terms, "my work explores and honors how Blackness and Brownness are porousness," and always already a coalescing everydayness that while seen and experienced can easily still be unfelt but consumed by other bodies.

Salt, Fat, Ashes, Heat is concerned with reformulating productions of difference, labor, and consumption that essentially swallow one into death as an entity of capital, and not necessarily an entity accountable to/for others.[128] These productions and responsibilities are interwoven within modes of difference, including the imperial and colonial mandates that dictate the very terms of race and consumption. Decolonial philosopher Daphne V. Taylor-Garcia tackles the interconnected constructions of class, gender, and race and the mixed-race *damnés* across the Spanish colonial Americas by underscoring the twisted collisions of movement, migration, difference, and colonial practices of subjugation.[129] In employing this decolonial framework, the author privileges an analysis of anti-Blackness and its colonial correlations to take on certain racist tropes in order to expose their significance in categorizing contemporary racialized subjects. Take for instance the trope of "Amazonian" cannibalism by Spanish colonists that has been consistently used to reinforce the savage-versus-modern-subject dialectic. For Taylor-Garcia, the question is not whether humans ingested other humans but how such an act established fixed representations of the people of the Americas. As she notes, "the earliest accounts of a savage, beastlike, man-eating people in the farthest eastern reaches of the known world are what identify and distinguish 'humans' from inhuman others."[130] This abstract, but commonly honored notion, between the human and subhuman, according to the author, has engendered the "conditions for articulating a coherent Western European Christian identity."[131] In doing so, it has also painted the flesh-eating savage of the wild as a counter-conceptualization to the modern subject of race and difference. That is to say that the modern subject's circulation as a stable identity relies on the savage-other's ongoing purchasable fabrication.

I turn to Taylor-Garcia's reading to think with and about how Eva Margarita's ingestion of her father's ashes reframes the significance of cannibalism against racist historical images that continue to gain legitimacy and currency across histories. And to also continue imagining how the feral, wild, savage-other, as positioned by dominant culture, transgressively counters hegemonic forces by undoing and recycling these powerful images themselves. This is where, I suggest, Eva Margarita brilliantly gains ground to re-govern the apparently ungovernable via recourse to loss through new grieving assemblies. In consuming, this artist-theorist abases the inherited responsibility to uphold those racist grammars that negatively shift culturally diverse and living spirits into deadened fires.

Funerary Textures of Suffering: Segmented Requiems

To be in the wake, at the morgue, at the people-of-color funeral, is to tend to the living and dead at the same time. In company with all sorts of bodies, from the one gracing the casket to those crying in unison, the funeral marks the spot where transition is held and emotions battle. Unlike the wake, where one patiently visits with the dead, the Catholic funeral promotes finitude—the covered flesh neatly buried and the spirit soon delivered elsewhere.[132] This ceremony presents a type of closure that in theory concludes suffering, but in practice, feelings remain as a deathless injury for those still breathing—an incurable wound that lingers across and through bodies.[133] The boxed body, however, as flesh and bones, is immediately a transitory entity that will, in both time and enclosed space, disintegrate. In this disintegration that no one witnesses, parted ways assemble more grief for those still living, still tending to a force "*only* known to ourselves and to each other *by* that force."[134] At funerals, everyone is both audience member and performer, engrossed like lights still glimmering amid an immobile box made of solid vigor and quieting authority. Those remaining in loss often desire to be like an inextinguishable fire, for in suffering we all become equally self-absorbed and extra compassionate, thinking ongoingly, when will our own fire burn out? Why haven't the dead materially returned, and what are the conditions for keeping on, which recondition the end of any ending's condition?

These inquiries do not remedy the internal combustions that make one feel like the dead have taken something with them, something one can never retrieve. At the funeral, we are all stabled instabilities, belonging to time's compassion. Thrown into suffering without specific location, and realigned nonlinearly in the moment's due, we yield to time. This suffering is both an invitation and an exit, a way forward into a way past, an entwined enterprise between individual and communal sorrow, or *a tear for a tear* given and received in an ensemble of entanglements, manifesting beyond Time proper. If the lost subject captures a piece of us in passing, and in turn we internalize them, or, as Jacques Derrida shares, "the dead are now only 'in us,' now only images 'for us,'" then what else is shared in these exchanges of suffering?[135] What becomes of the aggrieved in their unbearable loss and how do they see singular images as plural effigies? In Eva Margarita's case, introjected ashes amid already introjected images become layers of reproducible entities across linked forms.

If, as Eva Margarita argues, we are always already interlaced by inter-life matters and spirits hovering around, above, within, and beyond us, then her performances have drawn me personally in to grieve for and with our fathers. Often divided into public mourning versus private grieving, grief-work can seem apolitical, too personal, too ideologically charged, and indeed it is often never and always these things. Grief, too, falls captive to regulatory mechanisms that produce its legibility and extend its relevance as either collectively viable or singularly manifested.[136] Grieving "comes with silent temporal rules—both real and perceived."[137] Within all the tumultuous twists and turns, it is always "affective and embodied—sometimes private and sometimes public, but always personal"—always a special invitation to meet at the threshold of hauntings and disquieting sorrow.[138] The spillage between these absolutes is the accompaniment of conjure, where to feel the dead enlivened is to ask if they ever really left. This, here, is Eva Margarita's tender embrace of grief-work: the subtly forceful capacity to share suffering even as it endangers and consumes the living, impelling toward fire and more death. These are some of the spilled feelings I had as I attended my own father's funeral.

As the pallbearers gathered themselves to carry my *papi*'s coffin into the ground, I felt a surge of anger, shame, and guilt consume my body, not only because they were all cisgender Puerto Rican men walking him into his final hours, but because of the white gloves they wore to transport his body. These gloves felt transactional and distancing, a way to separate the sacred from the profane, a way to mark his entry into the dirt. With our lives still here and clean, unfiltered by finitude, the gloves morphed into the material grips of capitalist monotony. This, of course, is conjecture: when in grief, everything is an honest assault. In losing another, one violently loses previous representations of the self while living currently within a sequence of images, known and unknown to the self and others.

So how might our painful losses land us in para-grief, where everything is always already dead, everyone materially gone but still living to endure the passing of it all again, together, one image after another? That is to also contemplate that even as one consumes the images of those gone too soon, as Derrida declares, parents especially reserve the right to lift pieces of their own upon passing. In their doing so, the images left for us to see are never presented clearly or justly; they are not visible in their totality as we are neither entirely ourselves nor in touch with the lost entity itself. Now fragmented and harboring only copies of images, what we see is infinitely unseeable. At least these were my thoughts as I saw and felt myself becoming undone by holding onto images for dear life. Always an act of remembrance in a battle against impermanence, "grief paralyzes and cripples"; it endures as "it comes and goes in waves" of prolonging pain.[139] It is the copy of the entity's image that stubbornly lives within an already agonized heart.

In an act that was retrospectively injurious, I demanded to carry the casket and be one of two front pallbearers. The men (cousins, brothers-in-law, *compadres*) warned that carrying the front of the casket was the heaviest part and cautioned me to move to the center to hold less weight. I refused to move. I refused the white gloves. I refused to cry. With indignant arrogance, I placed my right hand on the handle, inadvertently moving the men to the middle and back of the casket with such conviction that other mourners whispered about Don Juan's youngest daughter staging a scene. In my mind, I imagined being beckoned to lead the caravan, for in this last act with his body, I might redeem our conjoined corporeality. My niece, empathetic to my indignation, offered to hold the other side of her *abuelo*'s body, and together we walked and trembled without blinking. At one point, I turned to her to see if she was indeed alright, for our drastically different heights made it difficult to balance the box. I used this moment to lend my left hand to my right, both desperately rechoreographing the ensemble of laborers and mourners, all playing their parts. We led the procession, not in typical cultural form, but we led him into the open air to eventually drop him into the ground with the silent desire to see him sneak out of the earth. At least, I remember telling my father during this long walk to his new dwelling that without fail, he'd have to muster the force to break free and back into this material plane. There was no other way to end but to begin again, and the choreographic authority from this moment forward belonged only to him.

The coffin, leaning downward and almost dragging to the ground, was unbearably heavy—our arms and legs shuddered, and the journey to the burial site was torturous. I could feel my lower back and legs shake so profoundly that my knees wobbled and knocked. This felt like the texture of grief-work and witnessing another man of color (our *papás*) lost to state peril, oversight, and systemic disdain for vulnerable lives always already marked for death. If he had lived a liberated life outside expendable labor, might this suffering have been less harrowing? Another one silenced, another one disposed of, another one who worked to get more work to become diseased to then die from work? I couldn't stop hoping for his life even when it felt as if the fire faded with each step across the pavement to the final resting place. "Grief comes like a suffocating blanket over the head" and even as one reaches up to grasp for air, the sharply drawn breath is still too faint to ever feel.[140] Everything is as heavy as the concrete and the casket; everyone is as out of breath as breath itself.

There's both a haunting and a political sociality to carrying a body to the ground that was already plagued by loss, a pre-conjuring if I may, that leaves open avenues for transgressive acts to assemble. I staged a scene of intentional politics that day that left my body undone and in perpetual longing. I didn't know if I wanted to drop the casket, drag him out of it, or jump in it, but I knew that his body was mine, not singularly, but a *light of ours* that I wanted to delay extinguishing. Like Eva Margarita, I wondered if every delay in closure could extend accompaniment, so that the adventure of death would be more than a series of durational torments—a co-opting of the means of production letting the intangible live on, or, in letting live, outlive their colonial expiration dates. Would my physical gesture transcend the planes silencing our inaudible gestures?

The day after the funeral, I sprained a calf muscle and was unable to walk without assistance. I bounced from the sofa to physical therapy for almost two months, unable to do much of anything but live in the denial of death.[141] My mother, convinced the injury happened because I demanded to carry the coffin, reminded me that it was the same leg my father injured months before he passed. Did this detail mean we were interminably joined? Was the consequence for staging a public scene the inability to move like his body decomposing in the ground? Or was this the first act of haunting? Avery Gordon contends that "haunting is a shared structure of feeling, a shared possession, a specific type of sociality" whereby "haunting is the most general instance of the clamoring return of the reduced to a delicate social experience struggling, even aware, with its shadowy but exigent presence."[142] Suspended by despair, like Eva Margarita, I tried to resuscitate my father through longing inaudible proclamations, silently recounting the departure as an insufferable extension of living. Did I eventually consume him like Eva Margarita ingested her father's ashes? Did we wear remains as injury, or were we now communal ether sharing space and time, in consequence, infinitely in accompaniment?

A Baptism of Fire and Infinite Flow: The Ongoing Visit

I did not know it until studying Eva Margarita's work, but my public scene was everything I needed to understand that the human body is both limited and limiting; death is not the body's afterlife, but the portal to immanent energy. And so, I rested, transformed, traveled in space and time, and in the process brought him closer, not as memory but as a spirit enduring across my body, injury, between and over everything I understood about tending to the dead, to my own living. If, as Gordon contends, "haunting is the sociality of living with ghosts, a sociality both tangible and tactile as well as ephemeral and imaginary," then my father took some of *me* with him, but as Eva Margarita explains in her work, it was done in accompaniment.[143] He, too, returned the offering by leaving a segment of *himself* behind: the injury, just the relational source joining departures and arrivals; and the body, just another vessel into the vortex of communal grief across a sociality of hauntings.

Grief is like that: it spills across lives, deaths, scenes, and haunted communions endlessly. It remains currently mobile and transformative even when numbing one into a deadened despair that resembles the aching fissures of finitude and the ethereal contours of immaterial energy. I return to the scene of my father's funeral often to recall all the details I must never forget, for in precisely remembering, he may reappear as a deep moan, a kind sigh, a tender touch, an affectionate surprise disintegrating the casket to reanimate spirits.

These recollections encircle like the fractal design of Eva Margarita's *Light of Ours*—flames turned on and off in repeated consumption and desire. Would he appear through the delicate gaps of light's repetition? Would Eva Margarita's father find a way to crawl out of her? If so, how would they both materially emerge? How would the emergence alter our remembrances of them? Questions are grief's prayer and testimony. And grief is labor that lives at the threshold of being untouchable and indispensable, manifesting multi-present interactions in which every motion is an everyday unfolding in conjure's name.

A year after consuming a portion of her father's ashes, Eva Margarita made the long journey to Guatemala to place the remaining ashes, secured safely in her personal urn, at his final resting spot: a grave site next to his own father's casket.[144] For Eva Margarita this act of returning home is as essential as consuming his remains. She candidly shares that there's incredible honor in being one of the last sets of hands to walk the dead to their resting place. In this way, her hands are privileged by his essence, life, and ongoing hauntings. Formed by historical admission, intimate meditation, united suffering, and intricate spillage, Eva Margarita's brave grief-work is always a personal and communal mission. Tending to all the energies that shift the fecund terrain of both life and death, this artist amalgamates singular and plural suffering by honoring their ruptures and overlaps. Across all attempts to cherish and amplify remains, she gently gravitates toward and from the transformative power of grief.

Has he returned to visit you since consuming his ashes, and if so, how did he emerge and how did you receive him? These are the questions I asked Eva Margarita when we spoke more than a year after the performance. Unsure of the inquiry's direction but open to being vulnerable, she nodded in acknowledgment, as if she'd waited to be asked these questions to have the opportunity to be with him once again. Silent at first but eventually trustful, Eva Margarita unveiled the following: "Maybe two or three weeks after the performance, I had a dream. I was in the office where *Light of Ours* occurred. He came to my doorway, and I said, 'You're here; you finally came. What took you so long? Why didn't you come earlier? I've been waiting for you.'"[145] As she spoke, Eva Margarita's eyes beautifully moved up as if beckoning him closer, or as if gazing toward the sky could surrender all matter in the form of the memory's materiality. He responded, "I'm here *now*."[146] But even with such an assured reply, Eva Margarita "could feel it wouldn't last forever." She reached out her arms to hug him but there was what she called a visual and sonic glitch; "he was a glitch, like a televisual glitch."[147] As the glitch began to fade, she could feel him quickly slipping away. In reaction, she secured one last embrace because, as she reveals, she "knew that was it."[148] I wondered what it could mean for her to respectfully grind down his cremated bones and flesh, consume them publicly, and then, in a private dream, hug a glitch, one that—in fading—was his final audible, haptic, and visual appearance.

Eva Margarita embraced a glitch; I hugged a voice as shapeless fog—the harder I squeezed, the faster my father dissipated. I shared with Eva Margarita that across cultures, *papis* obscurely return, and it is all so "unimaginable until they breathe again," until we learn to breathe again with them.[149] From a dissonant glitch to arid fog, they appear to remind us to be just "as careful with our lives as we are with our losses," for when we refuse this precision, we cannot possibly be "careful enough with what it means to bring something to justice by calling it grievable."[150]

2

Into the Still of It

Grief-Time, Viral Debt, and COVID-19

We are always looking at what to watch to ignore reality; this
is a type of grieving.
—Erica Gressman, in conversation with the author

Reclining with Venus: Distilling the Still

Just weeks after the viral pandemic swarmed the United States, avant-garde performance artist Erica Gressman performed *COVID-19/What to Watch in 2020*—an ominous new media artwork situated at the center of apocalyptic noise.[1] Streamed live on April 1, 2020, for the Experimental Sound Studio's *Quarantine Concerts*, this Miami-born, multiracial Latinx queer provocateur staged a grim scene in her Chicago basement.[2] Inspired by Alexander McQueen's 2001 *Voss* fashion show and wartime photographer Joel-Peter Witkin's 1983 photo *Sanitarium* (a starring image in McQueen's epic finale), Gressman traces and extends a rendition of their reclining Venus gripped by masks and breathing tubes.[3] Adorned in pandemic regalia, the artist satirically highlights danger under infinitesimal catastrophe to reflect an enforced solitude monitored by screens. For twenty-five minutes, the viewer's patience is tested by listening to amplifying ear-splitting sounds and watching titillating images set against the emergent pulsations of everyday survival. Within a tightening paradox of stillness among motion, attention is arrested through sonic panic and visual discomfort across frames. The decision about what to watch quickly escalates into terrorizing dissonance, becoming a reflection of our entwined lives under a global crisis.

What do these three distinct renderings of Venus, enacted almost twenty years apart, reveal about watching crisis as it reflects one's quotidian present in looping returns? In real time and screen time, mirroring realities realize material horrors in which the everyday becomes the staged event, and the staged event, a microcosm of quotidian cataclysm. Indebted to the social politics informing these historical scenes, Gressman turns back time to sample these images and echo terror's reverberations during global calamity. While each interpretation evolves from a specific political moment, every rendition unites light and sound to reflect relations across mediated meditations.

For instance, in McQueen's Vossian landscape, delicate and gaunt models walk a panoptic runway framed in one-way mirrors. These strolling mannequins gaze at themselves and one another, but never truly encounter the spectator's eye. Choreographed to house and techno

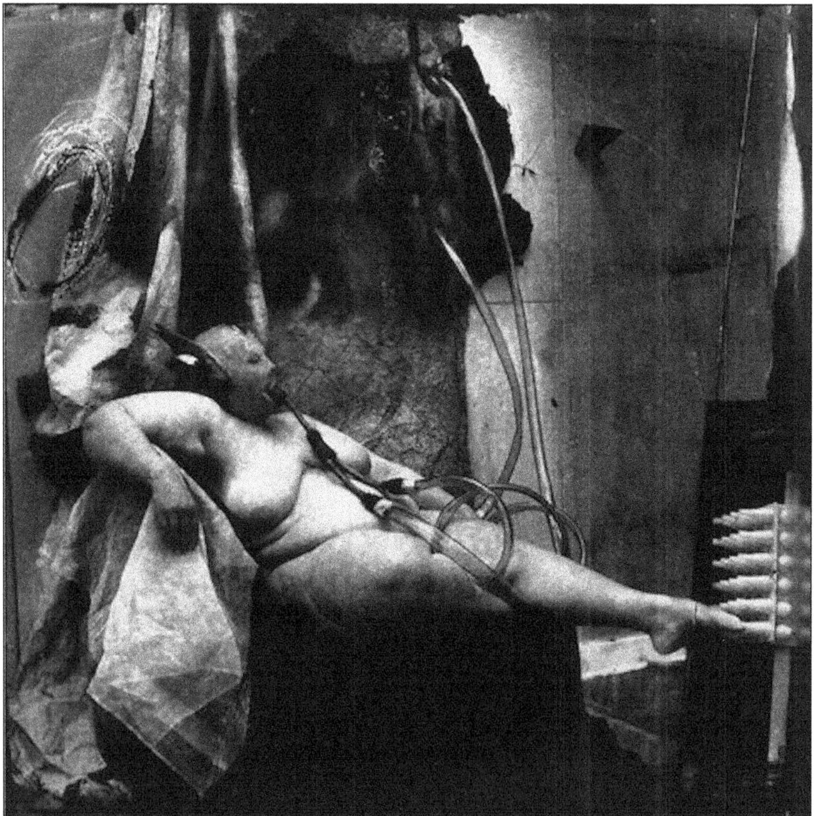

Figure 2.1. Joel-Peter Witkin's *Sanitarium* (1983), 3/3, 28" × 28" (72.4 cm × 72.4 cm), © Joel-Peter Witkin. Photo courtesy of baudoin lebon.

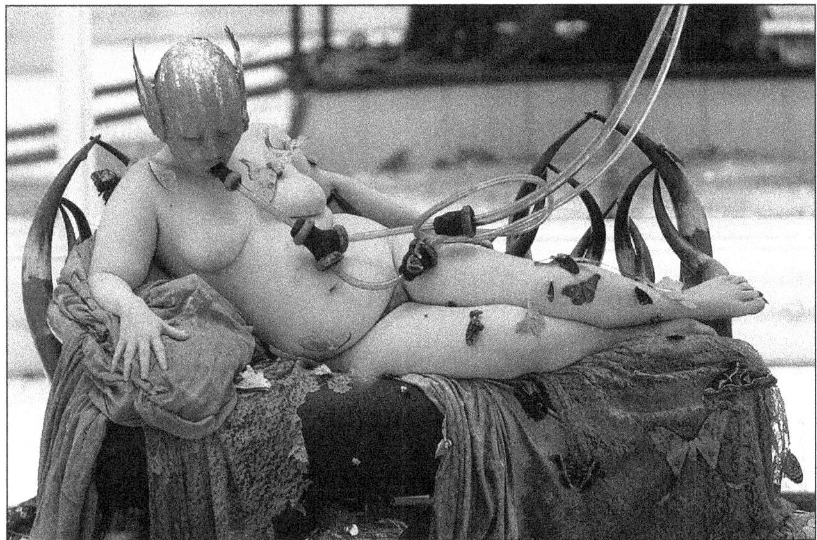

Figure 2.2. Alexander McQueen's finale to his spring/summer fashion show *Voss* (2001) featuring Michelle Olley and referencing Joel-Peter Witkin's *Sanitarium*. Photo courtesy of Hugo Philpott/AFP via Getty Images.

music, the show features towering cisgender female subjects dressed in falcon headdresses, feathered skirts, tree-trimmed suits, and electro-shock magnetic swimming caps amid traditionally crafted fashion attire.[4] Intermixing elements of the zoomorphic and nonhuman with high sartorial flare, McQueen's models resemble interspecies hybrid asylum residents strutting the line between sanity/insanity and nature/animal/human. Evocative of a psychiatric hospital, the runway is set with sterile white tiles and lights, compelling spectators to endure disquietly as McQueen begins the event two hours behind schedule in preparation for a spectacular finale.

In that finale, an opaque, still cube sits at center stage, enclosing a contrary model: a voluptuous leaning Venus reminiscent of Witkin's *Sanitarium* still-life figure.[5] In a classic art history pose, a nude model—Michelle Olley—rests in odalisque. However, nudity excludes the face, as a gas mask, joined to entangled breathing tubes, covers the model's head. With the centerpiece looking nothing like the sculpted models parading the sanatorium catwalk, McQueen's finale resists colonial standards of beauty and their deranged endorsement. In riveting form, the stationary cube eventually explodes and crumbles, offsetting the reflective mirrored frame to create connective lines through combustible projection. As we lean into the encircling mirror, will we eventually see ourselves, or only encounter mimeographs of one another slipping into finitude upon each frame? Where do we, as committed viewers, land in McQueen's *Venus* and Witkin's freakish outliers? And why does Gressman, a slender and androgynous contemporary minoritarian experimentalist, turn back time to re-enact this very scene with all its attached social relevancies during a pandemic?[6]

Like McQueen's incarcerating *Voss*, Gressman enacts a political evocation of her own by holding a two-way mirror to our entangled lives. Who are we singularly and communally as we see ourselves seeing ourselves seeing her? Who is watching long enough to charge the borders of inaction and activate the channels of still movement? In restaging this scene (reproduced from a previous image), Gressman holds the spectator's attention through quotidian sonic and visual dissonance experienced amid worldwide disease. Not attempting to offhandedly appropriate these historical signifiers, but rather to harness the political grammars devised within them, Gressman shares that "through these cultural references I perform my own interpretation of sabotage, decay, and panic by eclipsing it with a self-deactivated relaxing pose."[7] But this pose, as the artist also relays, is neither truly laggard nor relaxing. Instead, she plays with a self-devised concept of "leisure panic" through the manipulation of form to match the accelerated temporal rhythms of a borderless viral strain. Paradoxically conceived, "leisure panic" represents the dueling feelings of obligatory rest without resting, self-imposed interiority mixed with unnerving collective sentiment. Depicting a "leisurely" quarantined life, Gressman pretends to casually watch television "during a terrifying pandemic and presidency"[8] while finding it incredibly challenging to remain within her own body.

Like many of the versions of the leaning Venuses throughout history, Gressman lies casually on her side in *COVID-19*. Yet this artist is no art history prototype, still as any still-life should be. Following in the tradition of correcting outdated art history postures and social positions, like the Guerrilla Girls in their 1989 rendition of the *Venus Pudica*, Gressman twists aesthetic posturing into renewed political formation.[9] Counterintuitively and willfully, the artist portrays an antsy and fully clothed still

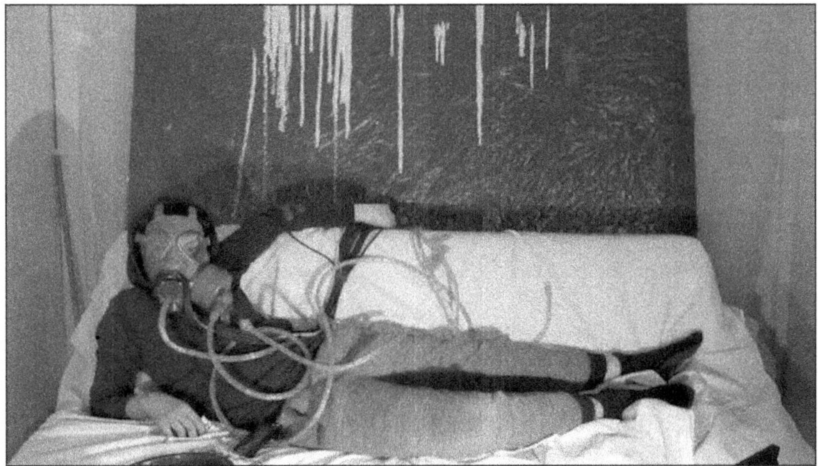

Figure 2.3. A photographic still from Erica Gressman's live video performance of *COVID-19/What to Watch in 2020* (2020). Photo by the author.

figure in seclusion. Sporting gray joggers, a red hoodie, and torn socks, she rests on a sheeted futon and stares into the set like a discarded athlete forced into house clothes. Her head is covered in a green and black military gas mask attached to breathing tubes and electrical cords; only her eyes peek through an enclosed windshield as a red hood veils unruly brown hair. Even with multiple coverings, this artist still normalizes the unformalizable through movements intuitively understood. Gressman picks at a bowl of popcorn atop a coffee table (kernels that never reach her lips), files her nails, and plays with a cell phone. With restless precision, she performs everyday activities to exaggerate the uneasy and common feeling of being locked indoors, doing ordinary things while attempting to extraordinarily stay alive.

With the threat of touch during a pandemic, Gressman remains inside to performatively summon the viewer into communal reflection. Lights flicker through the screen as the artist switches the channels of what appears to be a television remote control. As the lights shift in color from orange, red, blue, green, and yellow, white paint slowly falls down the wall behind her. Between dripping paint, bright lights, inharmonious sounds, and a fidgeting androgynously clothed anti-Venus trapped in a set, the viewer's senses are uncomfortably reoriented. Seen from within our own TV set, the sounds and lights appear to come from the television Gressman is ostensibly watching, but instead, the artist is contriving a sonic and visual score from everyday objects to multiply discordant stills into mediated cacophony.

Through mediatized manipulations of sound and image, Gressman controls what one sees, hears, and feels, as everyday items, like the remote control, soon double as apocalyptic props. Seemingly innocent objects are taped to contact microphones that trigger digital and dismal notes reminiscent of the pandemic sonic-scape—siren signals, alarm bells, speeding hospital wagons, and the terrifying hums of gasp upon gasp. Light-sensitive oscillators and a MIDI controller create a jarring composition for upcoming months fastened indoors for fear of viral contagion. Embodying "what it feels like on the inside"—the new interior and overlying landscapes of home, work, spirit, psyche, and body—Gressman entrenches one in dread and death through looping sound and image.[10]

Political propaganda adjoined, the artist imparts the feeling of finitude hailing subjects and encircling the living within a no-exit room as viewers simultaneously endure a similar adventure inside their own homes. Less than a month into our first global lockdown, this cultural worker telescopes time and foreshadows the atrocity of our prevailing existences by restaging the physical, sensorial, and psychological effects of the pandemic's imminent destruction of everyday life. This telescoping of time invites grief into the present, precluding it from being understood as an aftereffect of an event; rather, it functions as a co-collaborator felt over screens in real time. Arriving as quickly as the moving frames and flashing lights, grief travels like the borderless virus swiftly stealing lives and wreaking havoc.

Both mirrored proxy and noisy screenshot, Gressman is a simulation. The viewer, in sequence, quickly becomes an agent cornered in an entangled ensemble of mediatized debt and death under COVID-19. Yes, Gressman is one kind of projected portal into the pandemic's venom, but she is also a historical reenactment refusing to pass. Like McQueen's scenic design full of one-way mirrors, Gressman's performance threatens the normative protocols of peril in real time: *In watching her watching us watching ourselves watch this crumbling world*, who do we become behind the mire of mediatization in states of imminent death, crisis, and grief? Through the screen, this artist manifests how virtual connection supplants human contact during the rush to survive.

As an embodied aesthetic object, Gressman's *COVID-19* becomes emblematic of what visual and critical studies scholar Shawn Michelle Smith understands as the photograph's encapsulation; or, as she writes, it is always a "temporal oscillation, always signifying in relation to a past and present" but also prophesying a future, not merely anticipating one.[11] Holding up a looking glass to our overlapping reflections, Gressman engenders a poly- and arrhythmic sound video that vexes the presentation of self in this new everyday world. In displaying the past via reproduced images afforded new soundscapes, she offers the viewer the future's future in aggregated and culled stills. Each still as fragment becomes a frail screen for chance as an aesthetic mirage attempts to outpace viral velocity, and like involuntary muscle movements, we witness those caught by its venom.

Given the powerful currency of stills from McQueen's to Witkin's to everyday pandemic news reel shots, this chapter offers a series of *grief-time stills* (sonic, visual, historical, and embodied) prompted by Gressman's *COVID-19*; or aesthetic and performative snapshots that capture the vulnerable ways we plead with advancing loss to engage a new temporal grieving process. Prophetically preparing us for the perilous reverberations plummeting within this pandemic, Gressman, like many artists, foresees the future's future. To both survive and bereave simultaneously, pandemic grief lends itself as an obstinate force widening Time proper. For, as Gressman uncovers, grief-time is an indivisible duo on a tenacious spectrum. Repeatedly escaping the present and eclipsing the future while reimagining the past, this hyphenated pair crosses temporal states as a reconciliation with loss itself. To apprehend the temporality of the pandemic and its grief, then, is to surrender to time itself: to exist in the specter, tension, hallucination, and excess of crisis under COVID-19. Wreathed bedfellows, time and grief are incomprehensible (sometimes inconsolable) without understanding the conditions conditioning the other, precisely when crisis is both order and chaos, and death hardly finite. Even if, and especially when, the screen is both a limiting border and promising entryway, the pandemic shifts our attention from normative chronological constructions of time to a foreshadowing of its drive.

To revisit Gressman's evocative 2020 performance several years since inception is to re-record pandemic time and to rely on the still as a temporal heuristic for comprehending uninterrupted death and the politics of grieving—now, then, and always in anticipation. It is also to suggest that grief and time be analyzed as co-agents throughout this artist's work. For over a decade, Gressman has been crossing time and space, media, and genre to coalesce sound art with performance practice in order to experiment with embodiment "as a technology amplified by spectacle."[12] Fabricating "theatrical sets, interactive electronic instruments, and costumes to create a synesthetic experience," abstracted to mirror our entangled social and political lives, Gressman translates elements like sound and light by manipulating the body, a body refusing to ever be shown in naked form.[13] Building alternative technological worlds that resemble our own, this artist time travels, marking the oscillations of ongoing crisis and its time-warping grief. Grief-time, in this chapter, like the play on the word *still*, is deployed as an analytic for performance more broadly but also for approaches to studying everyday debt, disease, and loss within the context of a pandemic's aesthetic-life-world.[14]

Years after the piece's debut, survival and catastrophe capture new meaning. As we make room to grieve under foreclosing labor, we remain prisoners to future mutation and transmission, debt and death's debris, chronic illness and disability, and merciless and negligent governments. Despite the date of this performance and its dark satire, *COVID-19* is no April Fools' Day joke. Instead, this art piece mimics what we are and what we may become in our new quotidian practices of living together under global disease. While the artist foreshadows death, she (like the rest of us) could not know then that over sixteen million lives would be lost globally to COVID-19.[15] Yet she bravely embodies the contentious environment of the time by riding the line dividing ethical decency, states of emergency, the seemingly grotesque, and the threat of finitude. Refusing the spectacularism of the naked form, however, flesh is intentionally withheld, as this reclining subject is rather a biopolitical automaton, a sci-fi captive within daily pandemic world-making.[16] To protect herself against toxic infection, she animates and mobilizes the thresholds of restlessness, anticipation, fear, exhaustion, stillness, and grief under COVID-19. Preparing to stay alive and behold death as siren sounds resound as reminders of global annihilation, this anti-Venus shares a simulacrum of herself to access the interior copies of the viewer's multiple selves through grief-time's binding (un)still(ness).

Disruptive Fissure, Infinite Glitch: To What Is a World in Anti-Venus

From Witkin's terribly beautiful theatrical subjects in still-life to McQueen's moving mannequins and a reclining goddess, Gressman reanimates these controversial images to confront the tangled web of modulated existences within dangerous worlds. For this artist, the answer to surviving a pandemic lies somewhere between what she theorizes as "leisure panic," remaining still enough to still exist, and a kind of grief actuated by the virus's velocity and viral speed.[17] This grief, however, is not merely felt in consequence of or along normative stages of bereavement, but experienced immediately within the event, often prior to crisis itself. Grief's time, according to Gressman, is splintered. It courses through life like a sensorial glitch that happens before *it* happens. In returning the spectator to an event in two reproduced temporalities, she re-records these spectacular images as both distinctive moments and conjoined junctures in differentiated time. Images are record keepers and temporal mirages, but they also stare back to gaze forward, and in looking toward, epitomize a past. Yet the image, as Smith contends, "does not preserve a past that is stable and accessible. It delivers mutable and multiple pasts into a varied and shifting present," indexing beyond a trace and always prefiguring the future.[18]

By prompting one to confront the present by recording the past to foretell the future's future, Gressman foresees doom, destruction, death, debt, and disease, and, in seeing ahead, claims the potential within disruptive social fissures and glitches. These breaks and disruptions, while temporarily halting, are not unproductive interruptions strictly reproducing known social forms. Every moment in time is provisional and ever-changing, even if that moment bears the catastrophic feeling of forever. The interrupting glitch—a snag in time—cuts through the linearity of changeover and the singularity of social forms. Or, as cultural theorist Lauren Berlant notes of time and crisis, "politics is defined by a collectively held sense that a glitch has appeared in the production of life. A glitch is an interruption within a transition, a troubled transmission. A glitch is also the revelation of an infrastructural failure."[19] Failure, error, fracture, and a biting system hiccup require remedy and repair, even if that remedy is a "replacement of broken infrastructure."[20] Berlant notes that replacement is essential for moving forward but that repair should not take on the same structural forms. In deforming form's corruption, Berlant underscores how the glitch denies solutions to preexisting forms and rather rides its own irruption as an alternative path. Instead, Berlant calls for a "living meditation" that refuses to reproduce the same corruptible routines so that the glitch may be turned into alternative world-making practices. Invested in how the very fissures of brokenness welcome new forms of social life, Berlant advocates for a different, always moving, and living design for social reformation. Locking us into a screen to lock us deeply within ourselves, Gressman performs an anti-Venus reforming the glitches of crisis, one still at a moving time.

Regardless of novel intervention, every crisis leaves us in lingering debt to our own bodies, one another's bodies, the inseparability of worlds, and social forms—a chain of visceral ties longing for more time to be de-glitched into permanent replacement. Global postcolonial studies scholar Bishnupriya Ghosh smartly advises us to understand that "crisis is an epistemological cut in previous understandings of how things progress in time."[21] While difficult to pin down theoretically, crisis consistently breaks apart any temporal allegiances, splitting across space to provide what Ghosh proclaims is "a critique of the past" to expose how we have arrived at a passing present.[22] As well, it "compels new casualties for the past and future" even if and when "that impetus might well produce blind spots around what we continue to take for granted."[23] Ghosh provocatively asks: "Have we changed the terms sufficiently for it to never happen again?"[24] Or is this all just the cost of living?

These are just a few of the questions cascading across the artist's performative trajectory of disaster's everyday life. To reanimate the past, Gressman activates the future's future in combined stills, but this future's future, while an aesthetic destination, generates overcast answers. By casting into crisis happenings as they were, one will inevitably threaten the conditions of the event by dislodging sanctioned historical accounts to envisage a past by prognosticating a future to come.[25] At sparse odds with the terms of everyday life, the viewer sits in the seat of mediatized sensation as an embodied chimera endeavors to outdistance viral velocity and undo history's repeated stains. Attempting to outlive, to document, to share herself, to restore us into some archival repository that has survived the passing moments, Gressman opens the communal casket—letting in to let out, seeing in to see beyond. But this illusion, Gressman as "unstill still-life" and representation of a foreshadowed death, is known and unknown; a symptom of and a synecdoche for; a reference of signification that trails its own historical and temporal signage. Who is this anti-Venus giving herself up to thrust us into discombobulating interior landscapes?[26]

So, we sit, or maybe lean, and obediently watch the screen. In watching a version of ourselves, we inevitably envision those caught by the virus's poison, releasing a sigh of relief amid incredible sorrow. For in still living, loss reigns most present—just a tiny step away from death's door and grief's knock. While a crisis does not last forever, it certainly repeats to re-reveal that its terms and conditions have not been adequately changed or addressed, but in repeating, might have been somewhat reformulated. This includes the idea that although socially entangled, not all subjects inhabit the same cost of living under these terms and conditions. Some lives cost more than others. Some lives can never repay their inherited debts. Some lives only exist within the fissures of labor and cuts of neoliberal gain. Some lives are the mere sounds of lament caught within the glitches of imminent recklessness and brokenness.[27]

Or, as African American literature and cultural history scholar Saidiya Hartman notes, some lives are livable only through critical fabulation whereby a Venus is "both 'haint,' that is, one who haunts the present, and a disposable life"[28]—and, at least in Gressman's anti-Venus, a living apparition that foresees the future's future by mimicking figures of the past within the present. In seeing this way, Gressman cuts through established notions of the archive by sampling images, enacting a type of time dilation that swarms across dimensions and documentations. No easy task: this anti-Venus, dressed not to impress, reshuffles the given terms of repository by redefining co-responsibility. That is to also share that her home, like Eva Margarita's, is a site of safety and potential harm, a living archive and meditation of lived global time. Gressman, the archivist and performance artist, stores in the live the increasing threat of disappearance across worlds in real time.

Unwilling to separate political and ecological histories from pandemic conditions, Judith Butler, in the timely *What World Is This? A Pandemic Phenomenology*, meditates on what it means to share this world with others. Following a phenomenological compass that extends philosophy into everyday urgency, they demand a new type of global responsibility that invites multiple worlds to live amid differing bodies. In clever Butlerian form, they return to etymological positions to understand social conditioning. *Pandemic*, from the Greek *pan*, which means all, and *demos*, signifying people, extends into what Butler understands as "the people everywhere, or something that crosses over or spreads over and through the people."[29] Calling upon the exponential growth of the term itself, Butler understands the word *pandemic* to "establish the people as porous and interconnected."[30] By strictly dividing the lines between death and life, a pandemic reiterates existing social disparities across differences to refine human susceptibility. But no one is entirely immune; rather, we are "threaded together through infection," as the virus is resolutely borderless.[31]

Butler suggests that we—all linked through infection—can no longer think of grievability under traditional temporal structures. Instead, they caution us to see grief beyond those lives now gone, for "grieveability already operates in life as a characteristic attributed to living creatures, those who walk around knowing that their lives, or those they love, may well vanish at any moment, and without a proper marl or protest."[32] In this way, the pandemic highlights previous inequalities among the most vulnerable, disclosing how grief is not what happens *afterward* but what develops *within* and *toward* to inspire transformative ways of reshaping the terms of living. To know this is to understand the "unequal distribution of the grievability of lives"[33] and to recognize the inseparability of livability and equality in which those bodies still living safeguard the very conditions of living. Desiring an opening toward the world that includes multiple worlds and potential worlds remade, Butler declares that "we cannot really live without each other, without finding ourselves inside another's pores, or without letting another in."[34] Assuming no definitive place for individuation, Butler comprehends the *pan-demos* as the potential to share, to breathe in syncopated beats, recalling our responsibility to one another without foreclosing difference and present urgency.[35] But how do we carefully execute this responsibility under crisis when what is shared occurs through technologically modulated screens? Lending us a moving image of inseparable living, Gressman aggressively requests that we not only investigate the lens but wash over any illusions and delusions diminishing our layered interconnections.[36] To stare into the screen for this artist, like for Eva Margarita, is to refuse the option of looking away.

Through deliberate waiting, forced debilitation, and entrapment, Gressman advances an aesthetic threshold that, through the overwhelming racket of noise, becomes a form of stillness in motion. Requiring us to listen in detail to then listen-within, Gressman's kind of listening is an ensemblic process reverberating across time. It is a co-created invitation to capture those "disruptive fissures" that rupture the bedrock of narrative permanence.[37] In this cultural worker's mediated world, we make what we see together, and we hear what we live together. To inquire into grief's temporal delineations under COVID-19 involves surrender to not only one another, but to images, time, sound, technology, method, and corporeality, even when they present as unattached forms amid insurmountable interior suffering.

As a single shot in time and an entity without movement until moved into motion, the still, as Gressman extends, singularly and in succession, advances forward to pause the linear currents of loss into our interrelated future's future. Uncomfortable, and at times debilitating, this artist's work is interested not in holding one's hand through pain but rather in forcing one into discombobulating reflection. Uncomfortable aesthetic forms, according to scholar Jennifer Doyle, reveal something about not only the art object, artist, and the constitution of art itself, but our emotional capacities and vulnerabilities in a complicated and politically dangerous world. Or, as Doyle notes of difficulty as a productive aesthetic hermeneutic: it speaks "to quite fundamental aspects of being a social subject."[38] By creating from difficulty, Gressman represents social life, requiring us to restage corporeal relations of interdependency by looking deeply within to look deeply across, for what this world is recalls the world that once was and continues to reappear.[39] Even as Gressman remains locked indoors, *COVID-19* is an aesthetic act of communal agony through mimetic form, or we are all Gressman as simulation, conjoined as parallels, brave enough to thrust us into becoming one another, our worlds reflected across digital and global aggregate snapshots. This is Gressman's panoramic suffering in grief-time. This is suffering within a moving image. This is the collective gathering of sorrowing-together, especially when loss feels like a solo attack on one's tiny, afflicted world.

Let us take, for example, the technical characteristics of Gressman's lens-based performance that, in mimicking pandemic sounds and sights, pulsate a score that renders movement, light, technology, and music indispensable from the stillness of peril and panic. Although trapped indoors, Gressman finds sounds, objects, images everywhere, presenting one with not just an ear for loss, but an ocular gift for survival.[40] In typical artist fashion, all materials serve as nourishment, aesthetic exploration, experimentation, and intervention; for the aesthetic is inseparable from the politics it purports to uphold and distort in the everyday. This avant-garde performance artist and punk-rock musician is not foreign to creating musical compositions from homemade analog electronic instruments sensitive to light and susceptible to motion.[41] Producing live biofeedback performances (mixing science, politics, and aesthetics) for over twelve years, she has transfigured her body into different energies and entities in performances such as *Monster Wedding* (2010), *Full Frontal Biopsy* (2013), *Wall of Skin* (2016), *Tropical Frankenstein* (2017), *Limbs* (2018), and *Dissever* (2020), to name a few.[42] From animals, monsters, cyborgs, and witches to aliens and shamans, and now a biopolitical automaton anti-Venus, all of her figures comment on the interlaced constructions of sound, image, embodiment, science, and technology by unfolding the commonplace feelings of the racialized, colonized, sexualized subject (without ever lending flesh). The politics of salvaging objects, ideas, seemingly worthless items is also about participating in a willful act of disidentification and queer use—strategies developed to counter hegemonic demands for living in a hostile heteronormative world.[43] In recycling and repurposing everyday objects, Gressman regenerates valueless items into invaluable performances for surviving a fatal present manufactured by unpayable debts for minoritarian subjects.[44]

In all her performances, leisurely items become appropriated ammunition in which no object or sound is without purpose. Designed using a computer program and a drum module as the MIDI controller,[45] Gressman's *COVID-19* score blasts fast-paced siren-like vibrations on feedback, all sensorially resembling the feelings of horror, angst, despair, and misery. Enhancing the negative expressions one experiences during a pandemic, Gressman amplifies these wailing sounds through "an analogue instrument that responds to light waves of different hues and colors."[46] The lights, in other words, produce a series of high-pitched noises via "a color-changing LED light that illuminates the mood shifts of pandemic life, along with a new landscape of sirens." Stills, frozen in grief-time, shift in colors through blue, green, red, yellow, and orange to reflect the volume and aura of the score's feedback. These color-changing and flashing lights mimic the velocity of the virus, engendering musically and cinematically the current state of emergency. They also, as Gressman notes, abstractly mime shifting affective responses to crisis.

While the video lasts for close to thirty minutes, every minute feels like an elongated and sonically amplified encounter. As light resounds and sounds glimmer, "the frequencies of the sound waves increase its velocity over the course of the performance much like the infection and death rates of the pandemic."[47] This is to say that as the sound waves increase in frequency, the noise's pitch heightens alongside the quantity of waves. Or, as Gressman explains, "The waves themselves squeeze closer to one another over time to create the feeling of panic or anxiety."[48] Reproducing a state of emergency while living directly within it, Gressman blurs the lines between real time and screen time by forcing form to reflect quotidian content. In restaging the everyday as a barrage of panicked emergencies, the artist tosses the viewer into an assaulting threshold through form's details. In doing so, the dissonant sounds of a beguiling musical composition match the viral strain's velocity and visual peril.

Comfortable in the digital border state of mourning and destitution, Gressman stretches affective and sensorial edges by manipulating form. She courses through imminent death and prophetic grief to hyphenate us through a screen by mimicking the public's media consumption to perform lockdown. The screen as hyphen develops across the piece as viewers encounter the foreshadowing of a cadaverous velocity whereby many of us, just like the artist, will observe horror happening to others at the speed of light. Although presenting a casual posture throughout the performance, Gressman is no settled art object. This anti-Venus satirically disturbs cursory responses to violence, death, corruption through discordant sound and image. In form's defense, she describes the tension between normalizing danger and performing risk as having similar conditions to chaos and order. Invested in controlled chaos, the artist deploys experimental methods to echo political upheaval. This tension, in consequence, is visibly felt through the management of form in which the technical properties of the piece propel it forward. Gressman utilizes "light and sound to portray the sirens of ambulances and to comment on the state of emergency occurring regardless of how cozy one feels at home."[49] In doing this, she "attempts to capture truth in a world that ignores reality and covers it with conspiracy theories, the denial of science, and the prevention of care."[50] In an atmosphere inundated with fake news, the rejection of scientific thought rapidly becomes another viral hazard infecting the common senses/census/consensus. This spread of misinformation develops into another variant closing in and entrapping us all in the stillness of grief-time. For Gressman, the denial of reality produces instantaneous grief, shattering known space into splintered time through the very stylistic configurations of performing an urgent everyday life.

Grief-Time: Ineluctable Death in Unabridged Distances

In a viral adaptation of a virus, Gressman mitigates the presumptive parameters of time and grief by performing grief-time as an ideological countermeasure to normative fabrications of both. Understanding grief and time to be inextricable modulators for living, she metaphorically produces a hyphenated nexus of sliced but united entities through the manipulation of the screen. The hyphen, "never neutral or natural," works to designate multiple and loaded meanings even when it appears like an organic signal.[51] Occupying "impossible" states, often brimming with political and social authority, the hyphen unifies like a joint but also indicates social friction and historical tension.[52] In other words, this character divides signifiers while generating new ways of experiencing unstable and assumed terms like grief and time. In Gressman's piece, the hyphen's potential between grief and time operates like a dissenter to linear stages of bereavement and a consenter for reimagining loss as imbricated in controlled chaos. Used to join and/or separate, this punctuation mark indicates the opened and sealed cuts evolving from its very own generative fissures. In its vertical adventures, might the hyphen be able to chart an entryway for both grieving together and more interiorly intimate contemplations? Marked into relation across and between space and time, the hyphen leaves room for more than its inherent visual signification; it remedies silent pitches into cacophonous composition. Or, what it reveals to the eye it signals to the ear in possibility and invitation. In its disconnected connection, the hyphen, as Gressman understands it, allows grief and time (grief-time) to move into transformative cycles simultaneously untethered and tied to each other.

Take, for instance, the idea that in the silently hyphenated Freudian dynamic of mourning and melancholia, grief fills up negative space and noise. It is often described as a private and imminent misery that, similar to but not the same as melancholia, functions pathologically. Unlike mourning, an outward and public process that moves into the world to help the subject reconstitute the lost object, grief stays put to remain undialectically stuck.[53] Endlessly annexing suffering, grief is an unbearable attachment, a debt owed that can never be repaid. In grief, debt is always non-relational.[54] But what if this over-one-hundred-year-old mourning–melancholia dialectic, and its appendant grief, were more entangled than formalistically separated? What if the psychoanalytic distinction between the terms didn't matter as much during crisis, knowing that whether it is defined as a process or state, public or privatized, we will be ultimately rearranged, and as Butler suggests, reconfigured by loss into inevitably knotted engagements?

In Gressman's piece, grief-time is both a threshold and an aesthetics of the threshold. The artist performs a quarantined biopolitical automaton who attempts to outpace the speed of virality by mimicking our mutual lives during disaster, all while in leisure panic mode. Panic mode, even if sarcastically performed by a leisurely leaning subject, spurs decision-making from immediate disruption. This mode breaks open the presentation of linear progress narratives and the perceived incapacity to move into action. This hyphen in grief-time, then, might be understood as an invitation to act, sense, and move differently during states of emergency. It also might imply that time should not be removed from affectivity but instead be seen as leading the emotion into action and resolution. As the artist remains locked within a screen alone, and viewers remain to watch her pretend to watch us, grief-time could be experienced as both ours and theirs, yours and mine, everything and everyone in "unabridged distances" across a spectrum that evolves the moment one begins living and losing, for, in living, everyone eventually loses.[55] Unbeknownst to the stricken, grief-time operates like a bargaining master for hours stolen and days unencumbered across screens. Amid siren sounds, in the depths of despondence and stillness, we all experience its ineluctable casualty. We all already live in preexisting grief across preexisting times. We all ride the hyphen as mimetic and metaphoric line through and across lenses, an invisible divider, reflector, and uniter throughout aesthetic renditions of quotidian life.

Amid advancing disaster, grief takes on many forms, analogies, and proximities. It can quickly materialize into a futural feeling—something one experiences in the present or past, but unknowingly extends into another time and place. Here. There. Everywhere. Before. After. It lurks throughout time to morph into distinct energies across terrain and outside of any chronological order. From this perspective, pandemics must assume and shelter their own temporalities, often instantiating complicated grief, or "a prolonged, impairing form of grief wherein an individual gets indefinitely stuck in the incapacity to process the loss and move on in life, with a persistent yearning."[56] This persistent yearning is not like the seven stages of bereavement, but an expansive force field more like a "whirlpool of grief" that moves in excess of time—a kind of *loss timelessness* that reshuffles and reorients subject landscapes.[57] As an alternative to inflexible systems for comprehending loss and time, the whirlpool analogy relies on the currents of water (river flows, waterfalls) to reimagine grief according to the natural elements of the world. If grief is always disordered and turbulent, surrounded by the feelings of being "washed up" and broken down, but hopefully returned to shore again, then grief bears a time that also grieves.[58] This whirlpool analogy enables a malleable understanding of loss, one that, like a hyphen on a spectrum, shifts, bends, slants, joins, divides, and unrestrictedly reorients longing to account for feelings ranging from denial, frustration, anguish, and rage to an open-ended and disquieting desolation, sometimes felt through a masked anti-Venus. Grief-time, linked like photographic stills to create a cohesive video, is a nonlinear affective construct that vibrates in radio static to reverberate in anticipated feedback, precisely when our shared worlds evolve into horrific scenes.

Forever in motion and alive, grief-time expands in parameter even when it appears to be suspended. This is experienced in how the artist's musical score combines blaring lights and ritualized embodiments to hypnotize the spectator and, by consequence, metaphorically produce a metronomic environment that times loss into ongoing grief. Lights, sounds, movements in looped feedback, all created by Gressman, magnify a merciless aesthetic record of time's passing. Staring straight into the screen, this artist anxiously but forcefully confronts viewers to contend with and anticipate mortality across death's web. Fearing not our response to her aggression, she pulls us into the rapidly moving sonic and visual stills that recount isolated suffering. If at first death is a distant encounter, Gressman's aesthetic choices become our inconsequential and cruel quotidian experience under viral threat. *What to Watch in 2020* is everyone and everything pointed critically out into the world and back inward again, simultaneous pre- and post-post hauntings of death's residual grief as we attempt to stay alive.

While specific to the COVID-19 crisis, these looming specters of death are too often common conditions for those living with chronic illness, pain, disease, and disability in a chrononormative world.[59] With impending death underwriting various lives, those already susceptible to the deadliest terms experience harsher fates. Elizabeth Freeman and Ellen Samuels, in their coedited special issue *Crip Temporalities*, argue that pandemics expose and reproduce the parameters of crip world-making by undoing the ableist-capitalist measurements of time.[60] From waiting with time, slowing down time, borrowing and pacing time, the editors underscore the globe's forced departure from anti-crip time, or what Alison Kafer dubs the "temporalities of late capitalism," which include speed, accelerated precision, "productivity, capacity, self-sufficiency, independence, [and] achievement."[61] That is, "if pandemic time is crip time" for everyone, then "what if the temporal rhythms and their attached notions of normalcy, productivity, and community were forever cripped" and removed from colonial-racial-capitalist speedy mandates?[62] What if they were rather formed by the "myriad realities of bodyminds along a spectrum of abilities," a spectrum of temporalities and borderless bodies making room for being-together differently within new digital worlds?[63] As the pandemic quickly ran across space and time, the body's movements also took on new design. It became abundantly clear that survival required new pace and form; the pandemic rearranged the normative contraction of time and the body's obedience to it.[64] Digital time widened interconnection and extended a longer but slower, more capacious hyphenation of entanglements, that outside of capitalistic competition, enabled connection, care, compassion, and empathy.

For many artists who regularly performed live, the pandemic quickly shifted the terms of liveness and performance. As Gressman retrospectively notes, the global crisis challenged artists to think about the *live* as connected to being *alive*.[65] While it was a distinct form of liveness, the live video engendered a unique relationship to the audience, which included a more diverse membership. Seeing the aesthetic as an inherently political channel, Gressman communicates that traditional live performance is often framed by and shaped for able bodies—not merely in how participation is managed but in how the artist's body orients content. When asked if the pandemic has made us more aware of one another's time, embodiment, -ability, and by consequence more attuned to novel performance modes, she shares that crisis just reflects actual *lived reality* as an always already *live reality* for the most vulnerable.[66]

For Gressman, the pandemic merely amplified the ramifications of social disparity in full view for everyone to notice. To become more aware of and careful with one another through performance, Gressman advises self-interrogation to activate interior transformation. By looking acutely into the lens and into the self-as-other, she suggests that we must turn inward to advance infrastructural and institutional glitches into communal prosperity. A foreshadowing snapshot of our singular-plural lives as stills taken before all the numbers are tolled, Gressman's *COVID-19* presents the energy of disaster moving in future terms. The ongoing and incoming shot-reverse-shots of death, then, induce the widening paths of grief along a more elliptical temporal spectrum. That is to reiterate that grief is uncontainable; it lingers and resurfaces with subject, being, species, circumstance, and calamity across time and space.[67] Often particular to place and condition, but far-reaching in temporal scope, grief is no time and all time synchronously. Its myriad life is an interspecies phenomenon, which, at its core, is unique to the one bereaved but global in its execution.

By charting lexicons of grief, psychologist Dorothy Holinger espouses how forms of grief are constituted by individual consequence and constitutive of universal sorrow. Grief rattles the psyche and reshuffles the body outside of Time proper, laying bare the taken-for-granted and narrowly devised evaluations of mourning and melancholia. From ambiguous, resilient, forbidden, and masked grief to complicated, traumatic, and chronic grief, Holinger reveals how the structural and linguistic properties of suffering disrupt its emotive stages, phases often used to conveniently index loss, death, -ability, culture, disaster. Grief, as Holinger also notes, cannot be veritably cataloged into a theory of affective stages and terms, for its very linguistic structures complicate its respective time. In other words, how loss materializes affects how the bereaved experience death. Moving across common and less common types of grief, she reroutes the temporality of grief along a wider and more promising spectrum. At times, grief is prolonged or silenced into suspension; at other times it becomes the chronic condition that psychoanalytic thinking describes as mourning crystallized into a pernicious melancholia.[68]

While extending the spectrum, grief can also go unacknowledged to become what Tashel C. Bordere calls "suffocated grief"—a halting and unpermitted access to bereave under subjugation, further perpetuated by resource discrepancies for already marginalized populations.[69] If, as both Bordere and Holinger suggest, grief is fundamentally unconditional in its conditioning, then it attacks, joins, diverges, suffocates, transforms, and sequesters, affecting everyone and everything without exception and linear affinity. A forlorn captive in time's clemency, grief is always a stabled instability for minor subjects. A mixed metaphor, infinite analogy, and allegory for living, grief is too many things at once to pin down into one social order. Knowing this, Gressman grants us the still (visual, sonic, embodied, and abstraction) as a zone of mediatized intimacy and digital horror, transporting us beyond the everyday into the future's future new normal.

Zones of Mediatized Intimacy and Digital Horror: Transportable Stills

From the pandemic's start, digital images and sounds have inundated the everyday, creating chaotic and distressing stills that have paralyzed some, activated others, and forced many more into isolated submission. Often sensational in nature, these stills violently underscore the helpless ways in which we watch another pass on, essential workers risk their own lives to save another, piles of dead bodies await closure in hospital hallways, and some anticipate the end of the world while wishing against its demise. Where, in these images, have we been advised and compelled to share our grief as a necessary survival strategy?

Devastatingly haunting, these commonplace snapshots yield filmic and sonic scores of aggression, rapid and slow loss, disease and health disparity, and apocalyptic dread: all reminders that what moves now may ultimately be just one still in a succession to inevitable death. Yet stillness also mobilizes. It particularizes mortality's motion as one confronts immortality's pause. In this way, pandemic time functions as a looping intimation of "the overwhelming, ever-present reality of dying."[70] While images and sounds disturb, shock, "flip by as sensational clips," they also narrate stories about how being still, at home, is an antidote to death— yours, mine, ours, theirs.[71] On the flipside, they also narrate how death itself is the *eidos* of the image—a cultural atmosphere filled with an end and a potential escape, alongside gatherings with those already gone in which screens become "clocks for seeing."[72]

If we take the screen as a clock that sees, seeing becomes a rushed reminder to stay still long enough to remain alive, for as movement occurs outside the home, death emanates. As many suffocate by disease, closed windpipes arrive as someone else's asphyxiated grief, and someone else's grief extends into a chaotic lineage of global suffering. That is to say that stills, images, photographs, and sounds shelter cumbersome deaths and debt, often never settled by Time proper itself. For even the stillness of the pandemic resurfaces through other affects via the continuance of loss as "restored behavior."[73] The paradoxical essence of the image manifests both end and beginning; for in death, there is also rebirth and transformation.[74] As metonymic death, sonic images wound, but in puncturing, they also restore and transfigure.[75] Gressman's performative take on grief-time feels like this: reticent stills that in duration surpass the adventure of death to become a riotous and metaphoric scream blaring and heard in perpetual return.

Listening to and looking at stills are hardly individual acts as artist, viewer, subject, object, immaterial residue, and social context monitor the senses across digital borders.[76] One can be pricked by a sound or image into a sense and feeling, puncturing the audience's psychic life long after the aesthetic event ends.[77] What one brings to every image and mediatized event impels its far-reaching energy—an ensemblic encounter whereby stillness and noise resound in multiple ways throughout Gressman's piece. The animation of any still/stillness is incensed by the viewer: "whether or not it is triggered, it is an addition"—what one contributes "and *what is nonetheless already there*."[78] This potential affective piercing, or what Roland Barthes classifies as the *punctum*, acts as a wound, one singular to the experiencer but provoked by the entire scene and its cast. Enlivened by the spectator's ability to bring forth liveness at the intersection of stillness, the still (across the senses and genres) holds the power to pierce the spectator out of illusion and repeated mimetic abstraction. Put somewhat differently, Gressman's performance is a simultaneous introjection and projection of successive stills storing puncturing effects across lights, camera, and action. In turn, the viewer consumes these tainted veneers and discharges the excess back to her, back into entwining worlds. And in this ensemblic dynamic, stills summon grief in a time that perhaps has no exact time, other than beyond Time itself.

In every image and sound there is an anchoring death that gains mobility through reengagement. Let us recall that Barthes sees the still photograph along a paradoxical line of movement: it presents as motionless but, as he shares, "this does not mean only that the figures it represents do not move; it means that they do not *emerge*, do not *leave*; they are anesthetized and fastened down, like butterflies."[79] Even within this nondeparture and nonmovement, there remains the flutter before the enclosure—a flutter that in analogy emerges into the hands of those similarly sensing the gravity and timelessness of loss. Phrased another way by Barthes himself on stillness's movements across personal loss: "It is said that mourning, by its gradual labor, slowly eases pain; I could not, I cannot believe this; because for me, Time eliminates the motion of loss . . . for the rest, everything has remained motionless."[80] This is often the felt sensation of grief: a numbing currency without destination, but an affective ambush featuring the velocity of immobility. This feeling, however contradictory and incensed by motionlessness, is also a "that-has-been," harboring an ontological againness that re-apprehends the butterflies' flutter.[81] Inducing an orchestration of motion, the sorrowful layers of grief-time bring to light the illusory ways we appear to stand still while moving like the trembling flutter.

In satirically foretelling the future's future, Gressman grieves. Time grieves. We grieve as grievability grieves. The entire aesthetic scene presents the clock that not only sees but that in looking, moves into landscapes of attachment, indebtedness, and eventual rejuvenation. Across

Gressman's accelerated sonic, embodied, and visual waves, we commit to inseparable flutter, emerging through recourse to the reproducible, to grief as a kind of light to be repeatedly illuminated.[82] Gressman's piece literally lends illumination through flashing lights in varying colors— every changing color becomes grief's quickly pulsating energy. We may see these flashing lights as syncopated alarm waves hypnotizing us into ceaseless anguish: lights that, under Gressman's control, beget reverberating sounds in grief's resonance. Moving at timeless and unabatingly distressing speeds, grief-time is a durational happening, which Gressman embodies still upon still as we collectively anticipate the inevitable rings of death. Reckoned with indefinite feelings that like stills upon stills accumulate, recede, and extend from one another, under a pandemic, grief lives at the intersection of continuity and discontinuity; every recurrence, another gesture for memorialization. If grief-work is the deliberate way one tends to the living and defends the dead through commemoration and ritual against incurable melancholia, as we witnessed in Eva Margarita's cere-mourning pieces, then grief-time is a series of compounded moments that apprehend, aggregate, release, spiral, and re-temporalize like the seemingly immobile still.[83]

How still is a still, though? Stills are generally motionless singular shots that remain static in capturing a brief period or occasion. When connected in succession, however, their silence sounds and images animate to counter the idea that stills bear the flatness of death. To this end, stills are only as still as the stillness of the moment in time, and, as moments in time reveal, it only takes a moment to be a lifetime. Sometimes grief feels like this, too: stationary noise, arrested feelings, visual chaos, everything exacerbated by assemblages of death that Gressman precipitates aesthetically. Visual stills, like sound, are never completely without motion, as nothing can metaphysically be deciphered as completely still. Something, someone, some energy cuts across stillness into movement by the sheer force of gravity. Gressman's *COVID-19* supplies spectators with the illusion and abstraction of stillness by providing the public a still-living reflection of themselves in sound, body, image, and titillating lights. All these details produce the interior and exterior praxis of inherently interdependent lives. Explaining how the aesthetic is embroiled within every social milieu, Gressman discloses, "Like my body and bodies as stills, sound is a motion of waves, suspension, repetition; sound is always moving, always everywhere and in everyone, even if abstracted into singularity and stillness."[84] If sound is an omnipotent motion, then we are always in motion, too—an unseeable but inseverable connection to everything. Unsurprisingly, the friction between stills (sonic, visual, embodied) and stillness itself (including its metaphysical impossibility) sits at the center of this performance. The artist herself candidly shares this conclusion in our conversations: "I always welcome tension more than the context that rests on each side of a hyphen or digital border."[85] Laboring in the fissures of blurred lines, tensions rise from chaos into order and order as chaos across *COVID-19*. Polarities are intentionally discharged to eventually overlap as Gressman brilliantly mines opposition to divulge their emancipatory spectrums.

Throughout this chapter, then, I follow Gressman's aesthetic and ideological lead across the interplay between the still and stillness. In doing so, I do not intend to disregard the many courageous protestors who charged to the streets in response to the militarization of the police, the government's genocidal reactions to Black life, and perpetual racist, transphobic, xenophobic, sexist injustices, but to complicate how we understand the interrelated nature of stillness and movement, and the flat image/sound/body versus one always in motion during crisis.[86] The idea is to maneuver the still/stillness as a heuristic to engage the tenuous temporalities of grief and to advance that nothing, not even the still, is ever reclining in stillness. In fact, something as still as a historical moment in time reveals the accuracy of Walter Benjamin's notion of history: the past always interrupts and dwells in the present moment to lead one into the oncoming future, even if in reproduced events and signifiers.[87] In this historical dynamic, where does time recline? Does it lean like this anti-Venus? Time, like grief, is outside itself, an ellipsis refusing to pose nakedly, linearly, and, in this refusal, morphing into something altogether otherwise.

I would be remiss if I did not rehearse the luxury of stillness, however. Gressman's performance is privileged by a specific kind of spectatorship. Being able to lean back into one's futon (and watch another recline) is a sybaritic posture—a pose not everyone is entitled to perform or able to view, both under and outside of catastrophic times. Mediatization can often be a violent reminder of how certain realities are staged, portrayed, watched, and, in consequence, other life-worlds are made invisible, and forever uninvited to the screening. The mass mediatized subject transforms into an unseen but acknowledged spectacle/spectator on a screen functioning like a plastic-glass hyphen. This hyphen, horizontally positioned, remains within the frame from axis point to axis point, directing, even if unconsciously, modes and possibilities of relation. Forming relations both behind the camera and through the camera's multiple projections, this hyphen (as a type of screen) assumes the material conditions outside, behind, above, and around it. And we, as spectators, introject the splicing symbol projected as unifier, as an interlocking modality for life under crisis.

Drowning in apocalyptic compositions, we have learned to survive a seemingly natural disaster at the sounds, images, movements of tyranny amid virality. Insecure leaders and governments let the deaths of the most vulnerable become a measuring stick for valuing all life. As one attempts to stay alive, a new model for living develops as stills upon stills (often on loop) across news channels modulate how to survive, witness, and quietly escape death while seeing others die at accelerated rates. Hardly any of these images and sounds, however, grant the space and insight to render acts of collective grief valuable and necessary.[88] Despite this, Gressman offers a type of redress to such solitary brutality. At the edge of existence, she pays her debt to herself, to us, to our colliding worlds in a series of tensions tempering the collective ear and communal eye.

Like the siren sounds resonating throughout the day and night, *COVID-19* presents our quotidian mediatized debt—to ourselves, to one another, to governance, to loss itself in which we are prompted to grieve not in relational flesh, but in mediatized prophetic time. By creating a visceral experience that reorders the politics of touch and the very politics of politics by displaying automations for emotional containment and release, Gressman portrays a digital grief in futuristic debt, all indebted to time's illusions. Stills upon stills capture our collective feelings of helplessness, suffocation, anger, sadness, pain, dread, shame, despair, and always an extending and halting grief that both unites and dislocates, that reaches forward to turn back. While we conspire to respire together, one breath as your breath and mine, Gressman unveils the delicate vulnerabilities of collective and intentional breathing. For example, her gas mask ratifies her own life by consequently protecting others, but it is also an object expressing another type of indebtedness that warrants no reserve. In cutting off shared breath, the artist presents the limits of touch and respiration as every air droplet becomes a constant reminder of potential loss, of "suffocated grief," and new ways of both coexisting and perhaps dying.[89]

The Intermediacy of Viral Bodies: Objects Formed in Social Attachment

News of the coronavirus swept across US television sets and social media outlets around the time of Gressman's performance. At the same time, uninstructed and biased politicians used the unpayable debt of others to divert the emergency at hand.[90] If at first the pandemic was described as a silent one, it quickly enacted "the metaphor of the 'perfect storm'"—a cyclone capturing "the convergence of structural inequalities" and its "inhumanely authored trajectory."[91] Or, as medical anthropologist Kimberly Theidon notes, the "chronicle of a perfect storm" is intentionally "foretold by considering the possibility of holding Donald Trump and his collaborators criminally negligent, on a scale that might warrant a judgment of crimes against humanity."[92] In a move reminiscent of historical policies that advanced white racial purity, Trump vowed to rescue (white) US Americans who were seen as potential innocent victims of this virus. This, coupled with herd immunity, instantiated contemporary forms of what Theidon calls a "eugenics mindset," working to further cement a politics of disposability.[93] Through the material dispossession of certain communities vis-à-vis the materiality of labor, unpayable debt remeasured those essentially marked by death. Once again, the double bind of vulnerability reared its head to remind one of its metaphysical variances. Rapidly, the coronavirus brought to light racism, xenophobia, and anti-Black death as epidemic, sweeping infections binding us in reticent and assaulting disclosure. To ensure that the strongest survive, the disposables and those molded by and into unpayable debt labor to secure someone else's life at the expense of their own. The pandemic unveiled the foundational elements of most storms through the collision of underlying conflict and the perpetual disregard for climate—neither one inseparable from the systems surrounding the other across political ventures.

This virus, and its powerful mutations, continues to test our humanity, compassion, and values to consistently show how "China's dilemma" is always already *our* own indebted concern.[94] That is to say that colonizing logics can never be equitably relational in nature—one's valueless death is often someone else's racialized gain. In the collective venture to outlive this pandemic, we recognize viruses as accommodating political conditions even as they are enlivened by our very own bodies.[95] Their speedy vitality and virality notwithstanding, viruses, according to the consensus of scientists, are not inherently alive.[96] They require the "machinery of other organisms" to replicate and "affect the health and behavior of other organisms."[97] Intracellular parasites, viruses require a recognizable host cell to reproduce. Because viruses are without cells, to be alive they need an already living thing to propel them forward in spreading, mutating, and potentially exterminating life in the process. This, unfortunately, leaves no death invalidated by certain regard for life, even if securely locked indoors.

Gressman's performance prophetically epitomizes the powerful and speedy transmission of the virus. Let us recall that during her performance wet paint spills from the wall behind her and the vertical drips are meant to resemble the everyday colors of violent precarity. Sounds swell against a black backdrop covered in dribbling white paint that the artist describes as "dripping down over time to eventually cover [a light-triggered sound machine] and change the audible experience as time progresses" throughout the performance.[98] But the white paint is also an admonition of white privilege, indicating the multiple racialized epidemics lingering across place. Whiteness, for Gressman, is an exercise in property, or "white supremacy, capitalism, and colonization evolve by leaving Black and Brown communities even more vulnerable to illness, death, poverty, eviction, and police violence than they already were before the pandemic."[99] Metaphorically and metaphysically, Gressman prepares the spectator for what continues to befall: mass death, anti-Black violence and casualty, incurable disease, governmental corruption and terrorism, fake news, and global dissent. As Gressman foretells of loved ones, neighbors, and civilians disappearing at alarming rates, she metonymically encircles us in Barthes's perception of death, or the ineluctability of "*having-to-die*, which is exactly what it means to be mortal."[100] But she also invites us to become "with and against the tension embedded in the violence of a pandemic" to engender "a performative scene on screen in which the relational conditions of existence surface their reverberatory urgencies," even if, and especially when, the lack of touch is the common measure for affection.[101]

The virus's menace is indivisible from the governmental injustices plaguing the globe and excelling at the expense of defenseless constituents. Gressman's piece parodies quotidian brutalities while surviving the very dreadful scene one is actively enduring. To do so she relies on "sound and light as a synesthetic method for universally forging these images and sounds into our memories."[102] By mitigating how one standardizes and responds to crisis, she warns against careless responses to one another and aesthetic forms. Yet no matter how much one deformalizes the pandemic's context, one still lives under its reign, captive to whichever way it mutates and garners speed. Unable to "outrun the veracity of the strain," our "vulgar conception of human exceptionalism," presented by Trump and global colleagues, presumes to monitor its velocity and poison.[103] Nevertheless, "viruses, like pollution, work rhizomatically and galactically; they do not abide by the human rules of time and spatial order."[104] Like grief, "the virus's only border is its symptoms," at times dormant, fleeting, asymptomatic, and deferred, but, like the *punctum*, always already there.[105] Against the screen, one becomes the mortal and immortal speed of global catastrophe; and unlike the speedy movements of the virus, one must try to remain still enough to outpace the vibrational impulses of contagion. To intimately know the virus is to be an expeditious tormentor skilled in the art of universal mobility and attack.

Describing the universal liability of most viral strains in all her work, Ghosh demands a reassessment of the virus's global position. The virus, for Ghosh, is "an intermediate object" or a "*hyper*-dependent object, unable to survive in the unhuman form without a host."[106] As an "object formed in attachment," it is also one "constituted by debt."[107] This debt is galvanized by the verifiable truth that we are all "caught in a force field marked by adversarial relations" in which we have rarely triumphed over this "timeless antagonistic war" with viruses.[108] In recounting a nonlinear narrative of the virus as hyper-object, Ghosh stresses how *its needs* demonstrate *our connected neediness*—all joined in cycles of looming contact (and contract) that releases few from its hold. The expendability of certain life forecloses the advancement of others', encouraging the threaded positions of virality, accelerated death, and the loss of vulnerable lives. Or, as Ghosh insightfully remarks about the virus, "it comes; we receive."[109] It deliberately disrupts, invades, attacks, and conquers via a process of recalcitrant indebtedness; this inimical relationship makes one a reactive informant, catching on to catch the end—a state of perpetual vulnerability that, however informed, still invades any attempt to escape its outline.

Butler similarly extrapolates on the entwined compositions of viruses (in particular, the coronavirus), vulnerability, and debt. In an interview with George Yancy during the start of the pandemic, Butler unpacks the politics of vulnerability and unpayable debt amplified by this disaster. Speaking around the same time as Gressman's new media performance, Butler travels the silhouettes of grief-time under mass death to demonstrate how the pandemic reveals the hidden and layered meanings of vulnerability. From a global vulnerability to vulnerable populations, Butler depicts how the coronavirus produces a universal susceptibility to death. And, by consequence, it highlights the most vulnerable of communities with the latter positionality rendered as such by ongoing oppressive imperial, colonial, racial, and economic logics. If at once, one is universally defenseless to the virus "because everyone is vulnerable to viral infection from surfaces or other human beings without establishing immunity," Butler imparts how vulnerability is predetermined, making the already liable more vulnerable under viral threat.[110] Offering philosophical lessons for how to observe vulnerability, Butler homes in on how "it describes a shared condition of social life, of interdependency, exposure and porosity" and also "names the greater likelihood of dying, understood as the fatal consequence of a pervasive social inequality."[111] Under global unrest, Butler presents the double bind of vulnerability: "impressionability and porosity define our embodied social lives," for we intimately share breath, but plural breath does not ameliorate inherited indebtedness.[112]

United by universalities augmenting disparities, Butler establishes the category of "the unpayable"—the most vulnerable of defenseless groups whereby "their entire future is structured by their unpayable debt: it becomes a form of bondage, infinite and without end."[113] Existing prior to the rise of the pandemic, this debt further exposes how crisis amplifies injustice. While not infinite, crises magnify extant abuses and violations of laws, policies, and ethics caused by racist, sexist, and colonial grammars that replicate violent histories. These debts, Butler clarifies, are without recourse; in owing, one becomes fodder for those privileged enough to survive death. Underneath this unpayable debt dwells the inner workings of colonial, racial, and capitalist sciences of reasoning that labor to invalidate the facts of the material world and expose how a natural disaster is anything but natural.

If death is the greatest of equalizers, how do minor subjects settle their unpayable debt in grief-time? Butler's notion of "unpayable debt" compels one to search for this answer, but to also keep asking, like Gressman throughout her art, to what or whom is one ultimately indebted under grief? Singular feelings? The lost subject? Law's lack? The Other? The inanimate other? The temporality of death (life!) itself? The future's future in aggregated stills? The virus as intermediate, hyper, or para object? These questions lurk throughout this chapter as hard facts against the brewing disasters created by not only fake news, but an avoidance of grief's temporality under growing social and political infection.

Infection as Intimate Affection: Aesthetic Borders of Virality

Potential contact is never without indebtedness. In debt, there is always grief—something given, taken, and ultimately owed. Minoritarian aesthetics scholar Joshua Chambers-Letson teases out these kinds of debt in his analysis of artist Felix Gonzalez-Torres's body of work. In conversation with the AIDS virus and the consequent mourning rituals undertaken on behalf of those lost to the epidemic through governmental neglect and corruption, Chambers-Letson understands Gonzalez-Torres's oeuvre as a living entity, "mutable and adaptable to the conditions in which it existed." Metaphorically taking on the life of the virus to outpace it,[114] Gonzalez-Torres ropes the spectator in through various viral strategies that traverse bodies themselves. From bodies of thought to bodies as corporeal flesh, and bodies of the law to the embodiment of love, Chambers-Letson expresses how the multiple meanings of the term *body* operate throughout the artist's "alive and interactive" oeuvre, spreading across viewers like the virus it labors to demystify.[115] "Rather than regarding the body's susceptibility to infection as a weakness, Gonzalez-Torres structured his artwork to function as carriers of his viruses."[116] Or, "bodies—as sites of infection and potential vectors for infection—became necessary components" of his entire body of work.[117] As the viewer viscerally engages with Gonzalez-Torres's symbolically contaminated objects, they also commit to sharing infection and intimate affection. Intimate affection, as the artist predicts, however, is transactional; to give is to take and to take is to owe something in return: these exchanges are never immune to the possibility of contamination and death.

This queer Cuban American artist, like Gressman, withholds his flesh in all his work. Gonzalez-Torres (as lover, widower, civilian, queer subject) morphs into items and objects such as candy, paper, beads, and lights that he welcomes the audience to touch, hold, keep, carry, and recultivate in looping extensions of grief-time.[118] In doing so, the artist summons one not only to experience the loss of his lover to a deadly virus via a piece of candy, but to admit, even if privately, that anyone, at any time, can be swallowed by death, infection, disorder, and grief.[119] Every object the viewer handles (including the candy wrappers, candy pieces, and sheets of blank paper) is a still piece moved into motion by the audience's engagement. And every item is likewise an inanimate object made animate through bodies eventually changing shape to become other. Touch is the possibility of contagion, death, or consequential rebirth, but always infinite love across multidimensions.

For Gonzalez-Torres, to love is to refuse to see death as finite. Instead, the possibility of viral infection, even if metaphorical, is an act of continuance, an exercise in staying alive as empathetic entities against violence and end. But it is also a form of singular pain shared out in a practice of communal care. The artist's body of work moves us to see how we are ultimately responsible for one another, and by consequence mutually indebted within and to our shared existences. Grief becomes caught in this knotted encounter as engaging it "reciprocally is an ancient form of mutual aid" that bears witness to how one loss encircles mass death and how mass loss is connected to individual pain.[120] While one shelters catastrophic loss in solitary ways as Gonzalez-Torres and Gressman reveal, the "universal expressions" of grief apprehend us in our elaborate suffering.[121] Even when one's name is foreign, as Butler announces, "we are given over from the start to a world of others," we are given over to one another[122] in still briefs and still lives over and over again.

Although it is a singular window into a quarantined life, Gressman's performance epitomizes an image of collective sorrow in which grief becomes both ever-present and still to come. Grief, as a "deep and powerful emotion" cuts across many species like a relentless "chameleon"—a timeless and animated telescope, universal, intricate, "acute or severe . . . like intersecting circles in a Venn Diagram."[123] And grief "whirls like wind" and "reorients desires, sometimes fruiting in the form of lush antiproductivity" and sometimes initiates "anhedonia and joy, fug, and lucidity, desire and depression, to an alienated life."[124] It impresses analogously. It is a foreshadowing lens, a whirlpool, a chameleon, merging circles, eaten candy and leftover wrappers, mediatized mourning, and a reproducible still characterized by decades in decay. While the pangs of grief may sting singularly, its venom is felt cosmically across a series of analogies and interwoven social realities. Difficult to announce, name, and pin down, grief is many opposing elements, feelings, and forces all at once.

Leaving spectators with a sense of discomfort, terror, and blaring anxiety, Gressman's *COVID-19* is no musical score for the light-hearted, or those who imagine an easy escape from disease and death.[125] Indefinitely affirming Butler's reassessment of global vulnerability, Gressman models the sonic score of mortality—not as we wish it to be but as it is. As we attempt to survive a pandemic, under racism as epidemic, anti-Black death, global protest, historical health disparities, and the rise of fascism, whose emergency is now just everyone's quotidian survival strategy against the borderless ontology of viral strains? Whose stillness is and isn't someone else's motion into death?

Gressman creates and augments the arrhythmic pulse of inharmonious worlds. Moving viewers toward the dissonant forces at play in our current reality, Gressman describes *COVID-19* as an audible piece "that one should not want to relax to or listen to for pleasure." For this cultural worker, the performance "is meant to alarm and jolt the audience into understanding the facts and severity of the matter."[126] While she mimics the position of stillness corporeally, her musical composition presents the continuous and discontinuous chords of noise. Manipulating senses and antagonizing moods, Gressman disorients the viewer to then alert them to the discordant vibrations that unsettle any relaxed or resting body. In doing so, she forces the rapid progression of sounds to counter the supposed stillness of images. This tension, unbeknownst to the spectator on zooming in, extends into a conflictual assault across bodies and minds trying ever so desperately to abide by life's biting violations. Such confrontations enable Gressman to compose a series of minor moods and keys that foster a "general atmosphere of horror"[127] prompted by negligent empires and their gluttonous emperors. In an endless horror movie instigated and perpetuated by the Trump administration, along with his insecure national leader co-conspirators, minor subjects, for Gressman, inevitably always die first. The artist communicates that as the coronavirus spreads and terrorizes, public figures still continue to operate without regard for certain life in order to violently keep apprehending and destroying the most vulnerable.[128] This disregard for certain life extends viral contagion into social and cultural contamination, or it infects the political body and illustrates "disorder by disrupting economic activity, casting doubt on the effectiveness of political leaders, and potentially bringing down governments," but also exposes "how dead bodies are treated" and grieved as ideological responses to ongoing transnational disparity.[129]

A Quarantined Life: Stillness's Motion in Temporal Deluge

If grief is always a chameleon, changing color and shape like the speed of light waves propagating through material, its time is often both a repeated reencounter and foreshadowing.[130] These temporal shifts are where one experiences the stillness of the still as both an analytic and a coping mechanism for feeling the anguish of death under open-ended loss. Like the virus as a transitional object constituted by debt, global collective needs quickly became indebted to Zoom, FaceTime, Skype, or WhatsApp, some even forced to watch their loved ones die at the speed of a singular still during this ongoing pandemic.[131] Unfixed to one simile, grief is *like* so many other unnamed and unseen things across sites. In being able to present like everything else anywhere, its time particularizes to reframe the conditions of the living amid the recently lost.

Gretchen Eick describes this never-ending grief as an exercise in intentional stillness in her prose poem "Night Quarantine." Written during the first year of the pandemic, Eick waits with grief in a temporal scene that throws one into the darkness of death.[132] She describes in poetic verse what Gressman illuminates in sound and image: the very termination of sunlight by dropping one into the obscurity of solitude, artificial lights, and mediated stillness among the dying. The nighttime "is silent and chill as the bodies that fill the morgues, the ice trucks, the refrigerated trucks. It is dark and hollow like their coffins, like this city, this night."[133] Painfully, Eick elaborates the perpetual negotiation with death when light expires for the day: "I want to walk into it . . . I want to walk until I am covered, enclosed in its soft shroud that holds at bay the dawn and its questions."[134] In the necessity to reconcile with death and be safely shrouded by night, she woefully adds, "Perhaps, if I could reach them without choking for breath, lungs calcified, without suffocation, I would join them, those dead-too-soon. Especially now when the dark has arched from mountain to mountain, and lets me stand within its gigantic, impervious sphere."[135] But not even the safety of night is impenetrable enough for Eick to move outdoors. She candidly shares, "But I do not move. I don't want to miss the pulling back of the curtain for the last act."[136]

From the window, another type of hyphenating screen, yet another act in a dreadful non-play, Eick watches death move through the night whereby grief becomes something else, something akin to something else yet unnamed but potently felt. Like changing colors and tides, grief envelops, and its very encirclement appears like the paradoxical forces of mobility and immobility. Eick's window, as threshold, is yet another venue to rewatch reality as lived in real time. And this time, through the night's despairing glimmer, we are reminded that stillness is and isn't ever still. Lingering in this stillness, Eick survives her own death by swallowing the affective debris left behind by those captured by night's finality. Grim acts abounding, there are those who remain still enough to live and those who labor in motion to perhaps die at stillness's command. Stills upon still-lives, then, become a form of shared mediatized debt amid a pandemic, capturing us in the pangs of communal grief and yearning desire for more life.

In living and mourning over screens, through windows and across mirrors, we commit to an aggregate of visual, sonic, and embodied stills that unite and separate, wound and transform, but never, even in stillness, foreclose motion. Simultaneously eclipsing the present and future in a negotiation with the past, grief-time's modus is to foretell the future's future. While clocking us into existence, time can easily tick us into a place of finite immobility among mass death. Traditional notions of time, as we experience, do not calm the tides of grief, but merely help it drift along emotionally.[137] Like the pulled-back curtain, the clock that sees, or the pain of bearing calcified lungs, grief-time, permanent and erratic, ordered and jumbled, never flows linearly. Demanding and ubiquitous, it waits for motion to surrender loss into a recognizable emotion—one witnessed in words, verses, sounds, pictures, noise, flashing lights, siren wails, ambushing grunts, abated touch, and the residue of suffering over "unabridged distances."[138] Universal but singular, or plural but also individual, *COVID-19*'s grief-time, as Gressman performs it, is an exercise in political stillness at the threshold of mobile noise, a hyphenation of the senses loosening the borders' edges. Stillness is never without movement: "everything is always already in motion; therefore, everything is constantly emanating sound and breath."[139] That is also to reiterate that at the height of this pandemic, global dissent and anti-racist protests were made possible because of viral velocity as such physical stillness prompted political mobilization. The border between stillness and movement quickly became an antidote to the perceived linearity of grief-time, or every musical score made by conventional beats and normative melodies.

When offered screens for funerals, how do we reorient the politics of ritual, assembly, and commemoration in grief-time? Further removed from communal mourning, we become simulacrums under suffocated, arrested, ongoing, and complicated grief—all figures lent by Witkin, McQueen, Gressman, Gonzalez-Torres, and Eick to illustrate the intricacies of grief-time. Yet no image, still, practice, or performance is a secure method for feeling loss in the suffocation of crisis, regardless of the insidiousness of time.[140] When grief is arrested by advancing global loss, as Gressman's performance foreshadows, one must constantly negotiate the psychical and social resources to preclude suffering. Or, as the artist reflects on and reveals about her performance devised during high intensity, "while my piece takes place in 2020, we culturally behave like COVID is over even as we suffer new strains and mass death. We have become numb to the reality that people who aren't as able will die, and we seem creepily okay with that." She vehemently adds, "We are in denial. We accept that there is a disposable class, a mentality that people are outwardly buying into and invoking. These are the present terms of an infinite grief."[141]

A series of turbulent feelings that continuously reappear, grief-time bears the intermediate objects constituted by indebtedness. Our collective debt, unpayable and barred, remains irrevocably consistent throughout this viral horror, a foreboding scene that prophetically rearranges temporal landscapes.[142] In holding on, grief-time marks the attempt to pay off our debt, to survive loss at the cost of another life, another still, another destabilizing composition for both the dying and the living. Just one aesthetic window into disastrous sociality, Gressman's performance places pressure on how compositions rendered in traditional rhythmic patterns model the horizontal impressions of grief, a kind of grief always in reproducible minor keys.

3

Basins for the Bereft

Environments in Ephemeral Etchings

The grief that permeates in/around us should be exorcised
through a collective reconciliation with tears.
—Pedro Lopez, in conversation with the author

Surrounded by grief, how does one learn to lend a tear for another's
lament? For queer Puerto Rican multimedia artist and community
organizer Pedro Lopez, the answer prevails in the very shifts of sorrow's
percolations, its possessing, ever-present conditioning across time and
landscape. As dreadfully individual as it may feel, grief is a rather infi-
nite social undertaking that "should be exorcised" through collective
assembly and emotional vulnerability. Involving collaboration to propel
its anchored presence, it impels evocation, a premeditated and equally
improvisational summons to eventually be cast out. Or, it is *a tear for a
tear* that lands one closer to grief's settlement.

Since 2012, Lopez has been actively innovating at the intersection
of photography, sculpture, performance, and community advocacy
to rearrange repressive ways of being together in the face of colonial
violence, loss, and injustice. Interested in how communities under
siege publicly convene to gently hold one another through systems
of oppression, and the ensuing deaths of the most vulnerable, this
New York City–based cultural worker realigns grieving assemblies,
expanding them beyond presubscribed colonial scripts. In expand-
ing these scripts, Lopez recharts how counterpublics alter normative
sites of gathering while simultaneously amending psychic life and the
ground's inherited histories. By retracing these spatialized histories
to mourn and morph together, this artist devises various settings to
weep against these colonial logics. Crying together produces interior
cleansing from oppression's contaminations as well as evidence of our

co-presence across worlds, breeding invisibility, silence, separation, and inaction.

Driven by despair and promise, Lopez reimagines our capacity for fellowship through the conceptual and enduring art project *Tear Basins*.[1] Reformulating spaces of liberation by honoring our universal longing to cry away suffering together, *Tear Basins* pays keen attention to our neatly stored feelings caused by colonial coercion, governmental violence, communal separation, diasporic malaise, social agony, and imperial trauma. This project proposes that while socially transformative events frequently present as singular causes, they more commonly evolve from centuries of overlapping dispossession. These overlaps across difference and deprivation are layered with evidence of interdependence, mutual desire, and extenuating particularity, even if dissimilarity negates interarticulation. Equally material, co-historical, and metaphysical, *Tear Basins* evolves as a dynamic aesthetic-life-world across social reciprocity. Unfolding across mediums, the project also assumes multiple and coinciding forms, from a public sculptural stone series to a private collection of artifacts chronicling the history of tears, to a spiritual reunion with ancestors, and an online journal titled "When Was the Last Time You Cried?" Throughout and between these iterations, Lopez recenters grief gatherings by encouraging slower, tender, more benevolent, and "softer sides" of humanity, performance, and advocacy.[2] That is, Lopez establishes environments for weeping despite violent uprising, ancestral disappearance, and colonial destitution. Across genre and landscape, this artist traces interwoven pasts that, while consistently lodged within a divisive present, sketch paths for more transformative ways of being together.

At the same time, being together necessitates understanding systems of oppression as mutual violations across differences that, in resonance, endure across seemingly singular causes. For Lopez, targeted violence never erases reciprocal subjugations, but rather opens pathways for collective convergence. It is not by chance, then, that *Tear Basins* was initiated in 2017, shortly after Donald Trump's election to US president and the contentious selection of Ricardo Rosselló as Puerto Rico's governor. In following these appointments, one is immediately drawn into scandal, corrupt fiscal politics, unnatural disasters leading to mass death, and the ongoing violent colonial predicament between Puerto Rico and the United States, mired in debt, disease, and the possibility of statehood. In response to far-right agendas and centuries of subjugation, Lopez turns to the aesthetic to assume collective mobility, beholding grief's authority during national crisis as yet another aftereffect of territorializing logics built within the everyday.[3] As retribution to incalculable oppressive plights, *Tear Basins* emerges into a multidimensional decolonial performance project across people, place, and history to model colonialism's unremitting compositions.[4]

Like the Rican diaspora's colonially instigated tracks and trails, *Tear Basins* imitates motion across durational fronts to reveal how any election or situated disaster is not actually an individual or atypical occurrence, but a continuous process.[5] Unaware at the project's start of how tragedy would continue to befall this archipelago via further hurricanes, political scandal, protests, accumulating debt, and infrastructural disarray, Lopez foresaw the catastrophic future to retell its slighted pasts. But foretelling the future arrives with looking backward, for the aftershocks of any crisis, as Puerto Rican feminist scholars Yarimar Bonilla and Marisol LeBrón attest, often redisclose "its foreshocks."[6] Amid repeating crises and corruption, what we envision as progress is commonly tinged with looping historical recurrence.[7]

For Lopez, grief's historical temporalities are driven by dispersal, dissipation, and disappearance. With all these equally informing the *Tear Basins* venture, he reconsiders the relationship between grief's pervasiveness and diaspora's situatedness and singularity, and how both, in tandem, displace notions of permanence. By attending to often unseen traces and details of sites under siege, Lopez intentionally turns to underground motility amid ephemerality's above-ground counterpublics. Following the Muñozian rationale that the "ephemeral trace" is indeed materiality's matter and not just those "traditional modes of evidencing lives and politics," this cultural worker invokes grief as shared suffering found along those living outlines longing to be traced over again and again.[8] Similarly advancing what postcolonial scholar Julietta Singh signals as "an infinite history of traces without an inventory," Lopez's project charts the uncharitably documented by following flashes across sites under constant takeover.[9] If, as Singh contends, the archive will never restore us, then this artist takes to heart restoration by deeming ephemerality to be grief's redeemable channel for celebrating lives, stories, colonial histories, and their entangled silences.

In pursuing others by chasing residues, the parallel layers of this project aptly communicate the artist's desire to follow, harbor, or retrace to re-record testimonies and tears across existences, places, and bodies. In coursing remnants, Lopez conceptually directs spectators to track orientations to landscape across both spectral and material appearances, asking that we dismiss the ground as neutrality's resource. For if there are endless and uncatalogued shadows wandering above, below, and around, then they lurk not as diasporic archives but diaspora as improvisatory glints and erupting soils across, within, underneath, and always above land. Rather than a reserve and reservoir of material, the landscape for Lopez is always emerging. That is, the tracing done here is but one living account of Lopez's imbuing outlines, trails of tear(ing) gestures formed from coloniality's disquieting motions and orchestrations.

Unsurprisingly, this tracing motif appears throughout Lopez's oeuvre at the intersection of image, text, sculpture, place, and performance. His obsession with capturing the uncapturable sits at the center of a methodological commitment to artistic sequencing, patterning, collection, and seriality across genre as political dexterity. From color photography focused on the frailty of queer-of-color desire in *My Gay Agenda*, to remnants of disembodied lives as tresses in *Hair Piece*, Lopez looks to ephemera as proof, as the ultimate reproduction of reproducibility itself, even if and especially when the transient performs permanency against dispersion.[10] Like these aesthetic projects, *Tear Basins* draws out yet another way to unfasten colonial and heteronormative immutabilities foreclosing our communal sorrows.

Despite the relevant challenges to grasping any glimmer, this chapter follows promiscuous routes to catch Lopez remedying sorrow's splitting, disappearing, scattering, and hidden composers. By remapping diasporic landscapes of grief, Lopez animates collective consciousness and, in so doing, demands our despair along with our solidarity. Led by decolonial praxis as survival strategy, he also requests the collective consent to be more than one identificatory checkbox, one site under constant attack, one entity amid mass revitalization. For this cultural worker, any liberated Rican future evolves by bypassing the chokeholds of singular catastrophe to arrive at coalescing modes of difference. Across historical etchings and conjuring spells, grief's tears inevitably transpire to join, release to transform, and gather to liberate, falling in vertical counter-measure to oppression's inequitable leveling fields.

Into the Valley of Histories: Cashmere Tears and Borikén Testimonies

Lopez's desired tears, however, do not fall in singular shape, form, or fashion; they descend across aesthetic sites, people, and circumstances uniquely. On July 9, 2022, after years of research, planning, and documenting current events, Lopez and team install *Tear Basin (Vale of Cashmere)* in the northeast corner of Prospect Park in Brooklyn, New York.[11] This 165-pound basin meets the public's attention between the hours of noon and sunset. On this day, for close to eight hours, Lopez, team, and guests participate in a living memorial and grief ceremony without secured permissions for engagement. Yet this seemingly unassuming, plain, and empty stone is rather a historically, spiritually, and politically loaded object. Lopez mobilizes attendees around its presence into liberating action across study sessions and mourning rituals to honor those living in and lost by colonial destitution. By understanding the potential to cry together as an emergent survival strategy against state-sanctioned violence and oppression, he leads guests to closely interact with one another, guiding them to cry into and touch the basin while simultaneously reclaiming disavowed space.

The artist, nevertheless, has little control over the emotional release of others in attendance. It is the vessel, its internal force and knowing, that animates the collective to move and feel. As a basin formed from historical and spiritual intention, this vessel morphs from an apparently empty object into a liberatory channel for the people. It is the object's informed existence, not solely Lopez's labor, that instantiates animation across entities, even if its impression is straightaway unimpressionable to some. Created as an homage to Borikén, its full "past, present, and liberated future," Lopez submits that "the present is never enough"[12] for any of us. One must look back to shift toward liberation's futural motions, not by destroying shared worlds, but cherishing the earth's trails. Trapped by history's erasures in the present, Lopez places pieces of the earth on top of already layered earthly ground in both symbolic and concrete redistribution. These multiple layers re-concretize our mutual

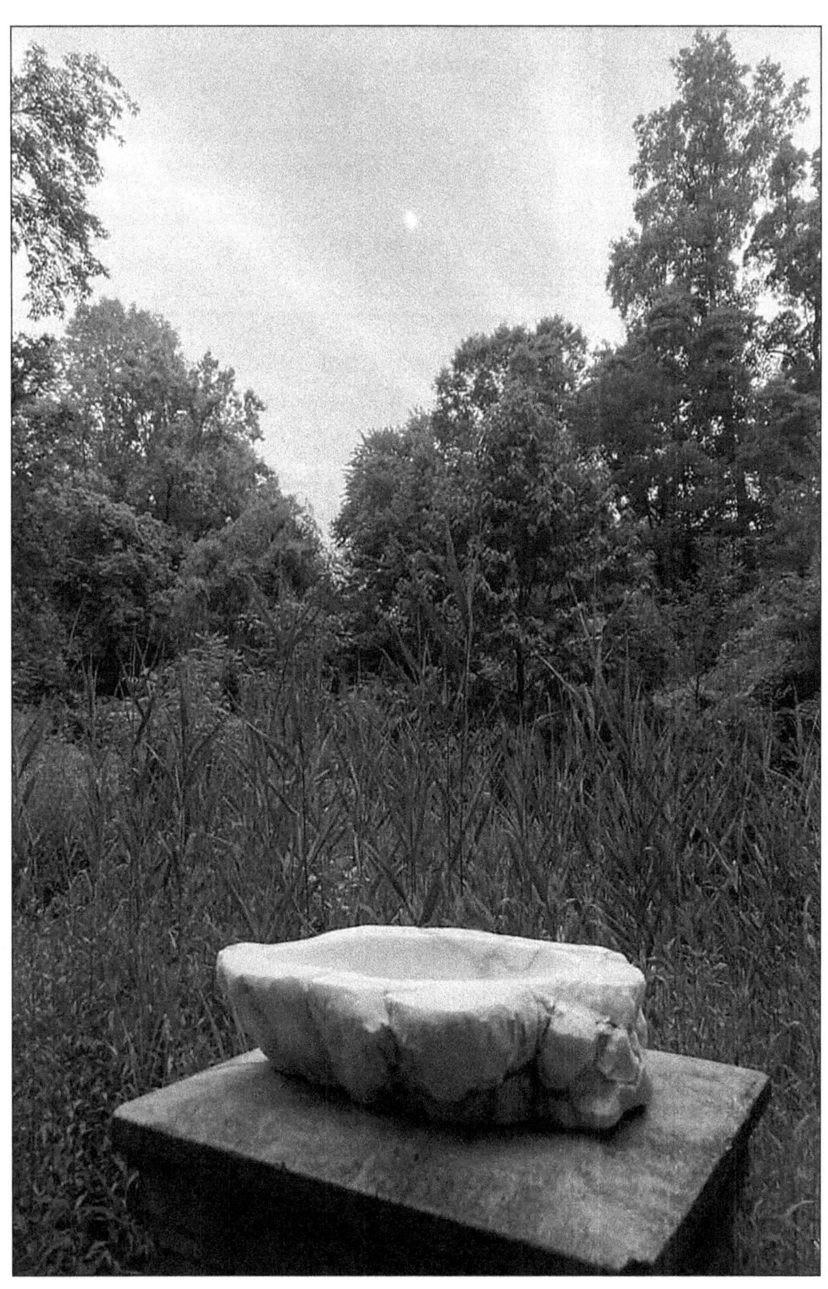

Figure 3.1. *Basin Vale Dusk*, 2022. Photo courtesy of Pedro Lopez.

grounds by reflecting our capacity to collectively rearrange them. Lopez extracts the earth's bedrock and soiled residues from the ground up, lifting everything underneath in preemptive stratification.

Playing with the dualities of situatedness and motion, flow of emotion and the hardened texture of rock, the artist places a decolonial and queer pamphlet at the foot of the basin as a corrective to colonial strictures mitigating interdependency, mutuality, and emotional intimacy in public spaces. By making additional copies of the pamphlet to distribute to those participating in the live act, Lopez attempts to gently educate and guide affective correspondence. Personal and conceptual, the pamphlet, or "placemaker" as the artist also dubs it, contains theoretical citations on the history of tears, reasons for humans to weep, the covert productions of place, and Puerto Rican anticolonial aesthetic interventions as accompaniment to the basin itself.[13] Apart from distributing this authorless brochure, this piece of paper that attendees may or may not carefully read, Lopez refuses to engineer this installation. Rather, like some in attendance, he watches, engages, and documents, hoping for organic movements to transpire. Far from controlling emotive expression, Lopez allows landscape, paper, and vessel to play the largest roles as instigators of sentiment and historical relation.

In providing space for skin-to-stone encounters, Lopez discloses that the basin extends "an opportunity for folks to be with themselves and one another through shared despair."[14] So, take, for instance, the fact that the shape and texture of the basin, which by no means is coincidentally composed, mirrors the solidity of endless subjugation and ancestral reclamation. Sculpted from alabaster, this communal basin is weighty, translucent, and a porous geologic material meant to endure but also to inevitably erode. Reminiscent of the Japanese *tsukubai*, a wash basin located in front of a holy site for ritual cleansing, the deeply concave container for holding mutual lamentation extends the tradition of humbly bending before objects.[15] Informed by gratitude, Lopez attempts to enliven the object's memoir via trace accounts by emitting spiritual meaning through mutual indebtedness. Offering praise before labor, he thanks the living object for its singular existence, harbored histories, and interconnected recitals.[16] Inherently relational through composition, *Tear Basin (Vale of Cashmere)* shelters legacies, some naturally embedded within the source, and others inscribed onto the rock by the artist after thoughtful contemplation. Like rocks lining the land to brace the waves, this basin is proportional, polyvocal, resistant, difficult to manipulate and move, but eternally dialogic in its composure and reproducibility. As in the *tsukubai*, one sculptural and spiritual tradition among the many intriguing Lopez, the basin communicates willfully with subjects and history, establishing spatial economies for weeping that include resonant engagements with nature, immaterial presences, and one another's inherited sorrow. By chiseling slowly and carefully over long periods of time, Lopez generates a spiritual relationship with the rock's textures, informed by both the interior and exterior landscaping of the object.

The Vale of Cashmere basin, like smaller ones made by Lopez weighing in at around thirty-five to forty-five pounds, is never meant to be mobilized and circulated for currency, however, but rather to be animated and reproduced by a collective spirit.[17] As an alternative to the commercialization of aesthetics, these basins, as the artist reveals, are never for sale. By refusing price tags, in addition to public permits, authorship, and managerial orchestration, Lopez and stone rearrange the terms and conditions of aesthetic encounters. In my ongoing correspondences with him, the artist shares that all basins and their subsequent engagement and circulation are offerings and mutual happenings, impromptu-rehearsed counter-hegemonic social scenes indebted to revelatory confrontations with grief.[18] These vulnerable gatherings, for Lopez, inevitably cross-fertilize, intersect, and intercede in stable ideas of place just like the very scattering movements of diaspora.

At the same time, Lopez reveals that this connection between object and history is enlightened by the artist's own interior tension with, and affinity to, place, space, and region. Born in California, but raised close to Cape Canaveral, Florida—near swamps, a space center, and conservative ideology—Lopez understands regional codes to shape interfacing identifications, advocacies, and aesthetic practices. Growing up gay and Puerto Rican in Florida required the constant negotiation of identificatory markers across disparate terrain. Disidentifying with dominant power structures meant moving between unstable identifications while often grieving socially oppressed and separated identities in difference.[19] How else, as Lopez shares, might multivocal experiences coexist amid hegemonic modes for living? In a world demanding the debarment of

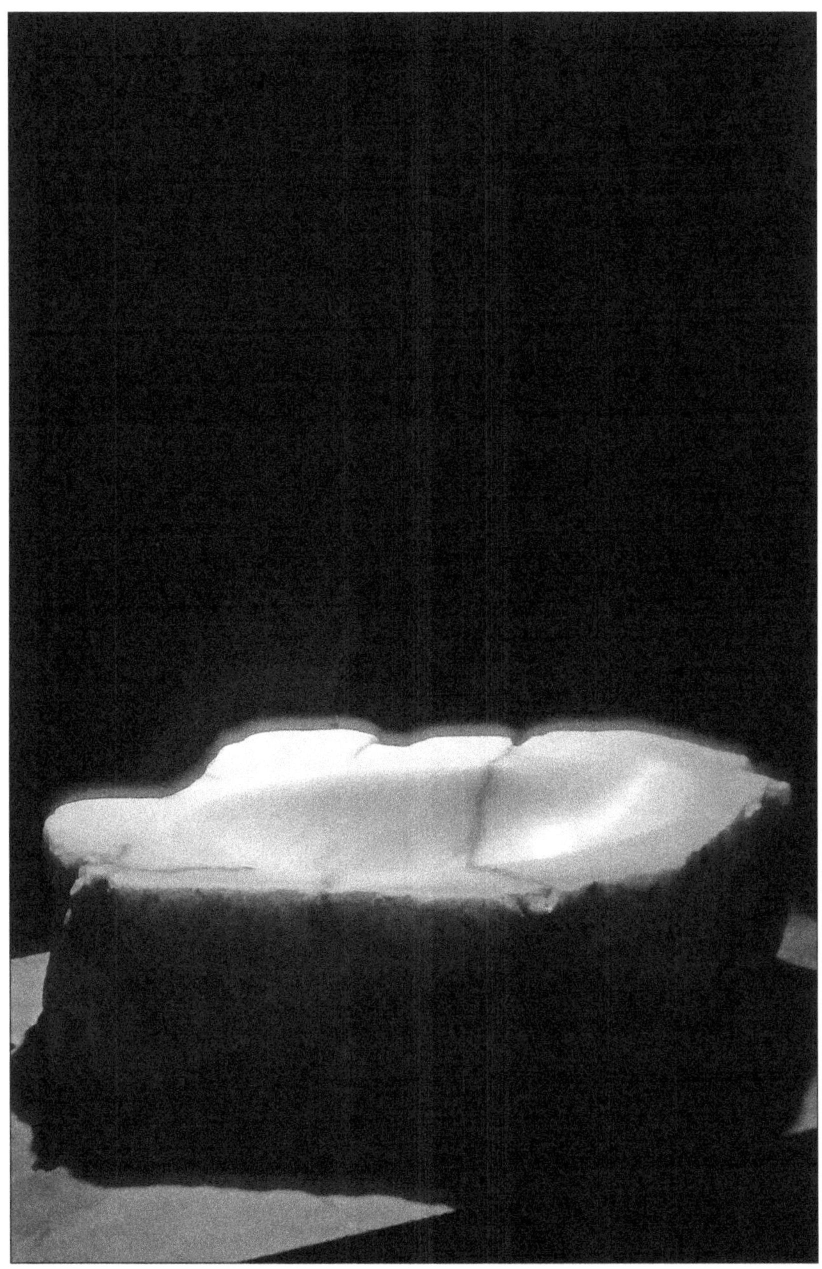

Figure 3.2. *Basin Studio 2*, 2022. Photo courtesy of Pedro Lopez.

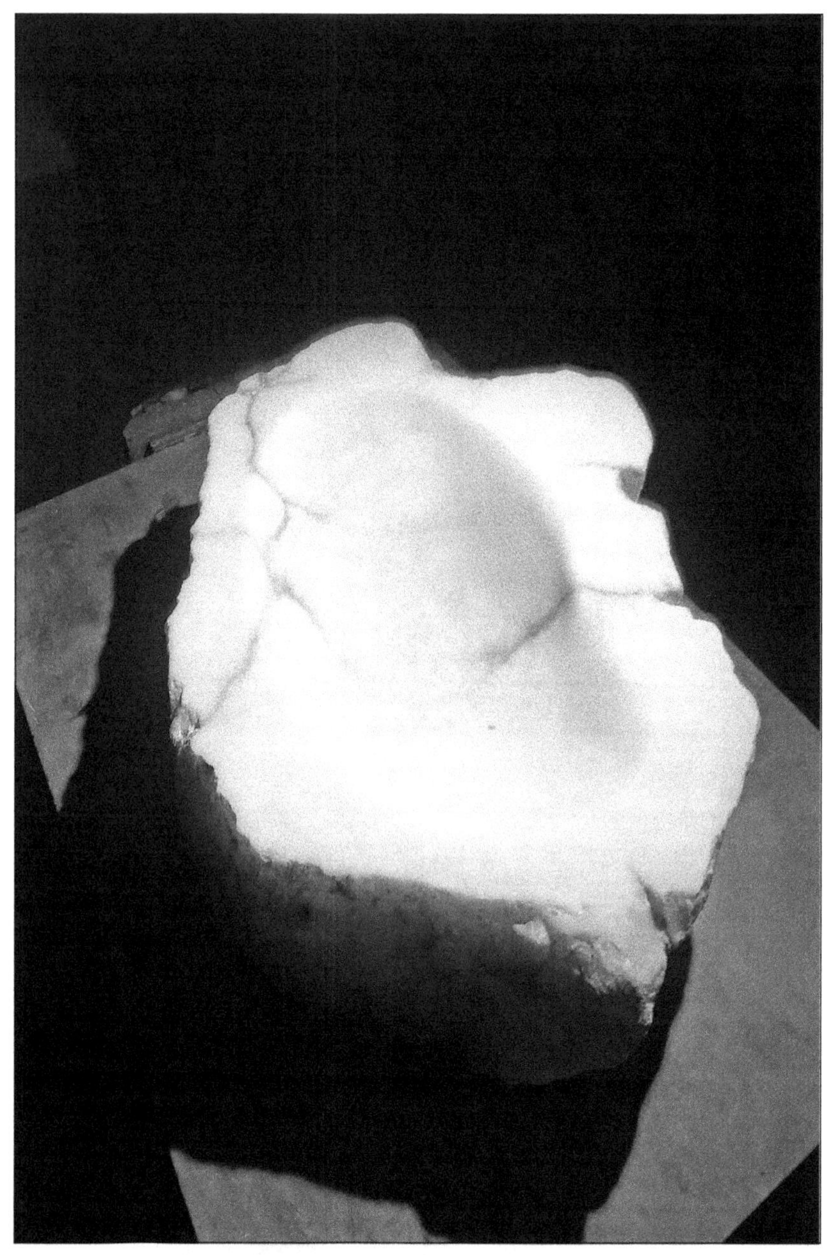

Figure 3.3. *Basin Studio 1*, 2022. Photo courtesy of Pedro Lopez.

intersecting differences, Lopez contemplates how queerness and Ricanness gently coincide within the violence of their separation. Moving to Brooklyn, New York, allowed Lopez to shift with place aesthetically and politically and to reimagine how to accommodate cultural collision in a city habituated to productive contradiction. Torn between land, gender, sexuality, ethnicity, and racialization while in the South, Lopez hardly underestimates the magical capacity of site to enliven untold stories while simultaneously manifesting new social formations. To these personal meditations on difference, he adds that the hidden demands of landscape simultaneously suppress, discharge, and scatter lives and histories. Longingly and uncoincidentally, Lopez deliberates upon every basin's placement, thinking not only of the basin's material evolution but of the location's underground movements. Committed to what sites contain and conceal to restore public space for the people, Lopez chisels the earth to chisel through history.

But of all the nuanced and intricate places in New York City, why the Vale of Cashmere? Now a cloistered ruin, the Vale of Cashmere once contained watering fountains, lily ponds, bucolic trails, and beautiful, rare flowers and plants. Due to the city's lack of infrastructural resources, over time the park became a wild wasteland facing a now ample and elegant Brooklyn Botanical Garden. With all feral waste, though, we might imagine a backstory filled with treasures waiting to be narrated.[20] Although deserted for decades, this site harbors incredible historical remains, in both narrative evolution and object material.

No wonder that this park was named after Thomas Moore's 1817 musical poem "The Light of the Haram," one of four narrative poems included in *Lalla Rookh*, a heteronormative romantic ethnic fantasy centering a fictional seventeenth-century Persian emperor's daughter, Lalla Rookh, or Lala-Rukh.[21] For instance, Moore's famous tale (written in England) is actually set in Kashmir, an idyllic dream for Western fantasy adapted into settings for musicals, plays, operas, and international films, all traversing the globe as both tangible site and ethnic fiction for centuries.[22] Establishing Kashmir (Cashmere) as a wonderland of love and ethnic-orientalist-mythical paradise, the setting represents the park as a space of ethnic and cultural illusion, primed intimacy, tamed pleasure, luxury, beauty, and wealth. Moore himself notes: "Who has not heard of the Vale of Cashmere, / With its roses the brightest that earth ever gave,

/ Its temples, and grottos, and fountains as clear / As the love-lighted eyes that hang over their wave?"[23] Mirroring the poet's verse, the Vale of Cashmere was originally known for its exuberant gardens, playgrounds, and clean pool beds. Through time and disregard, it evolved into an unmanicured valley that, instead of inviting visitors during the day, became a popular cruising spot for queer men of color, and a public dance club for minoritarian subjects during the pandemic.[24] Once accommodating bourgeois desire, this landscape transcends into a working-class social scene for pleasure and shared pain, queer loss and love, unmitigated movement and entangled decolonial affections. What lives underneath its ground produces the very series of vibrational lures reanimating narrative discontinuity and performative continuity.

While retelling this story may seem immaterial to Lopez's work, or a critical fabrication at best, it enables overlapping cultural fantasies and colonial histories to subsist in confabulation.[25] The act of retelling, itself, aids in extracting and rerouting landscape's details so that we might understand landscape as a type of archive, a site of surface connections and burial affinities, an act of underground descent and above-soil ascent. For those forgotten, erased, silenced, and forcibly dislodged, overlying stories remain tantamount to ephemerality's archival project. This undertaking includes an archive-in-the-making that is, as Singh indicates, an "opaque hope" but always "slipping away as though it didn't want to be found, plundered, excavated."[26] Challenging the odds of effacement, Lopez honors physical place and its placelessness amid ancestral etchings to be re-sketched among the still living and their inherited deeds. Tracing lines of connection across stone, land, history, difference, and interior terrain, Lopez cherishes elemental details to summon a commons by conjuring diasporic remnants. Put another way, invented palaces (sites filled with interstitial sounds, stories, and senses) should be continuously reinvented to coincide with historical dislocation and spatial dispersal. Or to deliberately activate the sediments of any element is to actively animate its reinvention.

Take for example that *Tear Basin (Vale of Cashmere)* bears an etching of the island of Puerto Rico in its center space. In a gesture resembling the spiraling movements of diasporic digressions, Lopez reconfigures the island of Puerto Rico through a renewed center etching, drawing it away from its territorial marginality on earth and catastrophic and discordant representations. From a representational body of land to bodily relations on stone to an alternative archival transcription on a historically charged site, the basin functions as a heavy object of transference within a place's stabled instability. Attached to the mainland with archives formed by colonial limbs, the island and its people oblige concentrated attention. If the island belongs both here and there, with and upon rocks and illusions, across bodies and waters, from fantasy to freedom, how might we understand diasporic cartographies as movements along ephemera's flows?

For Lopez, this rock both is and is not merely symbolic. Large, heavy, and firm, this tear basin is a site of exploration and experimentation in which to remark its contours is to further understand the obligations of both colonialism and decolonial praxis. The stone's centered etching is a representation of a representation of another place and time presented as a solid object that, in real time, exists as not the thing itself but the object's digressions across history and space. The etching is an aesthetic illustration of a colony across waters but redesigned, in yet another time, on the mainland's grounds. It is a material and immaterial tribute, at once porous and stable, and at other times ancestrally summoning and historically dispersing. While spectators are directed via the pamphlet to the dedication to Borikén, the indigenous Taíno name for the island before Spanish colonization, only the artist is aware of this sketch and its origins.[27] Holding this information close to his chest, Lopez hopes to model the inevitable turns and shifts of diasporic mobility and simultaneously summon the ancestors without visible conjure. Gently moving between the unarchive and its repertoires and across the imposition of permanence and the potentiality of transition, he expands body relations through stone, corpus, repository, representation, colony, and reference, even when bodies are no longer present or intentionally unseen.

To add to the narratives already folded into reproduction's inflections, the brochure escorting the *Tear Basin (Vale of Cashmere)* unveils any unclear motivations across representational forms. At the foot of the basin, Lopez hangs the pamphlet, almost hiding it within the grasslands of the park.[28] It is hung so low that attendees must once again bend before the object and others to learn about the basin's history and motivations. While Lopez made copies of watercolor brochures for participants during the live July 9th event, the placement of the brochure for future bystanders is intentionally meant to draw attention to the basin both as a singular object and as referent for other entities. What is most clearly conveyed is that the act of bending, also witnessed in Eva Margarita's work, unfurls as a spiritual and political gesture employed to rethink structures of social, cultural, and public debt and indebtedness.

The pamphlet—made of one thick white sheet of typing paper folded into three vertical sections—contains black lettering in the form of endnotes with dark blue lettering as the central text. Along with an abstract cover image of smeared blue tear lines falling from the edges of the words *TEAR* and *BASIN* in the same blue, the pamphlet abstracts the stone's materiality to conceptualize its purpose. Reminiscent of Ana Mendieta's 1974 *Untitled (Blood Sign #2/Body Tracks)*, the 8mm film performance where she traces her blood onto a white background that remains after the artist departs the scene, Lopez's tear stains hang like a series of pastel leaking blue streaks.[29] Inside the pamphlet, the reader is met with a short lyrical essay written by Lopez but driven by a repeating theme and epigraph, "The present is not enough." Engaging José Esteban Muñoz's writing on queer-of-color utopia along with the artist's own ideas for a liberated Borikén,[30] Lopez reproduces and cites across texts to trace over theoretical alignments, connecting those unseen dots often separated by manufactured difference. Moving between a Muñozian critique of the anti-relational to the Rican anticolonial and decolonial across aesthetic interventions, Lopez demands our entanglements in body, culture, and writing. Committed instead to creating a community of tears that fall over colonial anguish to tether us temporally, culturally, and physiologically, Lopez hails the horizon. This horizon, while never intended for subjects under siege, opens the futural gates to our commingling emotive presences.

As shown in the brochure, *Tear Basins* (project writ large) aims to generate sites where one can collectively "replenish emotional fortitude," for these vessels "are places to reassess and rest with oneself and one another." Devising them as "an intervention in uneven developments and public space," Lopez attempts "to build social bonding and coherence within communities by providing an environment unbound by colonial time."[31] By crying together, we move toward emotionally complicated and cherished intimacies "that can help upend individualism and seed change for a future built on mutuality."[32] This mutuality, however, is

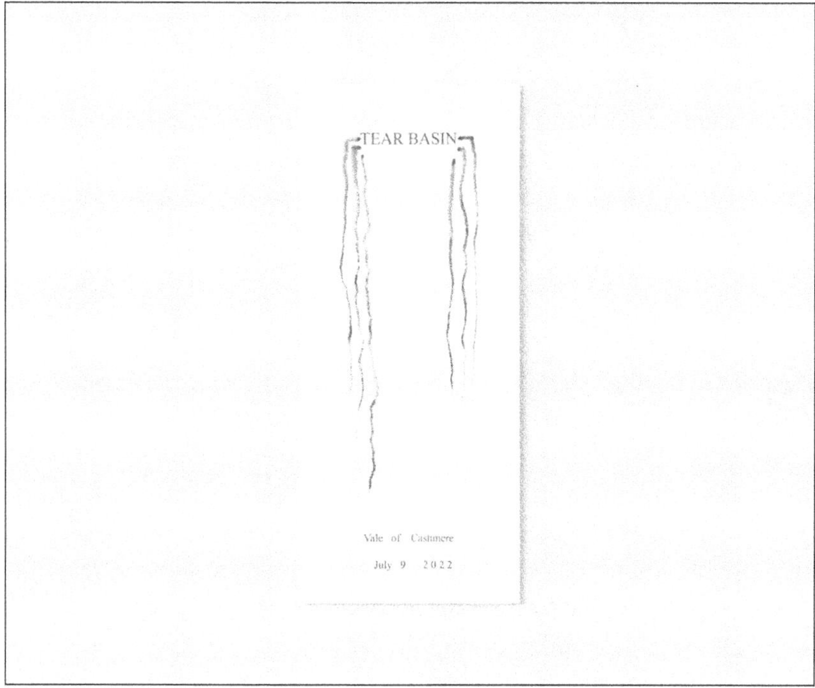

Figure 3.4. The cover of the brochure accompanying *Tear Basin (Vale of Cashmere)*. Photo by Steven Probert, 2022. Photo courtesy of Pedro Lopez.

built from particular oppression that, instead of dividing us across liberation fronts, unites across futural solidarity. That is, Lopez's future is specifically intoned and envisioned: it is where one meets the basin and releases "the tide within [one's] eyes" for all colonial sites, the island's indigeneity as progenitor of affairs, and the future as a queerly conjured and liberated one.[33] Along with proclaiming the basin's dedication to Borikén, Lopez declares a vision of the future that on the pamphlet descends vertically in terms of words and scope. "A future protected from the litany of languish" is the first line, read horizontally; below it is the following line, "a future where we can share vulnerability as a means of self-preservation."[34] Moving down the page, the reader is then met with the individual short lines "a future abundant," then "a future affirming" to "a future free." A large empty space rests between the lines (perhaps lines of muted silences and disappeared tears) to land us all on the last and tiniest verse: "A future."[35]

Refusing to instigate a totalizing, universal future with the article *the*, or to add his name to the pamphlet, Lopez invites a polychoral ensemble of voices and futures to manifest across ephemeral flow, sonic etchings that resound bodies and silenced histories. Committed to what *a* future may validate, this artist is under no illusion of the perpetual dominating forces and systems that colonize our day-to-day to counter our interdependencies by offering up only one kind of future. Refusal, and resistance, for Lopez, are shaped by communally working through grief to conjure the ancestors for guidance, without any state-sanctioned approval. Therefore, a signature of one or an agenda for all, like a state permit for a public park, is a careless attention to solidarity's potential. Lopez forcefully declares that we can refuse what has been imparted upon us and "resist by learning new modes to help encourage each other toward strengthening our collective consciousness."[36] Traveling toward a future that must be collectively rebuilt, he extends an alternative way of archiving solidarity—one that contends with the present's devaluation of entwined historical forms and futures. Like Muñoz cruising toward a queer-of-color utopia, Lopez's future is more than "a fantasy of heterosexual reproduction,"[37] the material negation of ghosts and their present ghostliness, memories without social reimagining, unrequited imagistic desires, or etchings and echoes without vibrating spectral lines. Instead, he advances ephemerality's presence across centuries of colonial anguish and diasporic disappearance alongside the possibility of more communal pleasure across all types of minor keys.

The July 9th installation coincided with an improvised dance party, unplanned but unsurprising, near the basin's location. Lasting until sundown, the fiesta organically materialized, according to Lopez, "with music blaring in typical Brooklyn Boricua style as Celia Cruz and Marc Anthony songs rang over the speakers and the people danced."[38] While not expecting a party to ensue under the basin's grief gathering, Lopez bears no allegiance to the protocols of any space, as they often deny complicated emotions to coexist in the name of one feeling at a time indivisible for all. Embracing instead the idea that space is always contested, nuanced, complicated, and remade by the people, he understands landscape to be a living entity as archive that, albeit situated, is always undone, and remade by moving bodies. Whether a slice of heaven on earth, hinterland, or public dancehall, landscapes bear continued historicity, for at any moment, as queer Puerto Rican performance stud-ies scholar Ramón Rivera-Servera contends, "a quotidian utopia" may emerge as a choreography of resistance in varying forms and feelings.[39] Although seemingly totalizing, every location shelters paradoxical ten-sion, along with teleological and chronological assessments of histories below ground. Comfortable working within and across this pressure, Lopez reproduces renewed historicity, or sites where inseparable bod-ies exercise multiple histories and enact radical and ephemeral nonlin-ear planes of engagement.[40] Following "alternate modes of textuality and narrativity" in pursuing "traces, glimmers, residues, and specks of things," Lopez's ephemera becomes diaspora as living archive.[41] That is to say that Lopez, chasing Muñozian ideas, is compelled by the very "traces of lived experience and performances of lived experience, main-taining experiential politics and urgencies long after these structures of feeling have been lived."[42] To think critically about each basin's location, and its potential disappearance, means taking no city grid, or its people, for granted. In every quiet crevice exists sound's historical resounding, perhaps heard across a dance party's elated roar and/or a funeral com-memoration's sobering wail.

Still, questions remain. Why place his tear basin, a panegyric for and representation of Puerto Rico's diasporic travels and colonial terrors, in this historically charged park? Why sketch the island onto a hard surface knowing that its immediate stability fosters its ultimate erasure? Rocks, like islands, are erosion's destination, and destinations are far from the end of diasporic movement. One might answer these questions in several ways (no answer opposed to the other but rather in affinitive condition): to witness how (dis)placement produces the animation of conjured an-cestral life; to understand landscape as living archival repository; to call forth queer-of-color ghosts still cruising against traditional national and cultural imaginaries; and/or to understand Lopez as enacting a version of what anthropologist Michael Taussig names the "space of death," de-fined as a portal, or a threshold, a very "wide space whose breadth offers positions of advances as well as extinction."[43] If we take the "space of death" to be all at once literal, ideological, metaphorical, metaphysical, and supernatural, might Lopez be reanimating a landscape filled with hidden loss in which the very act of grief sharing expiates the colonial demons repressing us all? Why else beseech, if not to cleanse? Why summon, if not to reconcile? Why create, if not to ephemerally score? Why sketch the dead if not to echo the desires of the living?

Yet, Lopez is not leaving behind customary tombstones in graveyards for others to mourn; instead, he generates a living memorial carved by his own hands of/for lives ravaged and disappeared by coloniality and colonialism's splitting of earth and spirits. Not initiating a strict hauntological excavation in the Derridean sense, Lopez readies the land with the ancestral living as if to also convey that land, too, grieves and still breathes.[44] Or, the land's spirits simmer off and seek justice, not through arrogant and vengeful ghost lining but through textured sonorities and immaterial gestures for more abundant gratitude.[45] Lopez's queer Rican basin is a diasporic offering imbued with multiple and still-living entities—conjoined, but never overdetermining the object's ability to morph into other energies. While seemingly an unextraordinary sink, it conceptually symbolizes a representation of a colony (an etching) within a rock situated within histories of cultural movement, all within a city park formed by subaltern travel, instantiating, even if unconsciously, diasporic sounds, fantasies, senses.

But Lopez is not invested in replicating tear basins across the diaspora to store tears; he rather encourages the diaspora to create and spread them together, removing proper names from the protocols of cultural circulation in favor of communal connection. If diaspora scatters, disperses, and displaces, Lopez desires the dispersal to rename individualism into collective action, not merely to cry together, but to store the memory into history's bedrock. That is to also suggest that if some sort of relief for the living is requested through the site, Lopez considers how places have historically offered, as landscape architecture scholar Karen Wilson Baptist contends, "a physical, sensorial, ephemeral repository for both grief and for the dead."[46]

Exactly how does diasporic travel, and even digression and displacement, recalibrate the spaces of grief, death, landscape, and their archives? For Baptist, the nonlinear rhythms of space, grief, death, and the living must contend with how both death and grief necessitate "a landscape to dwell in."[47] Not always a stable entity, landscape prevails more as "a reflection of the shared mutability of landscape and life," constantly rerouting our relations to time, corporeality, and space. Understanding diasporic movements "as death without the possibility of landscape,"[48]

Baptist exposes how land, like grief, is dynamically evanescent and situated within superimposed and contested stories, lives, and habitations. In saying so, Baptist suggests that negotiations with grief must involve the reformulation of space; for, "what death shatters, the landscape has the capacity to reflect, to amplify, and to redeem."[49] Although accessed across transient time, the stories embedded within the Vale of Cashmere redeem the broken pieces left behind in grief's demonic terror. Perhaps the gathering itself conditions our shared sorrow upon the distribution of common vulnerabilities. Otherwise, how might we reconcile ongoing loss amid unending subjugation and genocide on re-stolen land? In offering one's time and tears, as one redesigns mourning sites, an ensemble of lamentations rejects the foreclosure of multiple stories. In other words, how do we understand something like cruising as a futural navigation, a deliberate gesture of the present for the future's presence, an experiment with and across interlaced material and immaterial histories of subjectification? *Tear Basin (Vale of Cashmere)* shelters the residue of entangled identifications across historical parts united by cruising differences.

In Lopez's plotting of decolonial Rican rites of passage, diaspora is inherently queer, land is infinite indigenous disappearance, and colonial temporalities, producing grief's shifts, are equally spatial and historical disorientations. None of these political proclivities are antithetical to "cruising" toward a utopic future on land, that while always re-stolen, yields sites of overlapping re-memories in return.[50] Like Taussig's space of death, Baptist's diasporic excavations across ritual sites for grieving the dead, Muñoz's ephemeral and cruising gestures, and Singh's reformulation of the archive as living-body memory, Lopez carves places from within tenuous historical landscapes.[51] As an act of intimacy with grief, this cultural worker mobilizes ephemeral spillages to resculpt history in order to reorder our given inventories across stone and print without enforcing reterritorialization as an unliving archive.

Chiseling and Cruising: Skin-to-Stone Remains

Fundamental to Lopez's conceptual and ideological interventions are the details found across the sculpting process. *Tear Basin (Vale of Cashmere)* was made from white Italian alabaster, but most importantly with "an intentional and emotional discussion with the object before advancing its shape."[52] Only after this lengthy conversation does Lopez dare chisel, or, as he calls it, "spiral into the circular."[53] Via curling motion, his hands align with the object's history as he sands down the rock, conscientiously morphing it into a re-conceptualized island. The etching flags Lopez's citational attention to Ricanness and the loaded layers of dispossession, displacement, and diasporic digression by landing on Borikén's re-return. By seeing Puerto Rico's imperialistic conditions along the lines of Puerto Rican scholar Jorge Duany's proposition—as a *nation* always on the move to remodify cultural re-identifications—Lopez renders grief as part of colonial motility.[54] From mainland routes to the island rerouted in sketch, the motion is exhausting and emotionally cumbersome, mimicking colonialism's constant *effects* as living forces felt through debt, violence, policing, disease, and more death, all always propelling grief's active *affect*.[55]

Lopez retraces these movements and effects/affects by honoring all Boricuas with an accompanying tribute, or a call and response to/for indigenous Taíno life by returning to the island's original name. In doing so, the basin morphs as form within form, reflecting atmospheres of subjugation and the movements leading toward new futural predicaments. A gentle hail, the dedication also symbolizes a space for conjoining affections. The word *Boricua*, according to Puerto Rican writer and editor Roberto Santiago, conveys a "term of endearment, respect, and cultural affirmation; a timeless declaration," a dynamic diasporic word referencing the origins of Puerto Rico's people while acknowledging its violent and genocidal history.[56] This term is replete with courageous defiance, perilous political terrain, and the desire for a liberated future free of colonial languish.

Working from this indigenous cultural erasure, Lopez performs a Muñozian "hermeneutics of residue" by following the imperative that "after the gesture expires, its materiality has transformed" across indispensable ephemera.[57] Across various energies as sites of evidence, attainable relations become offerings between forms as gestures, and gestures inevitably mark "a refusal of a certain kind of finitude."[58] If ephemeral "gestures are where the literal and figurative copulate," as scholar Juana María Rodríguez smartly elucidates, then how do we re-study the stone's central etching?[59] With a gentle offering in the shape of a heavy rock,

Lopez captures the dichotomous tenets underlining tender ambushes and vehement revolts embedded within Rican colonial life. Playing with all sorts of polarities, from individual and collective grief to soft affectivity and hefty materiality, to language's recuperating touch as an emblem of decolonial discursivity, Lopez reconceptualizes the frames of duality through a stone. Between ephemerality and permanency, the fragile archive and glimmering repository, all settling between rocks and island etchings to be eventually washed away by time and tears, Lopez asks us to hold onto an evolving recognition as tightly as we clutch a given sentiment. While it may appear as if Lopez salutes disappearance in its colonial returns, he rather patiently waits with texture, history, and immaterial plenitude amid grief's enclosing *duende*.[60] In shared sorrow, deliberate decolonial praxis, gentler ancestral summoning ensues whereby *a tear for a tear* may become an intentional gesture for more capacious ways of living togther.

Finitude's refusal to end morphs into many forms across Lopez's project, demanding the distillation of trace and gesture as ongoing study. For example, Lopez describes the basin as harboring "a tactile duality that speaks to an understanding of self and other across space, location, and time."[61] First "raw and rough externally," the basin is eventually "met with smooth stone skin."[62] With time, the sculpture, according to the artist, will begin to feel harmless just like a "remade body with a womb" meant to be animated by the public, not hidden in storehouses with other objectified bodies and unable to partake in reproduction's reproducibility.[63] Not meant to be only visually engaged, the basin welcomes an expansive sensorial experience to be "pondered over in order to feel the presence of tears in the magical possibility of holding anything ephemeral."[64] For Lopez, each basin works to rotate lives, bodies, representations, sentiments, energies in its hardened stillness, with no entity as essential as co-experience itself, as both interior dissolution and communal reconciliation.

Skin-to-stone contact allows one to not only *touch upon* topics, but *touch* silenced histories, denied lives, and communal lamentations. Still, touching requires the company of other senses, including the uncounted mystical ones. It involves a sensing-with and a sensing-for bodies engrossed by the object's textured sounds. Never singular, it requires an ensemble of voices across moving forces. As performance studies theorist Hypatia Vourloumis suggests in a treatise about grief's permanent impermanence, "to touch is to always be touched in return"; "to touch is to alter and be altered"—or the want to "touch and be touched by the amorous other is always also the desire to touch another world."[65] Conveying how the palpable sense of touch radically amends temporalities, spaces, stories, and interdependencies, Vourloumis refuses the minimal transports of material exchange; instead, she encourages "expansive material ephemeral touch" whereby the immaterial embodies publics through contact against loss's haptic foreclosures.[66] Attempting to feel past the material's materiality, Vourloumis espouses a mode of touching in concert with Muñozian ideas along cruising routes. Touching, here, becomes less about perfect convergences between subjects or collapsing points of contact within orderly operations, and more about how touching counters the state's call, as Muñoz shares, "to keep us from knowing ourselves, from knowing our masses."[67] To know ourselves is to be open to touch's magical capacity to invigorate stories and encounters, for the haptic gesture is where one may find beaming constellations and emotive spills, in which non-lexical actions and tactile sensations stretch thresholds into the portal's opening.

The potential to touch and be touched is imbued within these basins through various calculated gestures. While creating *Tear Basin (Vale of Cashmere)*, Lopez repeatedly listened to a variety of music including classical chamber music, folkloric Puerto Rican music, and popular salsa tunes. Inviting a group of genres and instruments into the scene, including the stone's own sounds, Lopez communicates that every rehearsal attends the final performance, even through impossible material. The stone, however, is not the only material that advances in this evolving art piece. As one studies further, one begins to uncover Lopez's sensorial traces and research lines of flight as also main stage performances.

Yes, the basin carries a visual representation of Puerto Rico (a reproduction in a series of reproductions outside the island as place) that is stationed within a colonial valley named after an ethnic fantasy for heteronormative Western fancy, that, through time, becomes a cruising stop and utopic dance scene for queers of color. But the basin also produces its own internal sounds, beckoned between cuts and crevices and evolving for, from, and with the artist's touch. As Lopez's hands affect stone, the stone sounds back by drumming and lifting the body and ears

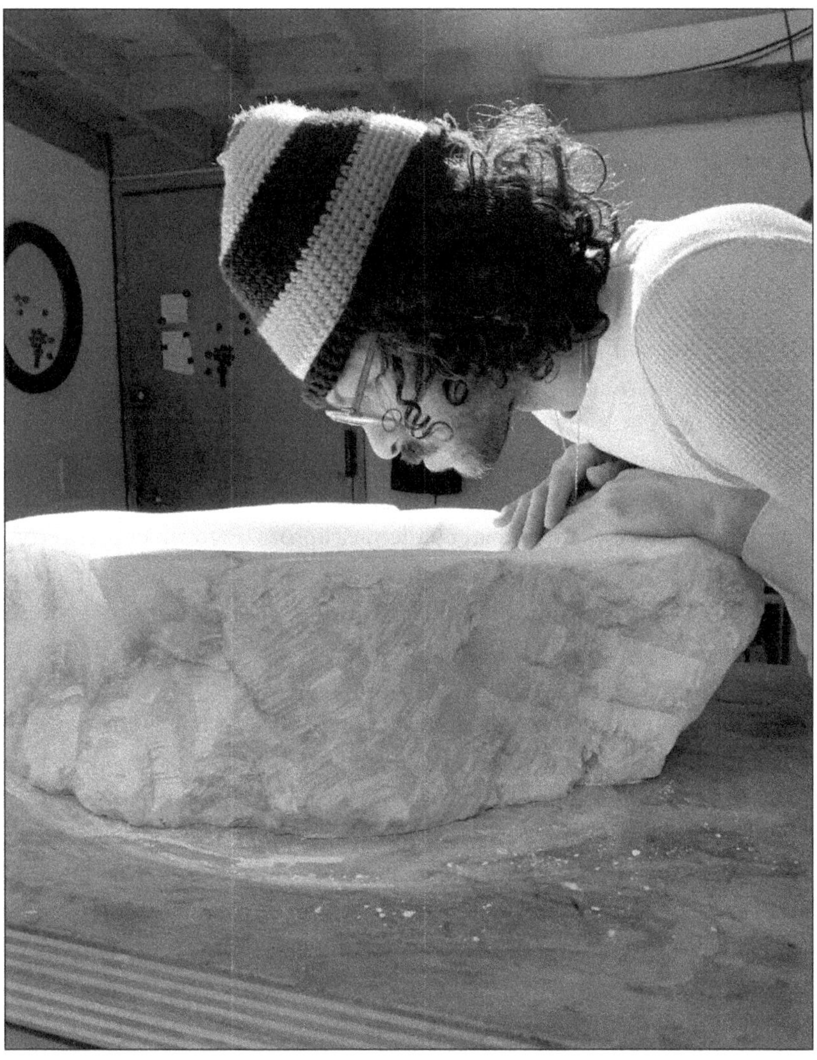

Figure 3.5. Pedro Lopez in his studio, looking into his *Tear Basin*, 2022. Photo courtesy of Pedro Lopez.

through quivering vibrations and oscillations. Becoming an extension of this stone through frequency, Lopez joins others, above and below ground, but always within fragile yet sustaining colonial histories. This process occurs as energy transfers from energy into an already energized magnetic field across dimensional landscapes. Within a public site marked by historical tension, Lopez extends touch across reverberating suspensions and traces that reimagine spaces of death into spaces for grief's transformative conjurations.

But how does touching itself touch the ground infinitely refusing its gesture? *Tear Basins* attends to this question by elusively sweeping across place via recurrent time. That is, while this project's start date can be traced to the status question of the island that plagues diasporic politics and corrupt party leaders, often reappearing via elections and referendums, this piece deliberately moves with the island's catastrophes and interfacing cultural and social challenges across ongoing events. From Puerto Rican cabinet corruption to debt disaster, multiple hurricanes like Irma and Maria, administrative scandals, and community protests to remove elected officials, violence against and murder of trans and queer people of color, along with mass death caused by failing infrastructure and colonial-racial-capitalist frameworks, Lopez's basin makes place for our entangled colonial histories and presents through the re-marking of both land, time, and community.[68] While initiated in 2017, after yet another corrupt election spearheaded by the mainland, *Tear Basins* bears every tear already fallen and every drop yet to fall. Put another way, landscape's history is a lifted reiteration and potential irruption: a series of citations and encircling breaths that recall history's multiplying and heavy condemnations, some above earthly concentrations and many others holding ground underground. The island is at the center of Lopez's basin, but the basin is not the island's center.

Indebted to the coterminous textures of density and depth across historical and spiritual proportion, *Tear Basin (Vale of Cashmere)* is energetically coded for this social advocate and artist. Although alabaster is an accessible mineral to work with, Lopez's engagement with it is tied to an ancestral earth ethic. This stone, dating back to ancient Egypt, is known for its rare texture and the warm glow it radiates. A fine-grained high-density sedimentary rock but still a quite delicate stone, alabaster has been said to exhibit healing powers as a rock of illumination and affection since ancient times. Known to bridge the intervals between material and spiritual teachings, the stone is said to activate surrounding rocks with its powerful energy.[69] A catalyst stone for animating nearby porosities, alabaster arrives with a series of inherent spiritual meanings. For Lopez, laboring with this stone is indivisible from the mineral's ancestral significance and spiritual and cultural practice of cherishing existences across disappearance.

Lopez understands his work as upholding an ethical and earnest "relationship with the earth's indigenous textures and voices."[70] This aesthetic-earth-ethic is inherently ensemblic for him as he "creates from and for the earth simultaneously."[71] While the object's material produces its eventual immateriality, Lopez revels in the porosity of this rock by sharing that "alabaster is a water-soluble compound" and "in this future world filled with ubiquitous tear basins nothing seems more poetic than a community of tears slowly dissolving a large stone."[72] Calling on the capricious expression of feelings across texture, he also reveals that he loves "turning to emotions to carve through an emblematic emotionless material."[73] Inspired by dualistic renderings across affect and texture, he also notes that the time "working with calcite is ancestral," for when the "light hits the basin it glows due to its transparent properties"; it is as if "the light calls you forward."[74] To be called by the light, or the ancestors, is a sentiment tightly lodged within the overall atmosphere of *Tear Basins.* And for anyone unsure of where to locate evidence, Lopez would argue that stones shelter ancestors as they also hold centuries of exploitation and resilient solidarities. Symbolically and symphonically, light shimmers through the darkness as weighty colonial contours deny liberated illumination. Light is a calling forth, yes, but light is also a reminder of immaterial insight. As Erica Gressman and Eva Margarita equally share in their performances, light bears the beautiful burden of awareness's voices across gestures, waves, and infinite traces. Like stone, light will eventually disappear, leaving etchings to glisten in outline, outlines for us to keep tracking and limitlessly tracing over.

If light renders an optic ensemble, then sound produces the symphonic and symbiotic collaboration between emanating energies. Be reminded that this cultural worker understands touch as a multi-relational (even multi-versal and omni-versal) return as he compares the chiseling sounds to a skin-to-stone full sensorial, erotic, and spiritual experience.

According to Lopez, "The stone chisels are like a metronome, where measured time moves and loses you within the object. The process is sensual; you feel the movements vibrating from your hand throughout the body then through your ears as you protect yourself from inhaling dust."[75] As the vibrations create a visceral score moving within and around the body, stone pieces fly wildly into space, generating a further ethereal communion. A trance that cuts any ties to conventional reality, the wild flying material exposes "how projectile the object is and how an erotic and erratic relationship is inevitably forged."[76] Committed to how this haptic and hypnotic experience shifts responsibility between entities, Lopez advances an alternative sensorial event in which to touch an object is to wait for it to touch back.

For this artist, transcendence is erotically spiritual, making transformations of any kind bound to the stabled instability of political, social, and cultural gathering. "I can feel it touch me," shares Lopez of the stone.[77] So after offering gratitude, he adds, what follows is a particular process with the rock to ensure communion: "I always sit with the stone on my knees to feel its weight in history. I cry on it and honor how its soft and hard edges produce a beautiful duality that activates the senses."[78] The activation of the senses conjures a series of coalitions and recalibrations mired in erotic affinity across elemental form—an experience Lopez never denies, even if we question the actual evidence found in such production.[79]

In answering the call of the elements, Lopez moves between the water within bodies (potential tears) to the collective experience of being with one another's internal ocean, soliciting the courage to rinse off suffering together by presenting one tear for another. For Lopez, this release of water is contingent on the possibility that others may not want to share their tears and may leave the basin as dry as it was upon creation. Unmoored by the potential lack of tears and rather committed to what offering and conjuring sites allow, Lopez's project provokes grief's expulsion. By understanding these offerings as ephemeral, he holds hope that attendees welcome emotional vulnerability but does not despair from any possible waterlessness. Between stone, light, and liquid, this cultural worker acknowledges the role of refusal in any offering. Lopez, alas, is not the basin's keeper; he cannot demand the terms of its ongoing engagement across elemental form. Still, in every offering prevails the conditioned conditioning of rejection's benevolent tyranny—a reality Lopez welcomes with assured dissent.

Names and Stones May Break Our Thrones and Place May Never Restore Us

Keep in mind that Lopez places an unpermitted and unauthorized basin in an unkempt park. Without signature or direct instructions for engagement, the basin performs its own rhythms and turns. A basin meant for human tears may welcome animation by other species and things but may never become a space for crying or reconciling with grief as the artist intends. Unable to control how touch and emotion develop, the basin epitomizes many knotted object relations left to be experienced without premediated direction. In other words, the basin is an endless possibility within several intentions and iterations, where not even Lopez controls the object's multiplicity, longevity, or hapticity.

As Roland Barthes communicates during his own grief, objects, inanimate and animated, bear and transfer sentiment, at times engendering "suffering, like a stone . . . (around the [neck], deep inside [one])."[80] The Sisyphean stone, rolled up to roll back down, recalls the object's intentional gravity.[81] One desires the object to work in service of the subject, but the object, made of its own condition and conditioning, bears willful course. That is to say that, as philosopher Martha Gibson similarly shares, "there are dead objects and then there are objects of the dead—those spectral, melancholy objects meditating, and signifying, an absence."[82] While we drift toward objects with personal intention, objects often move opposingly through distinct gravitational pull, intimating encounters between and across the immaterial and tangibly alive. Numerous psychoanalytic and theoretical insights spring forth under this speculation, primarily the role of objects as "metaphorical and metonymic traces of corporeal absence."[83] I might also add, in the case of Lopez's work, the operation of objects as synecdochical etchings, where simultaneous meanings across so many parts to the Rican diaspora as a whole leave room for digression, transmutation, sublimation, and supplication. In other words, how does touch *touch* across parts, particles, and histories, and how do interfacing gestures welcome residues of forgotten articulations across unmarked repositories and unassuming objects?

For Lopez, as for Singh, archives, where so many objects rest, are "enabling fictions" and disorderly depositories filled with overlying unrequited personal and communal desire.[84] By attending to the details of the body as an infinite vessel for thought, memory, and history, Singh declares that archives will never be able to restore us; instead, we must shift inward, listen to our very own bodies, and rethink and reorganize corpses of thought and discipline that promise narrative resolution. Following threads, traces, and ghost lines that remain across body memories, Singh honors what philosopher Erin Manning terms the "anarchive" or that peculiar and "stunning something that catches us in our own becoming."[85] In this conception of the archive, our bodies, like the objects, spaces, and relations we carry as body doubles, exist in difference's abundance. While attempting to trace tears and testimonies, Lopez recognizes that any archive, like grief, is a complicated container of excessive lamentations and pleasures that evolve as the body speaks and the unconscious joins the action. As Singh specifically notes, "The unconscious is the most evasive archive of all yet is pulsing right there inside you."[86] Built upon depressed histories, unreciprocated affinities, impossible subjects, and daunting pasts, simmering in unconscious desire, archives are polemical places. At times, they are just singularly drawn etchings calling forward new economies of whispering lives. Often, as Singh also reveals, the archive is none other than one's body operating as a site of remembrance through corporeality as continued study.

For Derrida, who follows a Freudian analytic to read the depository's unconscious, the archive's polemic stems from its relation to site, source, governance, and utility. The archive is predetermined by an etymological bind that produces its instability and constant state of mourning.[87] Therefore, Derrida turns attention to one of the smallest units of meaning (the word) to open *Archive Fever*.[88] Landing on the Greek term *arkhē*, which Derrida describes as signifying both "commencement" and "commandment," he delineates the dual functions representing the term's currency. As both a historical principle, where ideas, things, and entities originate and get launched (commencement), and a legal precept exerted by hegemonic and governmental force (commandment), the archive is a non-neutral and centralized site of privilege and power.[89] The archive is a storing house, a particular place from which ideas are born, and the condition by which these very thoughts and objects become disciplined, governed, and circulated.[90] As both site and authoritative jurisdiction, the archive troubles, shapes, and consequently directs our exchanges. Signaling, as Singh notes, "a series of secrets between the public and the private," the archive is a privileged and governed place, addressed by and with authority.[91] While Derrida's investigation does not yield a cure for the archive's disorder, he shares that archives might just be anywhere, everywhere, anyone. To find and engage them is to relocate our relation to its symptoms, or to suggest, as Singh does, that our respective bodies are at once archives. Perhaps the "time of the archive has passed."[92] Perhaps the archive's death is its life and drive. In renewed form, residue slips through data and fingers, becoming those facts in flow needed to steady the violence of all kinds of death drives to disc drives. Or perhaps the archive is continually re-cultivated by those ephemeral echoes that request disclosure between virtual and in-person traces, along with all those untraced histories living deeply within the body memory.[93] Maybe archival ghost lines whisper essences and, in so doing, reorient navigations of memory, time, space, and spirit.

But what, if anything, is Lopez's archive? His body identification as a basin? Our bodies as the basin's body? The basin as an object relation within a resumed diasporic landscape? A liberated island in future time mired in grief? Puerto Rico, free and liberated, amid queer time and space? The question concerning one's archive is haunting for Singh, who sees the question as part of the anticipatory death of study.[94] To even ask about one's archive is to negatively subsume interiority's potential to exist as one. What, then, is Lopez restoring in storing stories upon traces across bodies of water, and how might we listen in the act of etching a kinesthetic oscillation across whispering echoes?

A durational installation series intended to infiltrate city topography and the ownership of space, *Tear Basins* is a performance in continuous study across artifacts, sentiments, sites, sounds, interiorities, and remains. Since 2017, Lopez has also been privately collecting and archiving contemporary Rican catastrophic events along with pieces on the physiological, psychological, political, and cultural histories of tears and basins. From ancient Greek and Egyptian basins to Syrian clay tablets dating back to 1400 BC, to the Japanese wash basins and the natural history of crying, to public cruising spaces for minoritarian subjects along with photographic imprints of social, personal, and political tears, Lopez has religiously followed the complicated milieux of gathering, crying, and mourning together.[95] By seeing grief as an ordinary and endless enterprise inseparable from aesthetic and colonial histories, Lopez chases lines across meaning, form, and site. More than just a stone to touch and feel in public, his vessel discharges the weighty psychological and physical tides of imperialism and colonialism (and their waves of difference) across material and immaterial intimations. The question for Lopez is not how to *permanently* capture the fleetingness of colonial transactions, but where to *momentarily* situate feelings of dispossession and displacement that leave oppressed subjects in daily grief. Something like a trace is always left infinitely open to erasure, disappearance, and return; therefore, by requesting that we shift the trajectory of mourning by reorienting transitional objects across colonizing publics, Lopez demands time's space.

What exactly then does the Vale of Cashmere basin introject and expel, project, and disorient, let in and let go, to exist? In so many ways, *Tear Basin (Vale of Cashmere)* bears the vibrant residue of entangled identifications and historical parts that, while seemingly disparate, unite across difference's abundance. In Lopez's charting of decolonial rites of passage, Ricanness is disobediently queer, stolen land is an ongoing indigenous erasure, and colonial temporalities become equally spatial disorientations all at once. None of these declarations and demarcations are antithetical to cruising toward a future on land that, while stolen, becomes another site of ephemeral narration. Perhaps the only way to navigate terrain is to cruise against the colonial grain into spaces with and for others whereby gestures and traces evolve vibrant worlds.

Understanding the landscape's charge, Lopez elaborates a translation of Ricanness through Borikén, a kind of "temporal insurgency in the space of Empire" accounting for several overlapping subjugated histories across stolen land and time.[96] These subjugated histories are marked indigenously and ancestrally, for otherwise, the call to grief operates as an afterlife rather than those eminent pre-lives stolen into obliteration. If the demands of the Empire, according to Lopez, necessitate our entwined death, space, and everyday performances—from sexuality to race to class—then we must counter such violence with a collective consciousness that encourages a conjoined humanity rather than only distinct plights. Lopez's basin, whether cried into or not, nourishes legacies of tears interpolated and re-interpolated by its mere existence, for this emotionally charged sculpture memorializes mass violence and loss to reconcile with its never-ending grief.

Imbued with queer, diasporic, ancestral, and decolonial significance, *Tear Basin (Vale of Cashmere)* "appropriates space with new ideologies for social infrastructure across difference."[97] In this act, social and cultural context and texture and material condition become essential to any of his aesthetic undertakings. Like Henri Lefebvre, Lopez understands that space can never be neutral nor automatically given; it must be made, taken at times, but always refashioned by the bodies that inhabit it.[98] Or, the production of space is not merely a vessel for things, inherited and outlined by grids, but constructed culturally and politically via social intention. Space harbors multiple places within formidable and intersecting histories that, while sheltered in domain, often exact signifying infoldings across and underneath terrain.

As a social advocate for vulnerable populations in New York City, Lopez constantly works to reclaim space by acting as the finance officer for New York Boricua Resistance and the co-founder of Comida Pal Pueblo, a survival program serving the Williamsburg/North Brooklyn communities.[99] Creating food pantries in unconventional sites and distributing resources for neglected communities across the city, Lopez's advocacy is inseparable from his art practice. The call to vulnerability in *Tear Basins* is what Lopez envisions as the softer side of the revolution, helping to model a kind of activism that embraces both warriors and healers alike. Commencing first as a dialogue between community members, Lopez's basin is communally composed and informed by collective questions about Rican diasporic politics.[100] Thus, retracing the asymmetries of power within broken infrastructure is critical to any expression of grief, for such sorrow is not only formed by institutional disorder but perpetuated by the tacit restrictions placed on sharing global loss.[101] Grief, as demonically as it shifts and turns, can mark an affection for space, the public, and mutual mourning. *Tear Basin (Vale of Cashmere)* stores the sounds and senses of communal desire and longing, diasporic memory, and sentiment by transforming with grief as opposed to grief merely superimposing itself on it.

This is not to suggest that sorrow only produces communion and never develops into contentious relations. Undoubtedly, discord lands

Lopez in the realm of minoritarian aesthetics whereby quotidian survival strategies for managing a hostile present are hardly inseparable from beauty, joy, and catharsis. As bell hooks rightly says, "Aesthetics is more than a philosophy or theory of art and beauty; it is a way of inhabiting space, a particular location, a way of looking and becoming."[102] The minoritarian aesthetic is a way of imagining better worlds and pleasures, of intimately *becoming* through both space and time, and facilitating not only representations and categories of the social, but the ensemblic bonds forming between objects, subjects, entities, histories, narratives, dispossessions, and landscapes. It is where the ensemble performs resonance as "the ebb and flow of encounter; a concession to share desire while following a sound, a rhyming, a constant eruption in time, an appearance and disappearance in the name of imagination."[103] Within these minor spaces one experiences "the greeting of spirits and the tenacious agreement to hunger together,"[104] a tracing of formless forms that deny structural intervention and welcome the uncapturable. To chase and document the seemingly uncapturable across resonating forces, however fleeting, is an uncompromising tenet of the minoritarian aesthetic.

Chasing, capturing, and documenting minor life is at the center of Lopez's body of work; therefore, it is imperative to extend a wider lens to his virtual projects initiated almost a decade ago to further assert this point. The following two visual projects prompt the documentation of unrequited desire and death—these images, like the stone basin as a transformational object, contain and impel grief. *Hair Piece*, a 2012 photographic series, is an intimate collection of almost a dozen multicolored and multi-textured hair strand images.[105] From red and light brown to dark brown and black strands, hair is looped and laced, knotted, tangled, and at times dirtied, containing external and clumping particles. While strands are often presented as unruly, each photograph contains a sample of human hair neatly pressed between glass microscope slides. Composed carefully against a white background, each photograph is hailed not by a face, but a respective name such as Marielle, María Pia, Jennifer, Chris, and even Pedro. By apprehending the human trace of the sample's source often used in hair follicle drug testing, for example, Lopez preserves unadulterated lives by appropriating the tools of scientific analysis often mobilized to criminalize minor subjects. As the glass tightly frames each sample, the eye moves to the uncomfortable textures at the center's frame. With Lopez playing once again with complicated dualities, hair moves from being pristine to filthy, then neatly preserved under sterile glass. While some contain plastic or other foreign contaminants, all strands are infinitely and cleanly encased in these slides. Reminiscent of feminist photographer and performance artist Hannah Wilke's 1992 *Brushstrokes*, which contains the artist's hair against paper, Lopez commits to document minor subjects as a life practice for resisting erasure.[106]

Similarly, Lopez's 2015 online photographic series *My Gay Agenda* is a satirical take on queer-of-color adolescent fantasy among Floridian bromantic racecar drivers, sexually repressed high schoolers, and bi-curious underground punks.[107] A series of three distinct images and text located on Lopez's website, this project depicts the artist's racialized relationship to queerness. This work commences with a photograph of two cisgender men embracing: one wears a mullet, khaki pants, and a blue-and-red NASCAR jacket with a DuPont patch on the collar; the other wears a Daytona 500 hat, a Dale Earnhardt T-shirt, and jeans with his right hand grasping his lover's butt cheek. His left hand, over the lover's shoulder, holds a Budweiser can. In the background, stereotypical car racing posters grace the gallery wall, including posters of Jeff Gordon and South Carolina's 1976 Southern 500 with a Confederate battle flag along with car driver stills. Following this chronologically, the eye is brought to a yearbook page displaying fifteen young men, mostly white, in tuxedos. Superimposed over these portraits, minus the artist's own photo in the bottom right corner, are what appear to be metallic blotches. The metallic substance as stain appears to perform a series of reflections: it texturally mirrors the release of adolescent sexual fantasy and the literal camera lens as mirror, as the object's shadow is seen capturing the moment.

Across a series of voyeurs and lenses, splotches remain in place, refusing to cross the borders between images. In maintaining separation, this three-by-five grid echoes the layout of the final image in the series. In a triptych of three photographs superimposed with white block text, the camera snaps a group of men from the neck down. From a white torso in sagging jeans to a Dutch-angled torso in light denim jacket, jeans, and dark blue undershirt to a side angle of the same shirtless man from the first photo, Lopez overlays these images with nonlinear text from Michael Swift's 1987 *Gay Community News* article "Gay Revolutionary."

Pulling and pasting creatively from across the essay, the first photo, for example, bears the sentences "be careful when you speak of homosexuals because we are always among you; we may be sitting across the desk from you; we may be sleeping in the same bed with you."[108] Each photograph is separated, like both images preceding it, with borders between frames and words as conceptual markers. If every image is separated as a conceptual marker, then every word is a warning to pay close attention to that which one cannot see but that certainly exists.

Lopez shares that the medium of photography always offered him aesthetic freedom until he realized that its liberation is contingent upon and motivated by spatial politics. While able to capture life and loss, photography often reifies existence according to the mandates of the site. Or, as he nostalgically concludes, "*My Gay Agenda* is a reflection of my space and time at the moment of exposure; and in many ways, quite sadly, these photographs represent a regional unchangeability."[109] Understanding aesthetic practice to inevitably shift with terrain, Lopez cherishes the ability to capture events through the camera but also relishes how live performances, led by heavy objects and improvisatory audience members, compel people to experience art as social life among intimate gatherings. By moving across text and image, material and texture, genre and media, Lopez takes seriously the recovery of all kinds of epistemologies of the closet.[110]

Lopez invests in the trace amount found across cruising sites, from parks and clubs to schools, cars, sporting events, and even stills between stills captured in endless recovery even when documents do not exist in official archives. Perhaps, as Barthes suggests, sorrow and mourning eventually extend "into its cruising speed . . ."[111] Time without gentle pause is suffering's acceleration cruising across Lopez's objects. His photographic series, like *Tear Basins*, are evidence of silenced lives, ephemeral sketches that, in existing, extend touch across mirrors and mirroring immaterialities, even when it feels like nothing has changed or no one was caught cruising. Even though these distinct projects appear devoted to specific queer erasure, they invite coterminous gathering whereby cruising across sites of difference (queerness and Ricanness meet other sites under siege) becomes a methodological component of minor labor. For Lopez, difference is the inseparability of difference[112] and the minor aesthetic inseparable from its abundant difference.

Whispering Archival Objects: To Weep in Plain Sight

But Lopez's basin project is not just a concrete stone in a park; it evolves with and from several research investigations. Since 2017, he has kept a close eye on Puerto Rican politics while analyzing the benefits of crying under colonial duress. As a critical study originating from his own tears against colonial logics, the study has also led him to expand the basin project into various iterations, like a collective journal issue titled "When Was the Last Time You Cried?" With close to seventy-five entries as of October 2023, Lopez assembles a range of testimonies, some literal, others more poetic and figurative, that answer the call to publicly share a personal experience with shedding tears. Varying in length, detail, and scope, the entries entertain Lopez's other probing question: "Do you cry often?" Documenting answers into percentages, with 70 percent answering yes, Lopez installs another archival artifact—this time numbers are used to activate and connect the masses.[113] These statistics stand side by side with personal depositions to challenge the common misconception of the frivolity of tears. Lopez attempts to prove that crying, like grief, is an unexceptional undertaking that, while exhausting and challenging, is necessary for existing in equilibrium.

In normalizing tears, Lopez renders incapable the detangling of stones and stories from the tears that are made and that may fall within textured materials and landscapes. Yet tears are and aren't the means to an end here; rather, the idea of them, their process, the very summoning of affection in connection to grief, produces the possibility for vulnerable futural encounters. That is to say, and as Lopez reiterates often, minoritarian aesthetic work is not only about the product, staged performance, but includes the years of study, testimony, investigation, and searches across all types of lost and found centers. It is in the means and process where we locate transformative ways of being together and find that answers and questions are coterminous bedfellows.

Following weeping stains wherever they land, Lopez has spent many years studying the biochemical and emotional components of tears. Drawing on biochemist William H. Frey's *Crying: The Mystery of Tears*, Lopez tracks how the author attempts to uncover exactly why one cries.[114] By theorizing how crying helps "to relieve stress by ridding the body of potentially harmful stress-induced chemicals,"[115] Frey investigates the physiological effects of tears to understand their emotional force. Crying, for Frey, is a complicated but also very natural process of secretion and excretion, a process "like exhaling, urinating, defecating and sweating." These similar and everyday processes "release toxic substances from the body"[116] to restore the body's equilibrium. As chemicals leave the body, the body resettles into a type of conciliatory state—a negotiation of sorts between necessary emotions. In hypothesizing the bidirectionality of mind and body, Frey endeavors to demystify crying and elaborate on the social significance of tears. Similar to Lopez, Frey contemplates crying as an act done in accompaniment in which one should be assuaged when crying, not discouraged.[117] Both Frey and Lopez attempt to debunk the social notion that "big boys don't cry,"[118] for every tear indicates the emotionally cathartic and biological benefits of releasing stress.

Interested in how tears promote queer-of-color sociality, including a conjured Borikén, Lopez argues for a "culture of crying for men and the male population of color in public" so that "prosocial behaviors" are engendered to invite "softer," less imperially violent expressions of collectivity over racialized static pro forma identities.[119] As a queer Rican, Lopez learned that crying is frowned upon unless it is displayed as an act of force, rather than an emotional release or an impetus for social bonding. Crying together, as Lopez notes, "creates an emotional contagion that leads to systemic change," wherein outdated and dualistic gender constructions, operating in the service of colonial, racialized logics, seize to prevent the common formations of a "we," even if tenuous at best.[120] Seen from within, crying is psychologically and physiologically cathartic; it viscerally benefits the body by releasing hormones that elevate collective mood. Lopez's tear basins welcome communal weeping to "break down white-supremacist-patriarchal-capitalism" and achieve an overall sense of collective consciousness that exhibits a "softer side of the revolution."[121]

This connection between the emotional and biochemical in crying is also made politically aesthetic, furthering the idea of the aesthetic as both refuge and accompaniment. For instance, photographer Rose-Lynn Fisher in *The Topography of Tears*, which studies Frey as well, turns to the image itself to capture what tears look like when animated by different feelings.[122] In trying to understand the visual consequences of why we cry, Fisher uses an optical microscope to apprehend sentiments. Her black-and-white photographs document tears from all sorts of emotional releases: "tears of grief,"[123] "laughing till I'm crying,"[124] "resolution,"[125] "redemption,"[126] "possibility/hope,"[127] "compassion,"[128] "tears of elation at a liminal moment,"[129] "the pull between attachment and release,"[130] and "tears for those who yearn for liberation."[131] Combining science and art, these diverse images unveil the complicated landscape of why we cry, and subsequently, how tears manifest uniquely, conceptually, and visually. Ann Lauterbach, writing with these images, suggests that when we cry "all five senses collapse into a singularity: taste of salt, wetness of skin, sight blurred, ears filled with the rush of a pulsing, breaking breath, the thick scent of gladness for sorrow."[132] Though a reflection of our conjoined senses, "tears are intellectual" and "they come from thoughts that spill over the body's containing well; they are the secretion of excess we assign to emotion,"[133] and the emotion we follow in a haunting of communions, spillages, and unknowable vulnerabilities.

Lopez traces precisely these lines of thought by participating in a tradition of queer-of-color artists who turn to crying to sustain the hostile present. For example, queer Rican artist Ryan Rivera offers his tears to the viewer in *Goodbye Piece* (2002).[134] A less-than-a-minute black-and-white video of the artist in extreme close-up expresses a less conventionally masculine affectivity by crying into the camera. Without visible corporeality, moving limbs, or words, the spectator only sees Rivera's face pressed against the screen as he wails and weeps, calling us all to imagine a world in which queer sociality is pledged by a shared coordinated vulnerability.[135] And Nao Bustamante's *Neapolitan* (2003) shares similar sentiments. In this piece, Bustamante sits intimately with the film *Fresa y chocolate* and cries repeatedly over a love scene meant to tug at all our heartstrings. With the video playing on loop for over ten minutes, the viewer lingers with the artist as she replays the final scene of the movie.[136] Of this scene, the artist herself notes that two protagonists hug, "that's it, they hug, a plump moment of relief and connection for the emotional body." Bustamante also shares that as the scene's "music swells," her eyes follow suit: "I cry every time, inducing a momentary emotional response by technical manipulation of my psyche. An emotional vibrator of sorts . . ."[137] By considering tears as a conduit for social connection, Bustamante commissions our passions, asking that we endure her depressive feelings through extended loops within the screen.

Muñoz, writing about this piece, suggests that Bustamante's installation is an example of the rewinding, repetitive nature of the depressive position and its relationship to minoritarian aesthetic and political praxis.[138] This depressive position exists in conversation with what he calls brown feelings, repeated feelings that archive an "ethics of the self that is utilized and deployed by people of color and other minoritarian subjects who don't feel quite right within the protocols of normative affect and comportment."[139] Understood in this way, Bustamante's video art suggests that feeling Brown, like queerness, "never fully disappears; instead, it haunts the present"[140] in ways that are both repetitively ephemeral and inevitably quotidian.

To show how social accounts of grief can break through oppressive walls, I hope to *tear* a hole across worlds (in writing) and disclose the necessary light needed to share *a tear for a tear*, a flame for a flame, to locate the resonant calls of mourning that transcend borders, and in consequence, unite us in our common suffering, or our "apartness together."[141] I would be careless not to untangle these two words as they appear and perform in Lopez's cultural labor. This notion of an "apartness together" is developed by Muñoz from an ideological question posed by W. E. B. Du Bois: "What does it feel like to be a problem?"[142] In attempting to say something about Brownness, Muñoz turns to Du Bois's historical analysis of Blackness, not to conflate the two, but to try to answer, in earnest, Du Bois's question. To be a problem within the world, always surveyed, violently amended, and apprehended, punished, colonized, crushed into submission, we must understand the minoritarian strategy for living as an "apartness together." Muñoz argues that while Brownness is always a co-presence with other modalities of difference, it is at once an "apartness together through sharing the status of being a problem."[143]

But to feel an identification is not an identity, or a strict category for defining the self through others. It is rather a conscious praxis to be of a commons.[144] It is to remember that we are historical subjects tied to different types of utopian and identificatory ambitions—in ensemble with others, forming mutual responsibilities that exceed the immobility of indexicality in this here and now. Feeling Brown is about a "way of being in the world" that is not reduced to how one is perceived, but about "shared consciousness and even insurgent action,"[145] actions that Muñoz, like Lopez, traces throughout both everyday life and aesthetic practice. Moving past facile dialectics of us versus them, and identity as legible and fixed, both Muñoz and Lopez ask that identifications serve as vulnerable communion, intentional ideological investment, ethical integrity for one another, shared sites and objects, a "swarm of singularities" and powerfully nuanced "structures of feelings."[146]

How might Muñoz's "apartness together" help generate the conceptual domain for something like tears as the ephemeral evidence of being, being-with, and being-together, always spilling into our public behaviors and commitments? A collection of tears, Lopez's cultural labor suggests that crying is provoked by decolonial queer-of-color ensembling, sometimes through a lens, other times in public, oftentimes through a glimmer advancing the possibility of touch. For Lopez, "ritual weeping allows us to find the resolve within ourselves, enabling more time to focus on how we want to live in the future rather than being emotionlessly stuck in our present and past."[147] Grief, then, functions as a communal labor felt together in acts of meditation and transformation.

Let us recall that for Lauterbach, the word "tear" contains parts to its whole, evolving within and across the senses: "Tear. It's a neat little word, a single syllable, with 'ear' tucked within, mingling two senses, seeing and hearing."[148] The senses dynamically touch, broadening our capacity to collectively feel. This widens our encounters with "language as a type of touching"—an ear for your tears, those tears upon ears, listening-for centuries of muted voices and echoing silences.[149] Perhaps tears, like Eva Margarita's flames, are forms of aspiration, inspiration, and conspiration, a way of unmarking those charged by death and grief with renewed breath. For if the *ear* lives in *tear*, the word *eat* lives in *death* and *breath*, calling forward the entangled legitimations of the embodied senses that refuse to not be fused in their synesthetic, kinesthetic existence journeys.

Binding us in tears, Lopez's basins provide the environment and container for a Rican, Brown, and queer weeping-together that exists outside of state violence. Disidentifying to survive a hostile present, Lopez's wet basins store our vulnerabilities as ephemeral evidence of our communion of tears, for tears carry recuperative properties that both remain and disappear like Eva Margarita's flickering lights and Gressman's flashing visual-sonic stills. Lopez sees the material/immaterial consequences of death as an opportunity to create a culture of collective weeping. Through art and social advocacy, Lopez "builds new emotional communities" that extend the limits of "our colonial histories."[150] In countering oppressive narratives, this cultural worker studies how openly sharing our vulnerabilities is an invitation to elide our disappearance. Always folding the singular into the plural, he places his finger on activities collectively engaged, even if not consciously aware of the details instigating action.

Lopez is certainly not alone in his call for collective grieving practices. Moving from specific accounts of loss to a motley of sorrow across place, time, and difference, American activist Cindy Milstein maps collective stories of grief. Invested in "what it looks like when people collectively yet personally disquiet centuries of loss," Milstein conjures the past, present, and future to publicly disentangle loss from life.[151] In providing the space to not only remember the dead, Milstein impels mourning forward into moments of radical praxis and revolution that advance a common understanding of grief-work. To mourn rebelliously, then, is to accept the invitation to grapple with and sound out loss, even if the state labors to suppress communal grieving.[152] Opposing a universal plan for mourning and a singular prescription for heartache, Milstein assembles stories across consequences "from colonialism to incarceration, climate catastrophe to poverty, rape to chronic illness" to find common ground, the ways to rehumanize us into a great understanding of state oppression, global fascism, and the intimate ramifications of subjugation and restorative healing.[153] Meant to help us "better bear our manifold unnecessary losses when they are worked through in common, on commons: spaces that we create and sustain to use, share, and find comfort in, but also spaces that are ours to self-determine,"[154] the anthology moves with suffering across thinkers. In Milstein's assessment, these stories directly answer Judith Butler's evocative question in *Precarious Life*: "What counts as a livable life and a grievable death?"[155] All loss is also already life, for Milstein, and all expressions of vulnerability, from the heaviest to the most tender, are essential to public forms of grief-work.

For Lopez, being queer and Rican is a process, an investigation, a cruising and crying toward liberation, a way of dynamically becoming and unbecoming in both art and social advocacy, across body, landscape, and spirit.[156] The basin project is an ongoing cultural exploration, a public laboratory for coming and feeling together, enacting the "ethics of brownness" that include psychic and social approaches for understanding race, coloniality, and queerness "as a site of emotional breakdown" and transformation.[157] Attentive to the "larger collective mapping of self and other,"[158] that collapses simple relationalities into the ensemble, Lopez's work asks that one take on the *you* to take on the *me*—carefully attending to Butler's tenuous *we* into synchronicity's domain. This collective mapping of energy refuses to let the relational become the comparative to impel the impulses of multiple orchestrations across feeling, summoning ephemera as the necessary archive for queer Rican grief. Lopez sees this all as the decolonial Rican queer ensemble of the immaterial/material, never precluding race, sex, and nation, and always mitigated by both colonial logics and the people's will to advance a courageous alternative against such conditioning.

T(ear)ing into the Open: In Resonance and Welcome

Sometime on November 22, 2022, after more than four months of unpermitted residency at the Vale of Cashmere, Lopez's tear basin was removed, either by city officials or by an avid birder bothered by the basin's location. Having spent weeks cleaning the basin before it disappeared without a trace, Lopez recalls that he heard of its removal when a friend alerted him through text. Upon visiting the site, Lopez's friend could not locate the basin and wondered if it had anything to do with the Twitter (now X) battle begun by a Vale of Cashmere birder. As overlapping narratives often belie linear progression and facile denouements, let's retrace this story here as told by Lopez.[159]

A few months after the basin's installation, a Twitter/X feud was initiated by a birder who posted an image of the basin with a complaint about its visual obstruction. Aggrieved, the birder shared that the basin was not only aesthetically displeasing but interfered with their ability to capture clear photos of moving birds. Posting a photograph of a falcon resting on the basin, another Twitter/X user suggested that even the bird's expression revealed how unhappy it felt about the basin. As is social media's wont, friends sent these photos and message traces to Lopez asking if he'd like to respond or collectively charge the site. Lopez, still processing the basin he had just washed and cried into with his nephew in mid-November, declined the offer, but asked in serious contemplation, "When was the last time a falcon fucking looked happy?" This question propels him to share during our conversations that such a simple object produced incredible tension and conflict, linking the problem to certain people's delusional relationship to public space as personal property, and the city's investment in such racist and anti-queer illusions. Or, as Lopez vehemently declares, "the people, not the people for the city, create and animate the concept of place and belonging."[160]

Still thinking about the inter-species entanglements that may have gotten the basin removed, I inquired about city permits and the artist's right to reclaim their work. In typical Lopez fashion, he sweetly but confidently responded, "But the basin isn't mine to own . . . have you ever seen a falcon smile?"[161] Never having seen one express joy, I still probed into the basin's current existence. Staging an elegant dance of delegation between material, elemental forces, and textural history under heteronormative and colonial conditions, Lopez acknowledged its life as a very queer act and object. He shared, "I always knew it could disappear."[162] Its renewed and extended existences must now perform past the basin's removal. From documented photographs, personal memories, attendee testimonies, and Twitter/X war messages, the basin reproduces its own reproducibility across material and immaterial forms. Lopez, another attendee in attention, attends to a new series of trace accounts transforming evidence's markers.

Lopez intends to place another basin in the same location without a permit, conveying that the basin's urgency supersedes racist, colonial, and queerphobic city protocols presented as public urgency. The city's manufactured and supported public, not the people, perpetuates grief for minor subjects by restricting public spaces and gatekeeping invitations for communal gathering. This is why, as Lopez elucidates, against known policies and laws, people still cruise, people still make dancehalls out of swamps, people still search for one another when the lights go down and sonic volumes, once whispering, rise up. Thinking with Muñoz's work always, Lopez reads queer-of-color specters to "possess a

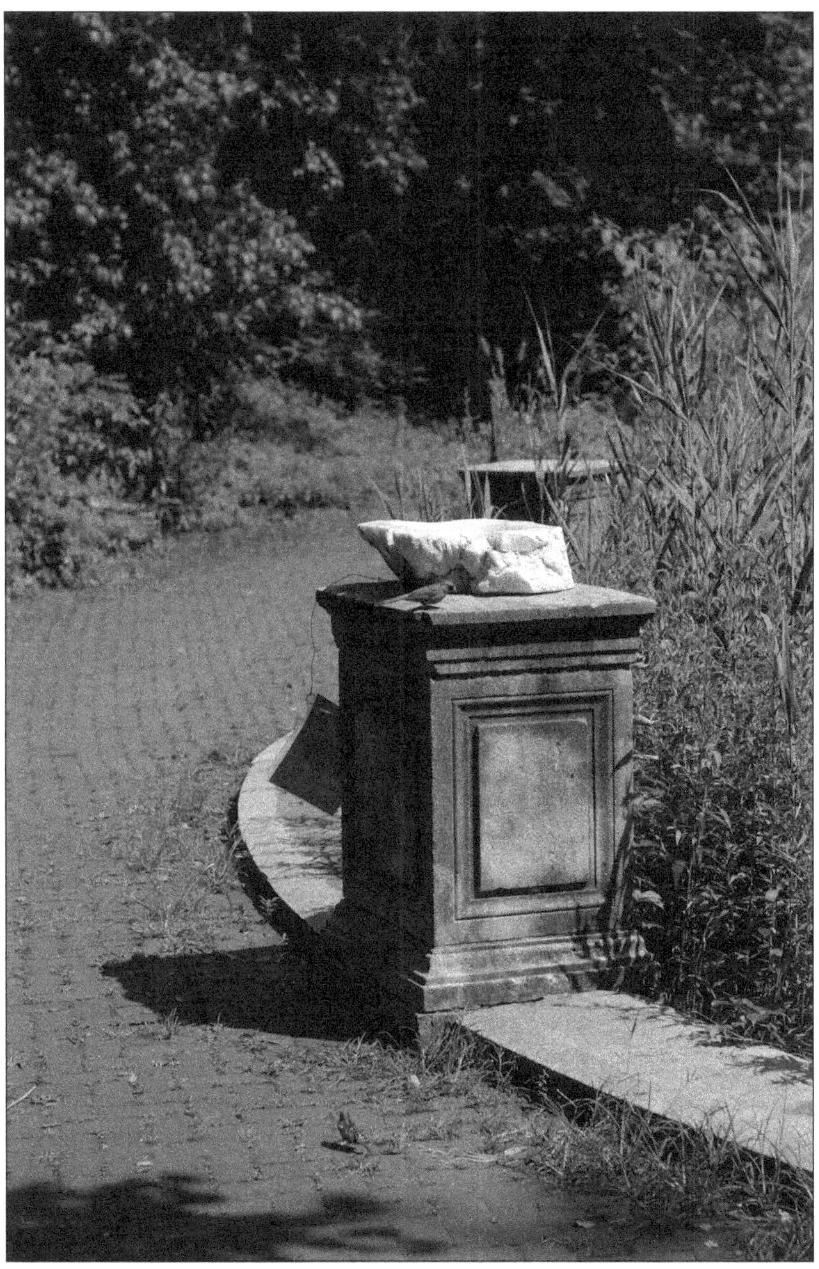

Figure 3.6. *Tear Basin* in its location in the Vale of Cashmere, 2022. Photo courtesy of Pedro Lopez.

materiality, a kind of substance, that does not easily appear within the regimes of the visible and the tactile."[163] Thus, while he may not have captured the tears that could have landed in the basin, Lopez reclaims historical remains and augments minoritarian stories by retracing their buried footnotes. Perhaps not the haptic gesture Lopez hypothesized in his original creation of this project, but the basin, and its removal, are other iterations of social life, still touching as touch arrives via pleading absences and residual presences.

This ensuing precarity is precisely what it means to deliberately hold each other (up) through the darkness, through the desired entry into light after loss, and to continuously adjoin singular mourning to public grief-work in minoritarian spillages and vortexes for new social orders. "Rocks naturally sit on top of one another, and this spiritually and communally moves me," shares Lopez, calling to stones for a tender embrace.[164] Committed to landscapes as living entities, not city permits and grids, the basin is an energy within spaces of overlapping historicities. It holds and cherishes presences physically unmanifested, and the transcendence of it all is bound to emotional contagion within dimensions of shared vulnerability and gratitude.

The ephemeral must be material, for it is experience over remains that captures retouching energies. Lopez shares, "The Taínos anchor me. Indigeneity anchors my practice. We are each other's keepers; not keepers of basins." And "one day I'll leave a basin for us, made with the spirits, on Avenida de Puerto Rico in Brooklyn."[165] Bearing witness to both an ongoing slow and rapid death, accelerated by global disaster and colonial racial capitalism inflicted on minoritarian subjects that we know as family, and those we feel in ideology, loss becomes our everyday, and the everyday a cyclical snapshot of *a future* that must be co-created. Even as the everyday leaves little room for grieving, the minoritarian aesthetic provides an ample and powerful countermeasure to colonially devised logics for living, allowing us to labor to hold on, let go, conjure, remember, enliven, and breathe together. From missing archives to uncovered landscapes and touching bodies, Lopez is less interested in redeeming afterlives as in figuring out how to share breath with ancestors, or how to bring their breath to life in reciprocal essence.

In turning to the aesthetic, then, he extends a collection of tears, contributing further to genealogies of minoritarian thought, politics, and practice at the forefront of grief-work. This is also to convey that queer, indigenous, Brown, Black, and feminist socialities expound the intimacies of mourning rituals across cultural resonances and spiritual endurances by being present as doing presently. An example of this is witnessed in how Lopez granted me access to all the details of his investigation, openly sharing his entire archive and artmaking process with me during our relationship that began shortly after meeting in New York City in 2019. By offering rough notes and reading materials as well as images, videos, inspirational music, text messages, details of the technical properties involved in making the basins, and even his intimate family histories, Lopez opened the door to unorthodox ways of study across disobedient methodologies. At times Lopez turned the camera around to compel a symbiotic relationship by requesting songs and readings, and asking that his own questions be answered. This has meant sharing research materials and feelings in entangled ways: recommended readings to current playlist songs to personal photographs and testimonies to the vulnerable expressions of personal grief.

As Lopez's words in the epigraph announce, grief is both an intention and a metaphysical force, metonymic reencounter and infinite energy. It is everywhere within everyone: a gurgling goblin to be conjured and expelled. In loops of haptic sentiment, this artist retouches the landscape, providing places for us to share our grief and negotiate its painful returns. In doing so, we are all left open to dismantling its archival borders while knowing that sounds, like all feelings, leak and spill across study lines as traces, living ever so dynamically in ephemera's remains as the most advancing of all repositories.

Lopez's project thrives in this spillage and tension, the pressure to hold on and let go through the material act of communally crying and the ephemeral stains of impossible tears themselves. So, *a tear for a tear* in his world-making is everything refused in h(ear)ing and found in listening, whereby the muted touch stone to feel integrated voices across texture, land, and the senses. From a tear lives the exit as opening: an expression of loss that is also a command for a new beginning. A perforation, another side, another perspective, a passage glistening from both lightness and darkness; something other, maybe something better than just a thing forcibly separated.

A tiny tear, *and a tear*, an ear, all waves passing through the body as a signifying chain, for tears are unifying lamentations for more than just grief; they allow the space and time to be vulnerable together. A *tear for a tear* is like a flame for a flame in this collection of aesthetic interventions that surpass minoritarian death traps and stabled instabilities. And grief is but a glowering hymn, a looping conjoined minor melody oscillated into ensemblic submission. Just listen. Just listen as touch. Trace over the sense's overlying embrace and there, like a voluminous note, prevails the melody of stone and relation.

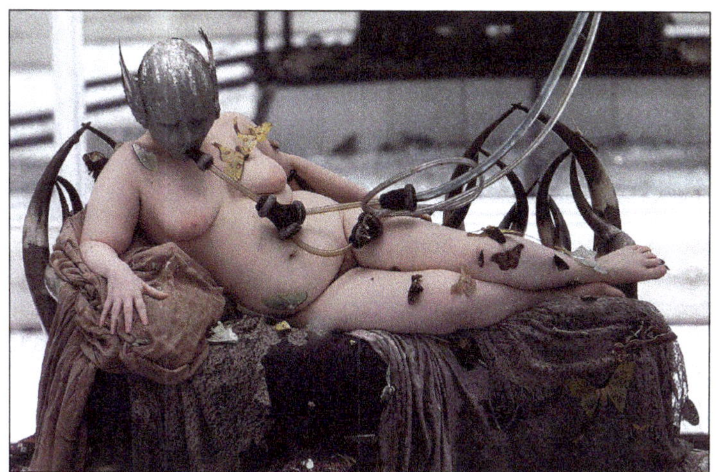

Plate 1. Alexander McQueen's finale to his spring/summer fashion show *Voss* (2001) featuring Michelle Olley and referencing Joel-Peter Witkin's *Sanitarium*. Photo courtesy of Hugo Philpott/AFP via Getty Images.

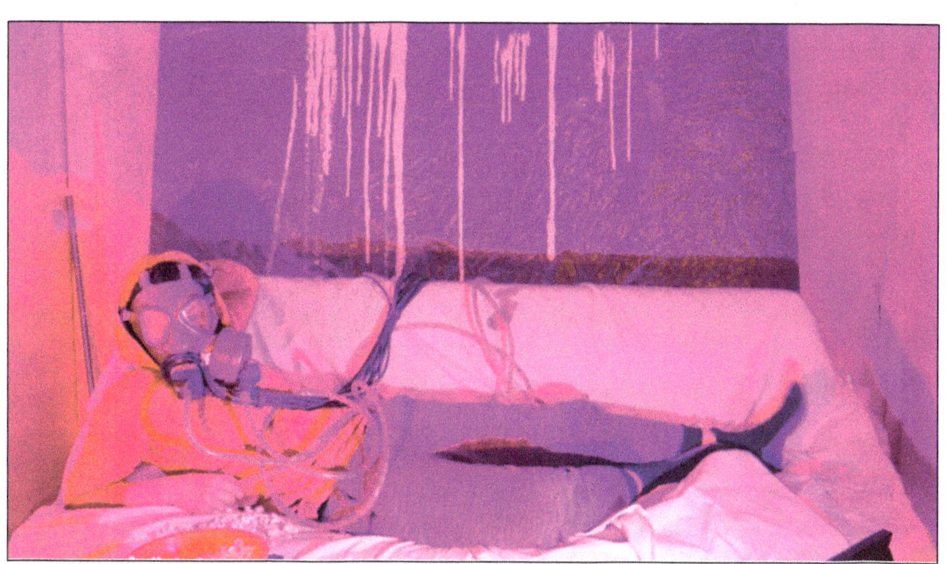

Plate 2. A photographic still from Erica Gressman's live video performance of *COVID-19/What to Watch in 2020* (2020). Photo by the author.

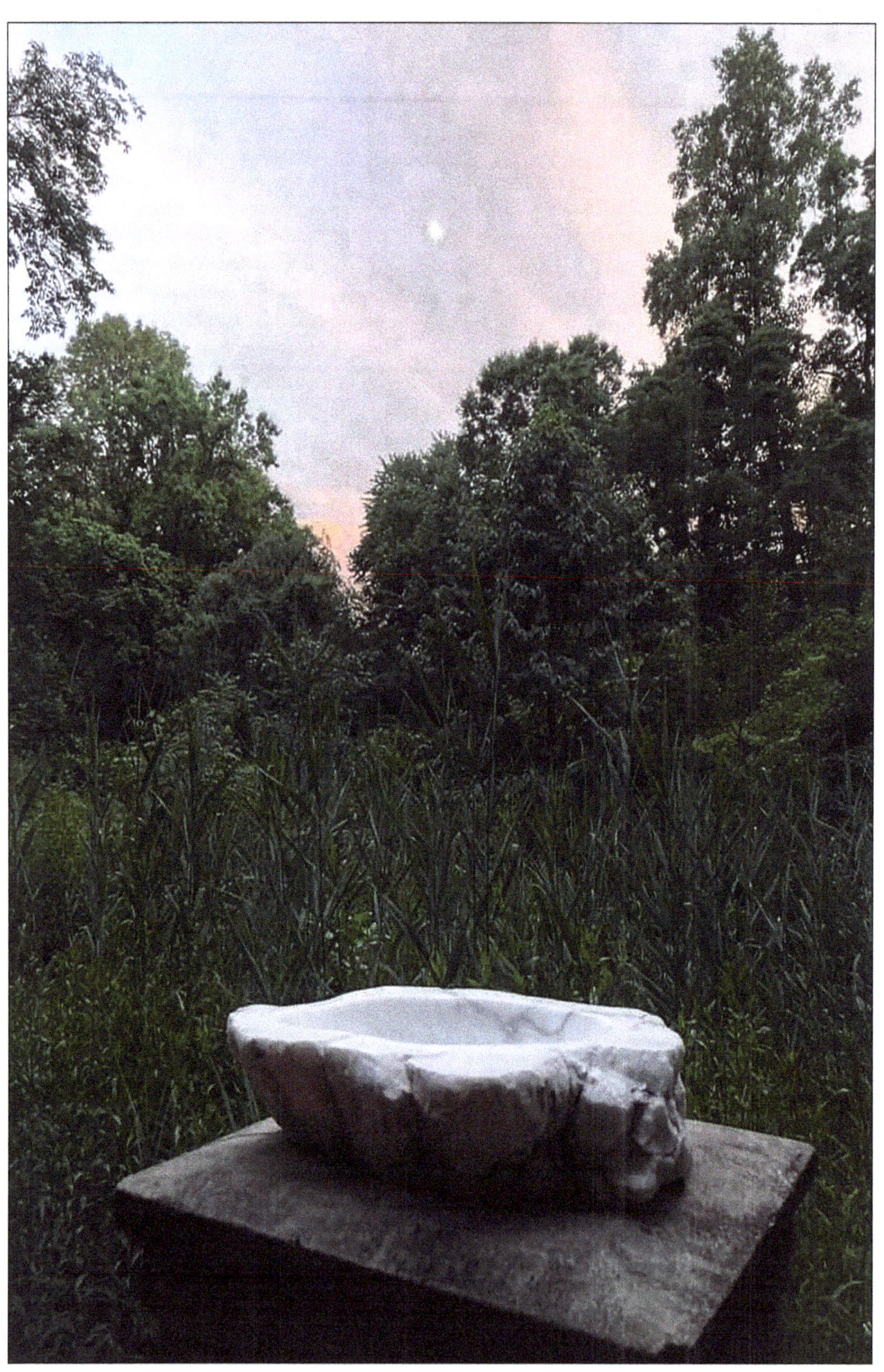

Plate 3. *Basin Vale Dusk*, 2022. Photo courtesy of Pedro Lopez.

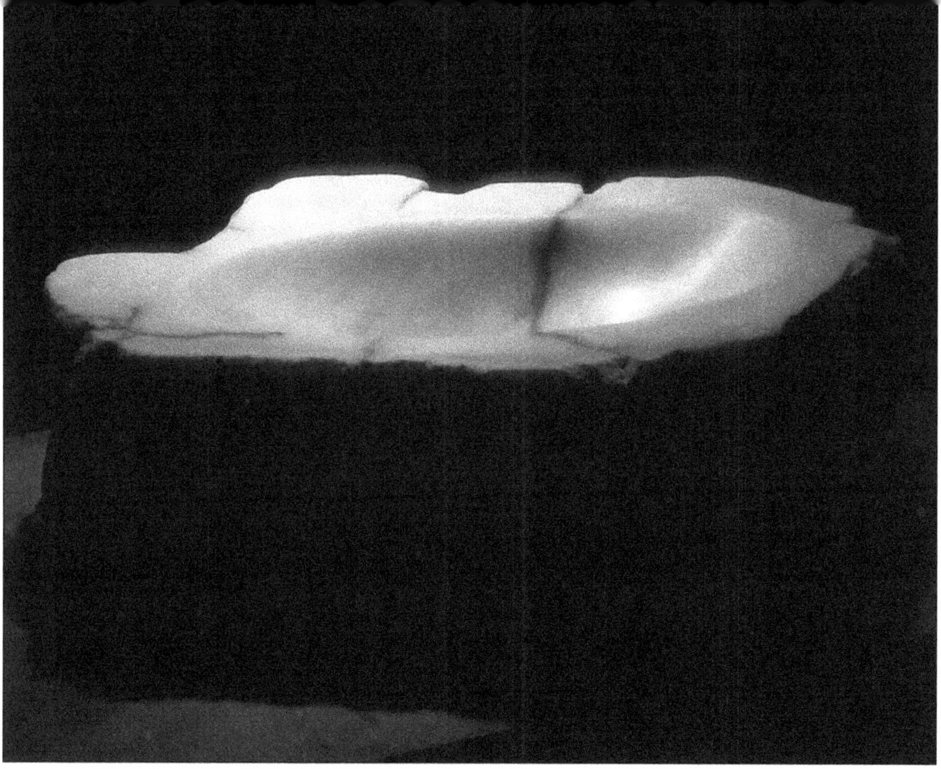

Plate 4. *Basin Studio 2*, 2022. Photo courtesy of Pedro Lopez.

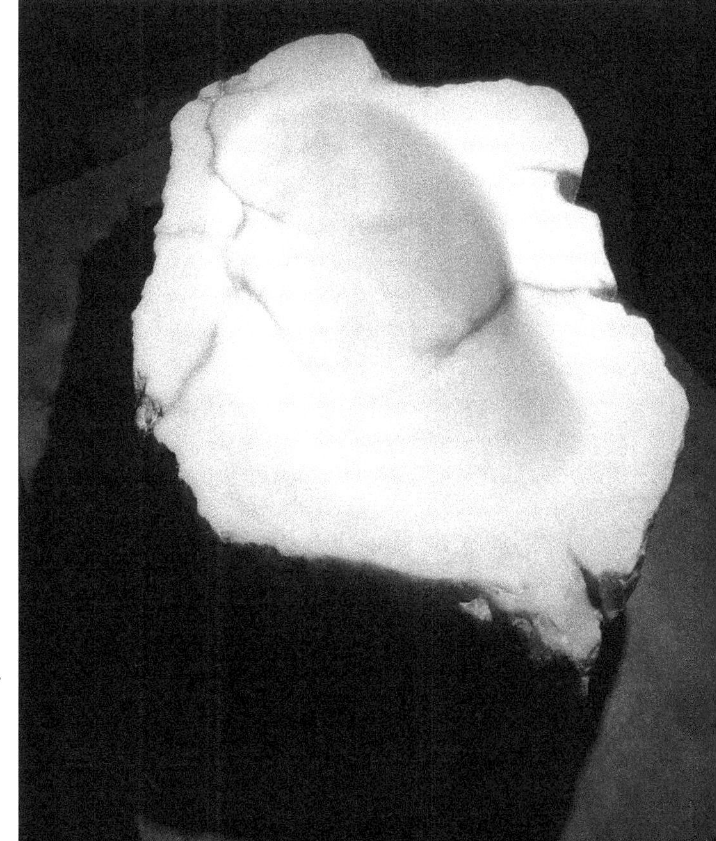

Plate 5. *Basin Studio 1*, 2022.
Photo courtesy of Pedro Lopez.

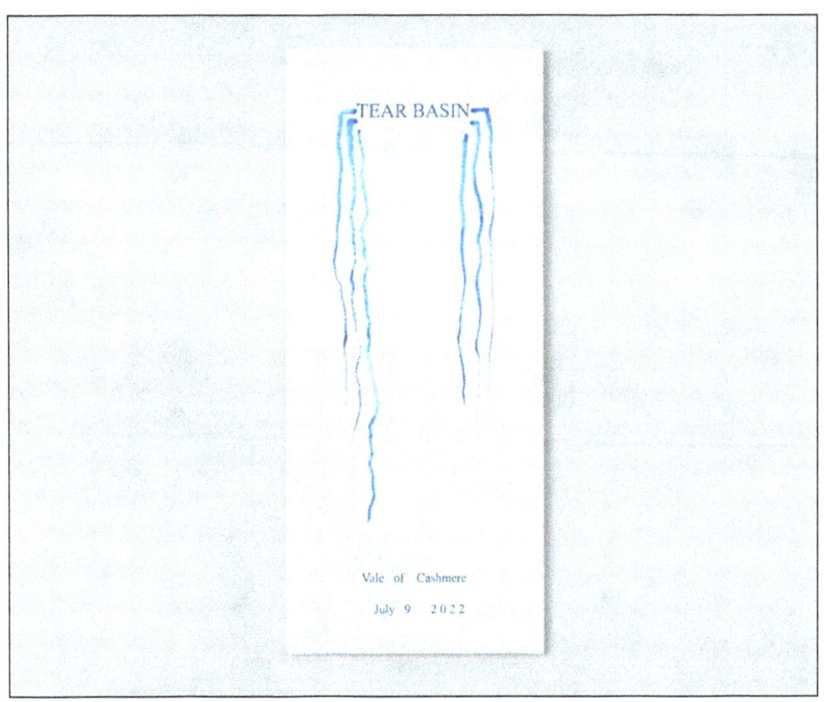

Plate 6. The cover of the brochure accompanying *Tear Basin (Vale of Cashmere)*. Photo by Steven Probert, 2022. Photo courtesy of Pedro Lopez.

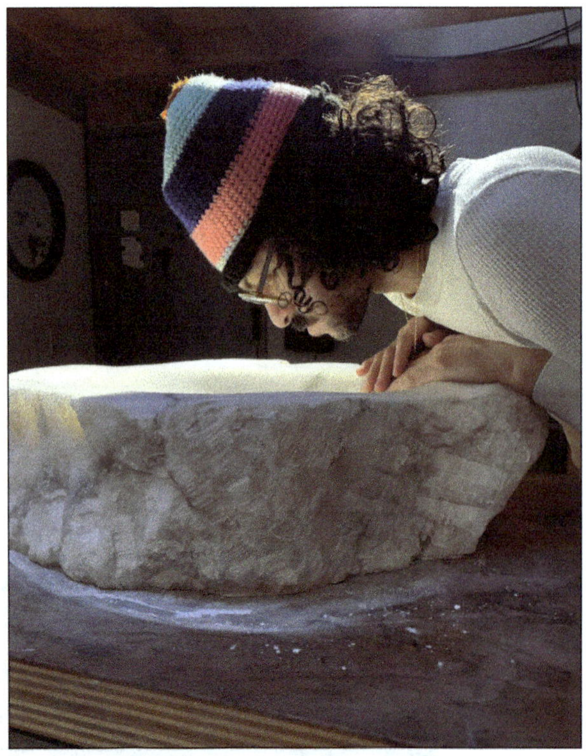

Plate 7. Pedro Lopez in his studio, looking into his *Tear Basin*, 2022. Photo courtesy of Pedro Lopez.

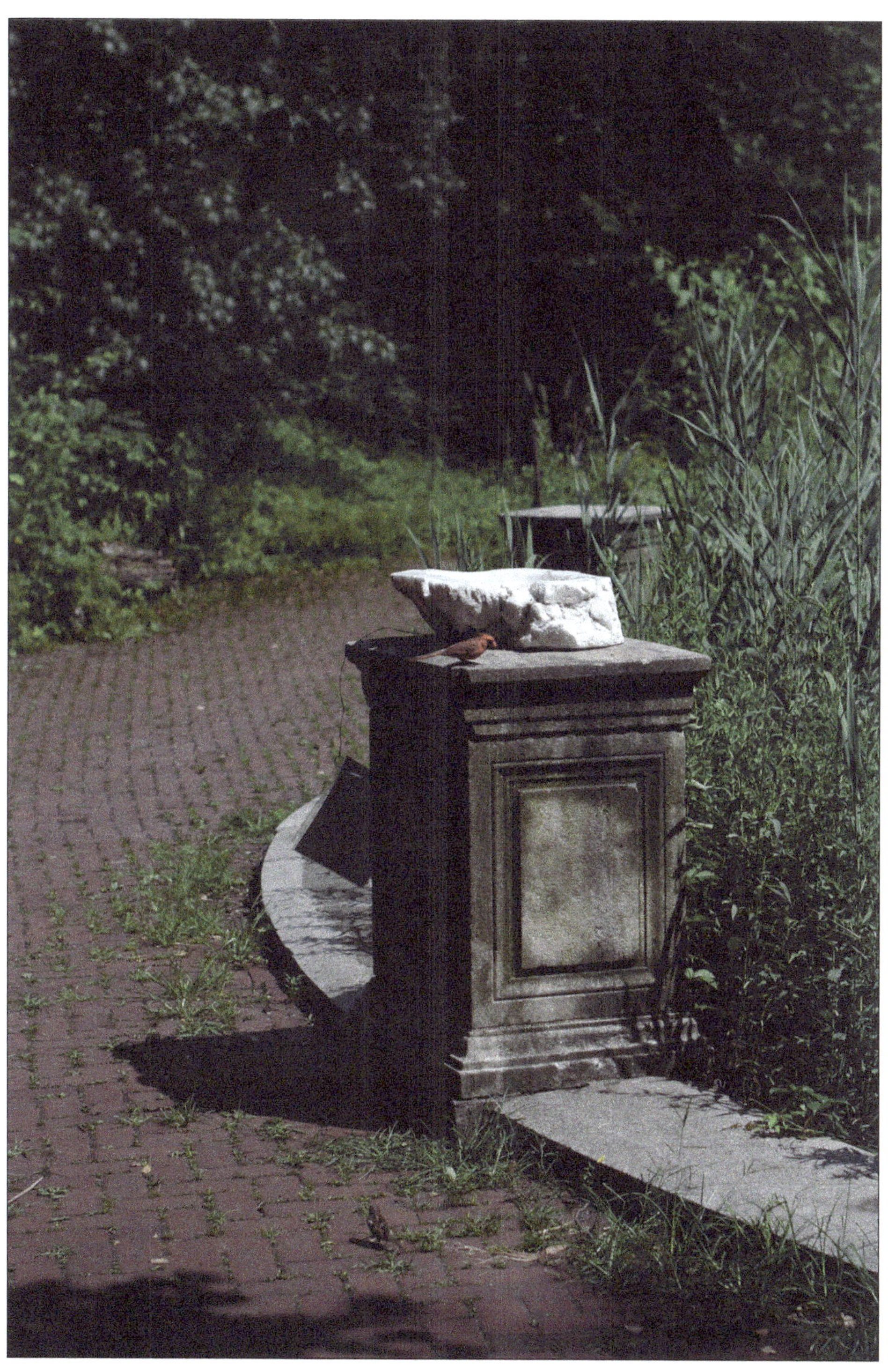

Plate 8. *Tear Basin* in its location in the Vale of Cashmere, 2022. Photo courtesy of Pedro Lopez.

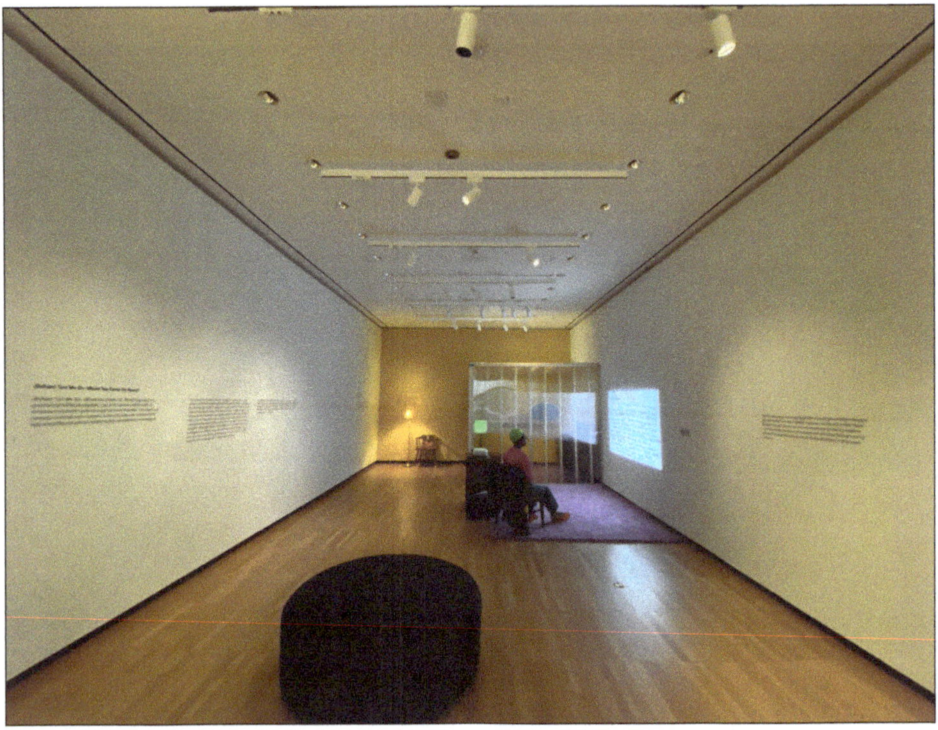

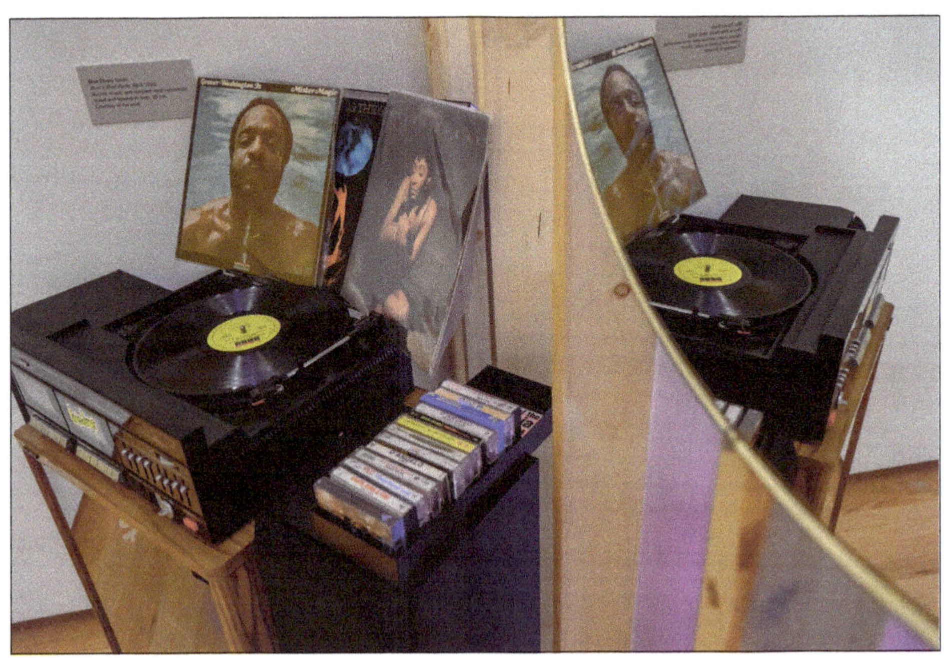

Plate 9. Long view of exhibition with the artist, 2022. Photo courtesy of Blair Ebony Smith.

Plate 10. *Listening Room*, 2022. Photo by Fred Zwicky. Courtesy of Krannert Art Museum, University of Illinois Urbana-Champaign.

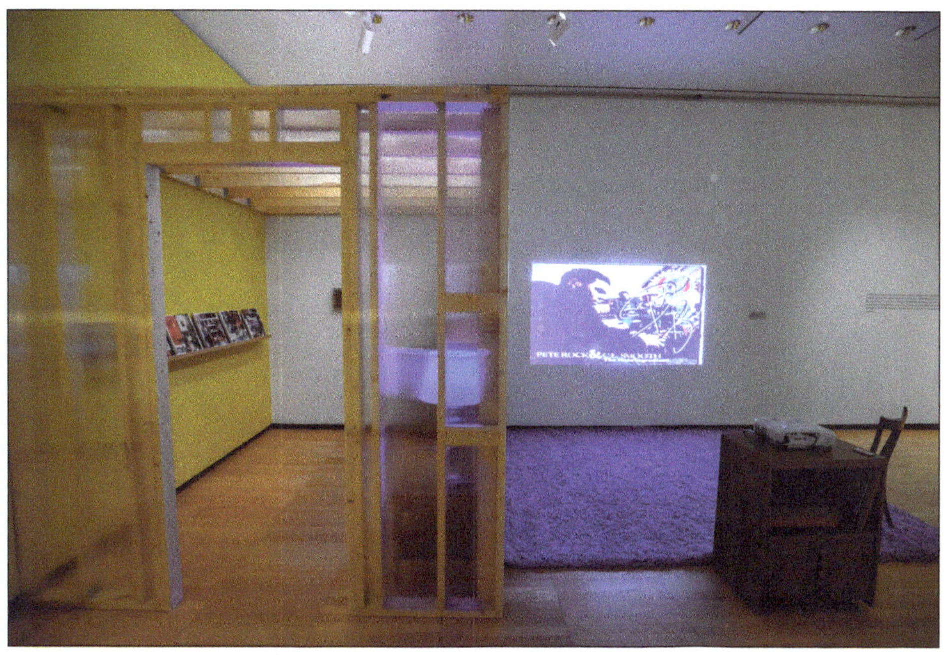

Plate 11. *Listening Across Rooms*, 2022. Photograph courtesy of Blair Ebony Smith.

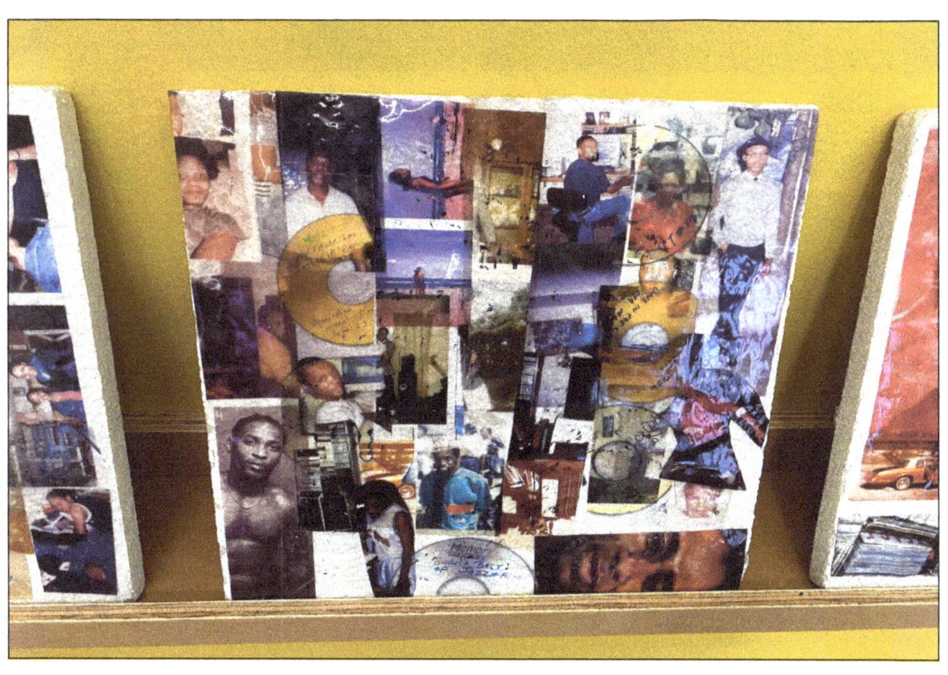

Plate 12. *Collage 2 (a series)*, 2022. Photograph courtesy of Blair Ebony Smith.

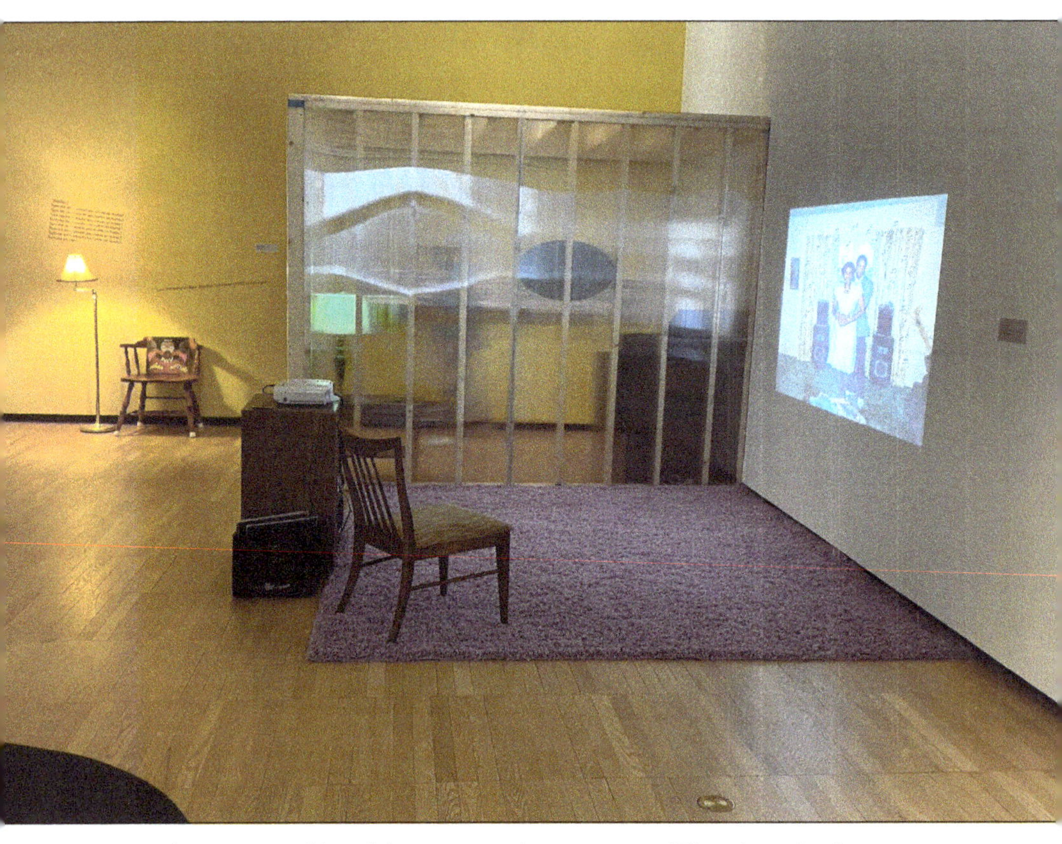

Plate 13. View of the exhibition, 2022. Photo courtesy of Blair Ebony Smith.

4

In Loops of Wistful Listening

When Hearts Keep Calling, Be Ever Wonderful

When I'm not leaning into grief and memory, I'm not leaning into myself. When I'm not listening, I'm off. It's a necessary calling to return to the archives.
—Blair Ebony Smith, in conversation with the author

Loop 1: To Listen in This Way

"Be Ever Wonderful"—these are the closing words on a birthday card to Blair Ebony Smith from her ailing mother. Writing a year before her passing, Beverly B. Smith encloses sentiment in carefully constructed penmanship, the cursive words elegantly swirling in blue ink underneath a traditional Hallmark script.[1] But this greeting card is more than a tender gift from a mother to daughter; it marks intentional lines of affinity and study by calling forth Earth, Wind & Fire's 1977 song of the same title.[2] It also indexes the inventories of kinship across Black popular music, everyday life, and homemade aesthetics. Written explicitly for Black queer feminist artist-scholar-curator Smith, this card evolves into a significant referential and archival aesthetic object over time, space, and memory to help trace endless existences across shared experience. Items like this pull one into the artist's commitment to preserve and patch together family artifacts as a type of grief-work while also advancing Black feminist and Black girlhood studies principles to broaden normative ideas of aesthetic value. Inviting sentimental objects to elaborate and perform aesthetic-life-worlds within prescriptive sites, Smith instantiates a dedication to Black feminist intellectual diligence across material-immaterial terrain.

This diligence, or what Black literary and performance studies scholar Daphne Brooks calls "laboring in listening," persists as a methodological counterpose to archival silence, disappearance, and blatant disregard of Black women artists.[3] As Brooks explains, laboring in listening generates counter-histories of Black feminist musical labor through an ongoing "discursive dialectical jam session."[4] Always improvisatory and rehearsed, this jam session is built on alternative operating systems for compiling evidence and piecing together data to reconstruct unique ways of relistening to archival documentation across hidden voices. Paying particular attention to the musical, anecdotal, and historical signifiers found within liner notes, Brooks reads and notates against the grain of fame. To listen in this way, then, obliges tending to the unyielding signifiers and energies dwelling within and beside artifacts, even when shunned into submission and recirculated across primed aesthetic sites. It also involves "listening in detail," to all the "asides," the tangential and digressive notes stubbornly breaking up linear historical narratives, as Latinx performance studies scholar Alexandra T. Vazquez proposes.[5] How might listening in these ways, across intention and theme, open other avenues for being together through loss and its vestiges, pushing forward communal reconstructions of social life?

If listening requires intentional labor and labor necessitates deliberate precision, Smith thoughtfully chases and chronicles every feature spotted within and embedded across family objects as significant containers of social life. While not specifically taking up Brooks's thematic charge to unite the sonic creations of Black women musical artists historically overlooked, Smith enacts a similar methodological practice by recording and remixing all types of evidence to summon familial voices and stories into documentation. Interested in specific messages within, between, and across items, this cultural worker pursues the transmission of meaning through overlying details. Seemingly unextraordinary, these details help build new archives designed from everyday Black childhood items that not only reflect but animate social relations and political affinities. From handwritten notes to poignant lyrics, Smith understands these objects as active members of an ancestral and political tradition of subversively developing new scenes for social awareness through alternative aesthetic manifestation.[6] That is, family artifacts are loaded with evocative energy, historical and cultural significance that, while inconsequential to normative cultural forces, break through conventional substance and intention. The matter at hand is to both decode the information within them, and to reproduce, sample, remix their messages into a transformative listening position.

Take, for instance, the stylistic and ideological qualities of Earth, Wind & Fire's song impressed on the seemingly ordinary birthday card. A little over five minutes long, "Be Ever Wonderful" blends uplifting lyrics with complex horn melodies, signature band harmonies across energizing percussive arrangements. Calling in funk, soul, rhythm, and blues with strokes of jazz, the bewitching melody elicits feelings of hope, enduring optimism, self-love, and reflection amid a tender call to "stay as you are" and "find your place among the broad daylight" beyond the world's destabilizing impositions. A timeless and soulful slow jam with a clear message to never sacrifice the singular in pursuit of love's unity, the song's intricate compositional components demonstrate communal harmonization and an ensemble's enlightenment toward more elaborate avenues for social gathering and justice. As the lyrics ring of "gonna find a few, who will always walk with you," the band encourages the expression of one's authentic complexity without fear of social isolation. For writer and poet Scott Woods, to listen closely to the band's contagious grooves is to listen to a type of Black solidarity counterposing the infections of racist beats. The band's albums, for Woods, are not solely composed of melodic, feel-good tunes, but written as "Black anthems" that evolve into revelatory, spiritual, and ecstatic experiences[7] on critical listening. "Half of their songs," according to Woods, "are about unifying humanity on higher planes of awareness and love" without sacrificing an appreciation of Black culture and solidarity.[8] Acknowledgment of these critical messages embedded in the band's musical catalog obliges tracing over systems of oppression falsely promoting the dualism of individual desire and plural rapport.

Taking a cue from the band's socially conscious tenets, Beverly B. Smith models a similar stance by advising her daughter to remain authentically herself by letting her internal light shine on and through regardless of political trials and social tribulations. From band to mother, the notion of the singular advances in accompaniment across a series of chords, references, and social solidarities. Smith holds closely these harmonies for being an individual in collective regard by receiving and assimilating these lessons as a listener, DJ sampler, and always a daughter. Led by references and cultural dictum, she attunes to the sonic annals left behind by loss, sampling details to remix listening, all lined by looping melodies, rhythms, and legacies.

Yet "Be Ever Wonderful" is only one of many decodable references cameoing across Blair Ebony Smith's archive, all carefully pinned and cataloged by the artist herself. Seen across artifacts like greeting cards, personal notes, posters, and re-recorded albums and cassettes, particular songs and lyrics like these trigger emotional intimacies and memories along with the political drive to recapture presences no longer viable in material form but mighty in cultural and historical significance. All these resonant objects become Smith's private collection unfolding into necessary archives across public sites often not designed for Black women and girls.[9] While this desire to collect and catalog is instigated by grief's personal tenors, it is equally triggered by the motivation to politically permeate regulating bourgeois spaces. Understanding grief's call as always already provoked by a communal and ancestral listening, Smith pushes forward with sorrow's ability to break open transformative ways of being together. And surrounded by all the death stored and displayed within most cultural storehouses, she wanders past institutional lifelessness into the domain of sonically compelling objects, turning anthems for being into a symphony of rousing artifacts. Despite how mournful it may feel to track and house these familial sounds, the course traveled is intended not to literally land Smith in her childhood home but to reassemble belonging(s) into alternative forms of listening. Committed to kinship's ability to morph and unite beyond loss, she articulates repetition and looping in listening as lineal practices made from the deepest conduits of love. Smith's "necessary calling to return to the archive"[10] requires experiencing the dead as living and returning the deepest affection to their spirited things breeding and traveling in wistful listening.

While wistful listening may be understood as a symptom of grief's remembrance trapped in a suffocating past, the process is not regretfully nostalgic, without political purpose or futural focus; rather, it is a type of listening that obliges one to tap into the collector's collection as an exercise in historical, epistemological, and familial excavation and deliberate documentation, all inseparable from everyday social suppression and its interruptions. If childhood relics carry the meaningful remnants of culturally expansive worlds, even if disregarded within normative sites like schools and museums, Smith's resonant objects endure the brutal to advance the socially beautiful. This chapter, then, follows the cherished items of a working-class Black family in Richmond, Virginia, with a keen focus on Smith's 2022 exhibition *(Refrain) Turn Me On—Would You Come On Home?* As a reverberating soundscape made of multiple listening rooms, this show animates the interior soundscapes of a Black home by charting how "Black girls and people collect, keep and resound music."[11] Pushing spectators to listen to "what it sounds like when [they are] played, turned on, and listened to,"[12] Smith enlivens familial legacy across nonlinear time to reimagine how objects store the emotional tenors of kinship within looping material-immaterial iterations.

To unlock an auditory portal that unites text, orality, photography, and cultural history, Smith samples the past into alternative refrains. By employing a sampling method dating back to the late 1970s, she articulates the loop as one creating endless musical texture, unforgettable motifs, catchy beats, and circular sounds that begin to end in time's present sector, as well as a mechanism that sensorially overlays multiple waves (sound, text, image) across spectral dimensions as psychical and social transmutations. And to reproduce a series of loops into familiar but also unfamiliar energy, Smith travels across space and time to innovate collectively, with and from multiplying evocations, including the object's sensory memories. In the process, these loops transfer and counter-transfer, introject and project; always stimulated by release and shutter, they encircle to transform through grief's transfiguring refrains. Likewise, these loops pull temporal energy inward to expel other spatial frequencies outward as these rotational motions are eventually animated waves in recurrence. Or, loops reform and re-perform in commonality and commonness, mirroring and appropriating original sources into renewed copy. With a transmissible home archive formed by digging across many interlayered loops and evocative objects, Smith challenges the conventional stiffness of majoritarian historical practice, eschewing sideways glances and hardly heard hums at the visual and sonic tensions blinding and deafening Black girlhood expressive culture and their collective makers, both here now and gone too soon.

Loop 2: In Auditory Arrangement: Disciplinary Drives and Drifts

Before diving into a reading of Smith's exhibition, I want to rehearse the specific conceptual and ideological sounds reverberating across the artist's oeuvre. To do so is to locate how these positions line and motivate varying but connected missions and purposes across aesthetic illustration. Smith—a Black girlhood studies and hip-hop feminist scholar and curator, Afrofuturist, DJ, bandmate, and SOLHOT (Saving Our Lives, Hear Our Truths)[13] collective member—is driven by Black feminist pedagogies and her parents' teachings to document quotidian life as critical Black aesthetics. Taking these lessons seriously since the late 1990s, Smith, also known by the alter ego lovenloops, continuously mitigates *what we know by how we do knowing.* Moving thoughtfully between multimedia as an act of disciplinary transgression, radical love, and ancestral labor, she traverses the senses through genre-crossing and genre-looping. These overlying and repeating turns across form, from sounds to images to text, are never one-directional; instead, as the alter ego name expresses, they loop across Black feminist thought and are always inspired by remembering who has been denied sight, sound, and sense, and who has overturned such silences and erasures. More than a crafty alliteration, then, lovenloops is "the conceptual and method-ological grounds for work"[14] that extends unfielded love and collective intention throughout every single loop.

Equally important, lovenloops models the social, political, and aesthetic practices enlightened by her mentor and SOLHOT creator, Ruth Nicole Brown. Brown's incessant lesson to reshuffle disciplin-ary demands to channel the past to transform the future in one's liv-ing present/presence[15] is a staple tenet of collective labor. By opposing dominant institutional ways of learning, knowing, and doing, Brown advances a Black girlhood studies approach to being together by seeing little separation between applied pedagogy, theory, ancestral knowledge, and collective living. Something like a classroom, for Brown, is always a re-manifestation of the outside world, and the outside world a rotat-ing classroom to be read and reassembled continuously by collectively remaking place. Yet SOLHOT is not a prescriptive type of study, for to celebrate Black women and girls is a nuanced exercise in which love and pleasure often meet the pitfalls of grief and pain quite fugitively. Knowing all too well how Black joy can be usurped and individuated by normative spaces, work by SOLHOT denies no emotion or social position; instead, it thrives along a spectrum of complicated sentiment across an even longer spectrum of immaterial-material precedence and presence.

While the creation of SOLHOT can be historically traced to 2006, Brown reveals that the collective enterprise began before it arrived in documentation via centuries and legacies of Black girl intellectual excellence.[16] In a sentiment analogously shared by Brooks, Brown creates and leads from oftentimes undocumented time, knowing that relistening ruptures any easy claim to epistemological certainty. For Brown specifically, this intellectual excellence is joined by forming formless conditions for creative knowledge production that move beyond academic prescriptions to honor Black childhood. More than a celebration of Black girl visibility, SOLHOT is an epistemological, genealogical, and aesthetic countermeasure to dominant knowledge infrastructures as it exposes how Black girls, often erased from archives, have always generated rigorous thought by superseding traditional scholarly boundaries. By unveiling the facades of empirical evidence, SOLHOT cuts across discipline, method, form, style, and various forms of creativity to cherish every thought by Black girls rendered insignificant under systemic racism.[17] An independent collective that also actively travels across cultural sites like museums, cultural centers, public galleries, high-school classrooms, and outdoor venues, SOLHOT has produced albums, virtual texts, aesthetic symposia, performance pieces, and plays, while fading the lines between pragmatism and creativity.

Activating theory via praxis, these alternative modes of communal learning feature in every SOLHOT event, from Black Girl Genius Week to live musical performances, whereby gathering in Black girlhood is a labor in listening and re-knowing by doing-together differently. Often creating live recorded music with on-deck SOLHOT DJ lovenloops, these improvised rehearsals in Black study are fugitive, undercommon, wildly communal, and emancipatory.[18] Any knowledge produced by Black girls, according to Brown and enacted by Smith, often lives outside epistemological legitimacy, and so to create new ways for reading and listening and being together is not only counter-institutional but an exercise in solidarity. In instituting against all kinds of institutions, SOLHOT moves in Afrofuturistic time and sentiment to promote a formless collective whereby hip-hop feminists travel fugitive routes as homegirls, together, to reinvent new archival repositories informed by improvisatory but also very rooted reverberations. An embodied ancestral orchestration traveling across time and space to preserve voices often silenced into the unknown, SOLHOT's praxis is forever an exercise in endless Black sound, image, and embodiment.

Taking to heart the command to be ever wonderful, Smith creates and cultivates with and beside Black feminist thinkers and collective cultural makers. Moving with luminaries like June Jordan, Sonia Sanchez, M. Jacqui Alexander, Ruth Nicole Brown, Audre Lorde, J. California Cooper, Lucille Clifton, Alice Walker, Zora Neale Hurston, Toni Morrison, Bernice Johnson Reagon, and her first encounter with a Black girl genius, her mom Beverly B. Smith, lovenloops refuses to overlook the labor accomplished by Black feminist diligence and instead chases these beaming lights across intellectual and aesthetic material. *To be ever wonderful*, as the artist also touchingly reveals, is to recall the ancestors and parents as dreamers, doers, and cultural makers who paved the way with testimonies and references to herald a conjoined intellectual history. To remember and listen in this way is to also articulate research beyond its legitimizing scope to respectfully recount the stories of those deemed unimportantly minor. If citational practice is often delimited by historiography's normative proclivities, Smith tunes in to references learned outside of school, listening tenderly to stories and sounds within the home.

A prime example of this is experienced in how Smith reiterates the trajectories of study by proudly revealing how her mother was a zealous reader, a community advocate, a caregiver for Black women and girls, and a staunch studier of everything Black world-making. Encouraging her children to study across platforms, Beverly supported Smith's endeavors from sports to music classes to artmaking to community activism. Like her collector and collage-maker husband Clarence, Beverly understood the call to gather in one's authentic light as evidence of the most precious glimmers deemed inconsequential within dominant social life.[19] From mentions of books and songs to citations of uplifting lyrics and poems, Smith inherited the lesson of quotidian referential signaling. While both parents "did not come from or have much in the form of material resources," Smith declares that her childhood, "while not without struggle, was rich with acceptance, encouragement, and a deep love for learning and self-growth."[20] Always schooled outside of school, Smith recognizes the co-creation of celebratory spaces for Black girls by enacting these lessons and blurring the lines between the living and the dead's living things across citational practice. Even silence, a tiny chord, a fainting sound, a glitching image, a passing verse, a smirk between energies, or a song on repeat—those things we inherit and hoard—are anything but mementos; they are loss's living vibrancy, never merely its dangling appendage.

In tracing Smith's tracks, one finds an intervention grounded in ideological, social, ancestral, and aesthetic weight built upon honoring lessons across and within several intellectual traditions. Engaging what J. California Cooper calls "homemade love"—a love ethic "usually done from the bottom up, with care, forethought, planning, and consideration for others"[21]—Smith locates intellectual excellence and affection inside the home as both a practice in place and transformative memory. This type of affection, as Cooper notes, cannot be purchased and sold or "wrapped in fancy packaging" but is rather organized from the most magical things, "many more things, the best things," that "were all made at home, first."[22] Unpurchasable but dynamically accommodating love, the homemade object is hardly a consequence of production but, rather, the thing that infinitely resonates across sentiment and relation to gain immeasurable value. It is here, through Cooper's words, that Smith celebrates life through the dead's evocative objects across lines of affection and affinity. Enacting a minoritarian aesthetic practice that privileges creative acts engendered from personal terrain, Smith places an unextendible price tag on Black art and sound. From her mother's avid reading of Cooper's work to her inherited understanding of Cooper's homemade praxis, Smith understands study as lineage, as Black feminist praxis moving from someone's story into a communal narrative to be interminably recorded, stored, and endlessly reshared.

For instance, Smith's 2022 show *(Refrain)* traces and cleverly parallels her 2020–2021 solo exhibition at the same museum called *Homemade, with Love: More Living Room*, a tribute to her childhood residence, Cooper's ideas, her mother's love of Cooper, and SOLHOT collective principles. In this self-curated exhibition, Smith asks, "What would it mean to co-create and be in a homemade space of interior world-making imagined *for* and *with* Black girls, women, and femmes as part of their everyday creative livelihoods?"[23] In co-creating these spaces, she participates in a long interdisciplinary aesthetic practice of treasuring the everyday and its resonant things for remarkable display through collective reformation. Being a collective member of SOLHOT has meant observing singular desire through communal sharing by attending every gathering as a homegirl and DJ, Black feminist creative and sound-maker, amplifying voices even when the volume is socially turned down.

For close to ten years now, Smith has generated spaces for "sounds to open up listening, slowly and voluminously."[24] By paying keen attention to quotidian objects and social encounters that emanate sound, she employs a homemade love aesthetic via wistful listening in which reinvented sites cut across aesthetic forms and any deferred feelings to land on creative organizing by Black girls. Listening in this way has insisted on a learned responsibility to the self in tandem with the communal good, inviting one's whole entity (as one is in that time and place) into spaces made for collective reformation.[25] Being a SOLHOT member invites fugitive and feral study, shares Smith, in order to "do together" and "be together" and to decide on what calls for co-creation. This occurs not by observing a prearranged agenda for how to engage one another, but by looking to "the gifts, talents, and ideas of those who show up."[26] Over several correspondences, Smith reiterates that one of the essential tenets of collective work is "showing up as one is" without any prescriptive ability or plan, and without denying ancestral guidance. From collaborative writings with Ruth Nicole Brown on Black girlhood and visual arts to serving as a DJ on albums like *How I Feel EP* and *We Levitate Presents: Black Girl Genius Week 2016* with SOLHOT'S band We Levitate, to curatorial work in *Homemade, with Love: More Living Room* and *Black Girls Are Forever* and compositions like *Cherish: A Love Letter to Gwendolyn Brooks* (directed by contemporary artist Yvette Mayorga), and singular projects inspired by communal desire in lovenloops's own *Don't Ever Forget It*, Smith has shown up across music, sound, installation, and design for over a decade.[27] In line with Black girlhood studies scholar Crystal Lynn Webster's notion that Black girls "continually face disbarment from ideas of childhood and girlhood"[28] and are often criminalized prior to existence, Smith articulates her body of work as one wittingly citing and tenderly engaging the past to land in emancipatory futures—futures that treasure, rather than degrade, the youth.

Since joining SOLHOT in 2014, shortly after her mother's death, lovenloops has diligently pushed the boundaries of knowledge infrastructures and aesthetic practice by privileging Black girls and women as intellectual agents and "as archives."[29] Always ensemblic, multi-sensory, and multi-aesthetic, this cultural worker joins a community of women-of-color artists-scholars-curators honoring self-devised archives by cherishing an aesthetic of infinite value across systemically repressed or unknown repositories.[30] By permeating conventional aesthetics with homemade sounds, Smith reflects a hefty tradition of unveiling aesthetic presumption by listening to everyday sounds as musical compositions. With a political intervention motivated by SOLHOT's performativity across analog, text, bodily, and digital form, she sounds out the lost residues of kinship as a practice of place, solidarity, and re-knowing. Dubbed the family archivist by her sister Toni, this deliberate record-keeper reinvents the ordinary, cutting the spectator's ties to any aesthetic, genealogical, temporal, and epistemological certainty.[31] Smith counteracts conventional ways of knowing, feeling, seeing, listening, and enacting memory by observing kindred affiliation and advancing nonlinear approaches to aesthetic time. Building familial archives into minoritarian aesthetic sites, often left open to appropriation by the very institutions simultaneously uplifting Black expressive culture, she never separates praxis from place, personal feeling from public display; instead, she moves toward a documented future by holding all these tenets and the dead and these objects in deliberate presence and highest regard.

Many of these commitments are reprised through kinship as epistemological and study as intentionally wild. In thinking about kinship and epistemology along these lines, fahima ife's maroon choreographic shifts bear witness to the experimentation of Black study in the afterlives of Black fugitivity. ife suggests that these fugitive movements are anachoreographic, or "the feral spirit of study," in which everything is already happening or might have happened as a series of intimacies and durations in refusal.[32] Taking a cue from the fugitive logics of Harney's and Moten's undercommons by enacting their theory into practice, ife dismisses conventional methodological approaches to learning.[33] Instead, she offers multiple scores for reimagining movements in tameless exploration. ife encourages one to think of ritual, repetition, and rehearsal as sites of improvisatory expansion whereby the improvisational becomes the necessary archive, formed and deformed in entanglement to repudiate embodiment's learned disciplinary structures. Pushing forward exercises in the inseparability of forms, ife turns study on its head, questioning the logic withholding minor aesthetic inquiry as fundamental to social and psychic life.[34] As an alternative, ife proposes "another mode of movement, one not reliant upon choreography as rule or dictated orientation, but a movement born in wildness, in fugitivity, in refusal."[35] This movement, formed materially and immaterially, is bound to a lineage of field laborers, workers, folks who worked in movement without "compensation or nourishment."[36]

To release study from colonial imposition, ife records "black study as something otherwise, some wiser configuration other than an argument."[37] Moving away from thought as problem and writing as solution, ife asks, "What if our sense of inherited subjectivity is sound? What if the reality we think we inhabit is nothing more than oscillation?"[38] By thinking of sound waves as both displacement and grounding, formlessness and lineage occurring in simultaneous time and inherited disparity, ife, like Smith, tessellates across forms, feelings, and senses. In doing so, a sensorial mosaic challenges every corner of study and its documentation to such an extent that what one understands as seeing becomes what one never knew about listening. Rearranging any slick notion of the senses as singular and the archive as a stable entity for justly recording lives and their things, these thinkers contemplate repositories as desirable mobilities, continual haptic sound loops, traveling through particles against the boundaries of Black death and the isolating geometries of nostalgia and grief.

Asking us to tune in to multi-layered textures of kinship, study lessons, and abiding grief within wistful listening, Smith leaves herself, the listeners, and even memory open to incoming spectral messages and psychic breakthroughs in acts of feral intonation. Through wistfully listening in fugitive attention, she occupies the public with personal attachments lodged tightly within decades-old songs reprinted by the mother, re-recorded by the father, and sampled in collective reconfiguration. These interwoven endowments solicit corroboration and aural and oral attunement across unearthly planes. Smith, the living progenitor of this inter-historical affair, morphs into an acoustic vessel for the dead and their things, returning to family archives to transmit the energies of childhood, not as a nostalgic reprint, but as a facilitator for transformation. Or, as she shares about and through every artwork, to remember them publicly ("here in spirit, always") is to remember histories of the self.[39] A familial acoustic channel, this cultural worker tends to both the dead and living self, spawning an aesthetic movement impelled by childhood experience, ongoing love, longing, and sonic sociality across mitigating spaces.

Loop 3: Ubiquitous Display: Vibrating Returns Across Repository and (Refrain)

Led by ongoing grief and a collective mission, Smith turns death's objects into extended life in her 2022 soundscape exhibition *(Refrain) Turn Me On—Would You Come On Home?* This self-created and curated show invites a working-class Black home and its multidimensional items into a white cube.[40] In collaboration with the Krannert Art Museum's inaugural all-Black faculty group show called *Black on Black on Black on Black* inspired by Black Quantum Futurism, Smith responds to the larger exhibition's call by refusing to untangle the categories of artist, curator, and ancestral member. Alongside esteemed colleagues Nekita Thomas, Patrick Earl Hammie, and Stacey Robinson, Smith shares the museum floors with each artist-scholar-curator singularly and collectively by leaning into the meta-exhibition's aim to undertake the intricacies of "Black experience, time travel and imagination" while exploring the depths and edges of "identity, positionality, healing, innovation, and education."[41] Like her colleagues, but uniquely in her own way, Smith generates a "multi-dimensional immersive, critical, and openly reflective space" for audience members to experience.[42] As a student of Black feminist study as communal listening, she specifically responds to the show's call through the technical particularities of form, or through the refrain's repeated refrain—a practice turned on and off through many correlating exhibitionary details.

For example, Smith's exhibition title *(Refrain) Turn Me On—Would You Come On Home?* is a riff on yet another Black popular song composed by one her father's favorite artists, the socially conscious Roy

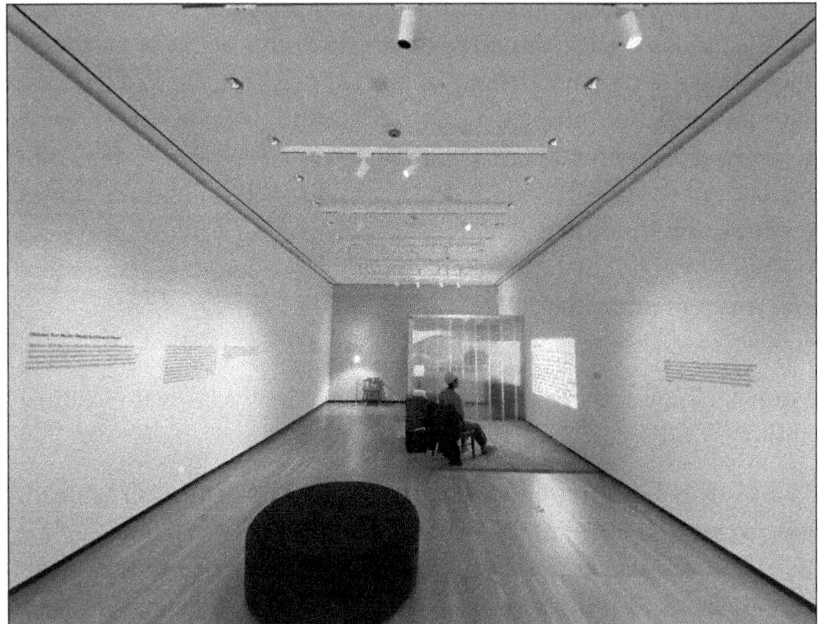

Figure 4.1. Long view of exhibition with the artist, 2022. Photo courtesy of Blair Ebony Smith.

Ayers. This title is sampled from the actual refrain of the song "Love Will Bring Us Back Together" from his 1979 album *Fever*. The catchy melody, '70s snazzy bassline, and repetitive lyrics set the scene for intermingling sounds across jazz-funk, disco, and soul. As one of the best and most prolific "jazz-funk musicians of our time," according to music producer, DJ, and record collector TJ Gorton, Ayers "released a string of groundbreaking recordings" that somewhat defied genre, crossing and mixing styles "to create his own signature sound which some have labeled 'neo-soul.'"[43] Marking form-as-content via this genre-crossing, the vibraphonist and composer extends repetition as a socially mobilizing endeavor. From the lyrics in verse one that long for accompaniment in "you seem so far away / please don't stay astray" to the chorus's sentimental drop in "teardrops just keep falling / my heart just keeps calling" to verse three's "I just want you near me / why then can't you hear me?," the six-minute seductive song is led by fervid and velvety vocals that run infectious grooves across Smith's gallery walls.[44] Delivering ingenious but lissome key changes across beats and hooks, this popular tune leaves Smith listening for the tiny sounds within every refrain to catch chords for curatorial expansion.

But the show's title is not solely a riff; it develops into the exhibition's framework, technical capacity, and conceptual layout—a *(refrain) from a refrain in constant refrain*. Enacting her trademark looping and sampling praxis from title to object to event, Smith smartly joins familial reverence and theoretical mission as the title also honors her father's favorite song played faithfully throughout her childhood. Clarence Orlando Smith, also lovingly known as "Burn" and "Landa," passed away almost a decade before Beverly B. Smith but spent a majority of his time at home listening to and creating mixtapes composed of jazz numbers, funk, blues, soul, R&B, and hip-hop jams.[45] As a young child, Smith learned about the performative power of music and was encouraged to listen closely to the messages gleaned across material and otherworldly sonic terrain. After losing both parents at a young age, she turned this practice into a deeper aesthetic, emotional, spiritual, and intellectual mission.

A direct quote from the song's refrain, the exhibition title enacts the first citational nod in study, a long line of nods in a familial practice of acknowledging the work of others as a type of ethical and lineal labor in one's singular-plural development. Conceptually guiding the audience through archival relining and tracking, the title also performs sonically, engendering a listening-scape through inquiries and commands. Posed as a question via the band's lyrical direction, the title invites the audience into Smith's memories, not as a flattening nostalgic experience but as one in which resonant objects expand growth and new world-making practices. If love can truly bring us back together, the call enacts the refrain as affinitive duty whereby repeated phrases, syllables, notes, and harmonic grooves legislate an intimate and prolonged affair with the dead. Notwithstanding the song's infective groove, Smith's aesthetic decisions are rather spiritually motivated, for the entire process instantiates attuning the ear to messages within objects loaded with spectral accompaniment.[46] In listening to the track carefully, slowly, and repeatedly, Smith claims to have been pulled into aesthetic creation by the song's musical and lyrical instructions. Of this spiritual encounter she shares the following memory: "I felt my father was speaking to me through Roy Ayers—asking me to turn him on and come home."[47]

Yet what does it sonically and sensorially entail to return home to turn the deceased on? Smith suggests that it assumes a certain strategic offense to be "open to the signals, messages, compositions, notes that transcend home as a place into a practice for memory, honor, and celebration."[48] Or, as she tearfully reveals during our multiple correspondences, "being open means being available to them still being here." This idea of "still being here," while appearing like the toxic immobilizations of nostalgia whereby everything remains trapped in the past, is rather a productive process in mobilizing from the presence of memory into transfiguring and emancipatory futures. By employing plaintive listening as methodological refrain, Smith mobilizes grief to initiate transformative ways for being together again; at times this togetherness is felt in immaterial sway, and at other times, it develops across aesthetic landscapes through the direction of a title. Being open, not without vulnerable risk, always entails embracing the portal's cleft across spectral discharge and vibrant sonic import.

A reverberant soundscape turned on by found objects, music, video film, sculpture, text, and collage, Smith's (*Refrain*) intermixes the politics of dwelling and cultural beats into a "soundhouse" where various listening rooms hold love, pleasure, loss, and longing as inseparable sympathies. With a keen focus on Black popular music, family photographs, and mementos, Smith explores how Black people, and specifically Black girls, record and "resound music."[49] Yet these familial artifacts are and aren't entirely owned by Smith; they dwell across a spectrum of material-immaterial Black cultural production, multiplied in sentiment and historical retracing. Or they belong to those sounds between sounds in which those gone too soon undo their muted inattention by coursing through the visceral receptors of energy and entity. In answering the call to "come on home," this cultural worker increases and alchemizes the dead's volume to decrease historical silence, and in so doing, echoes forward in homage and interminable appraisal. Every artifact shared, however inconsequential to the institution's categories of aesthetic worth, is a "structure of feeling," an aesthetic-life-world linking the dead to the living in endless closure.[50] Seeing grief as alchemy, Smith leans into grief and memory to lean into herself—"a necessary calling to return to the archive" to foster more substitutive, capacious, horizonless, fugitive, and emphatically Black girl repositories across wistful listening.

Meant to capture the directives of everyday sonic transference, Smith's wistful listening invites sorrow and pleasure, pain and longing, love and loss as co-conveners to every scene—no sentiment, however negating, is ever denied or dichotomously imposed. Skilled at running across opposed sentiments, Smith intermixes the brutal and beautiful, pushing grief to respire within coterminous crevices made and amplified by Black girlhood frequencies. Knowing all too well the pitfalls of joining nostalgia, gender, and race in any institutional art production, the artist vulnerably shares the following about this show: "It's easy to categorize my work under pure nostalgia. But it could also be understood as portals for incoming messages following histories of sounds and stories."[51] This artist is incredibly clear that subsuming grief-work into the pitfalls of conventional nostalgia renders obsolete the political practices of grieving and making while Black. Nostalgia is often presented and deployed as a defense mechanism against the inevitable and crucial processes of mourning, or as something pathetic and pathological that snares one into the infinite past.[52]

I suggest, instead, that Smith's work builds upon the productive relationship between nostalgia and grief by reworking nostalgia to multiple ends to reframe both grieving and aesthetic practice. By trying to understand how grief is evoked by nostalgic memories through resonant objects, Smith endeavors to transform both internal and external forces mitigating transition and change. I do not understand Smith to be assuming that nostalgia disavows mourning but that, when considering a Black girlhood studies praxis, it is imperative not to subsume any reflections on childhood as superficially nostalgic, as this, too, can evolve into another type of pathology—the infantilization and patronization of Black feminist thought and anything Black girlhood studies. There is something unsettling about discussing race, gender, and nostalgia in tandem for this artist and it involves how these categories when deployed together often undervalue certain aesthetic work by Black feminist thinkers. When asked if these objects remedy homesickness, or if the practice redeems loss, Smith responded by questioning the category "home" itself, as her work, as she explains it, is never about trying to get back to any specific domain but rather attempting to instantiate an aesthetic praxis as a practice of place.

Challenging the melancholic overexposures of race and the ongoing infantilization of Black girlhood studies, Smith regards her show as a celebration of sounds and a dynamic hymn for new portals into listening. These incoming messages turn the concept of home (often an immobile nostalgic station) into an entryway, an evolving opening, a potential two-way doorway for something yet to come, as opposed to something one occasionally visits down memory lane. Still, "yet to come" and "come on home," while bearing dissimilar directions, symbolize similar directives—to arrive is to also return, to return is to await the portal's access; every motion made of looping movements in eternal recurrence. Energized by harmony's funk into conjoined rhythm, ensemblic presences call out in answer to question in chorus, for in every (re)turn home, the "heart just keeps calling."[53] As the lyrics invite us to envision, coming home is where everything still lives across familial archives composed of bodies and the bodies of things we infinitely animate by remaining vulnerable to unknown dispatches.

Both celebratory and extolling, communal and personal, *(Refrain)* is filled with desires multiplying across feelings and memories, words and sounds, amid liner notes and bellowing objects. Composed of five interrelated and overlapping art objects, the show's range includes visual collages, musical samplings, sculptural pieces, remixed recorded conversations, and referential textured walls. From art pieces dubbed "Would You Come On Home?" to "Landa's Joyful Yellow" to "Burn's Best of Jazz and Funk" to "Untitled (mixed media film)" to "Burn's Best Radio.MP3," the exhibition ebbs and flows into duplicating listening rooms within a larger soundhouse, in which each art piece and space reference one another.[54] Like Ayers's extended refrain sung to the same tune, Smith deliberately replicates rhythms across every aspect of the installation to pull the spectator into the political and social logics of repetition. Incorporating words across the riff, chorus, hook, and bridge, the refrain, while working in accompaniment, singularly calls forward the ethereal loop as a concurrent and infinite existence, or to repeat is to come on home, back together again through the refrain's continual hail.

Upon entering the gallery, spectators are sonically propelled by the echoing sounds of funk, jazz, soul, rhythm and blues, and hip-hop playing over speakers. Sade, Roy Ayers, George Benson, Grover Washington Jr., Erykah Badu, Mos Def, Parliament, The Roots, Earth, Wind & Fire, Oneness of Juju, Bill Withers, and Plunky, to name a few of the artists, direct the body's movements, providing ample space to shift and sway with sound. These named artists, according to Smith, were consistently listened to during her youth, not as background noise but metaphors and signs for how to live, create, and cultivate love.[55] In creating this looping playlist from her father's pre-recorded mixtapes, lovenloops invites the spectator into childhood songs once heard over the family's stereo system. Taking seriously this music on rotation, Smith recalibrates many voices into an aesthetic practice that rings across institutional space transgressively and counterintuitively.

These musicians heard over the speakers are not the only voices prodding the ears, however; Smith's smooth and silky voice moves in and out and between songs in a pre-recorded narration that "includes samples of separate dialogues with family members." Sampling previous conversations with her Aunt Dana (her dad's little sister), Gran (her dad's mom), Aunt Netta (her mother's sister), and her own sister, Toni, Smith performs as narrator and actor and inhabits multiple voices. In doing so, Smith powerfully suggests that kinship is sound's ensemblic eardrum.[56] Positioning the familial conversation as an operable sonic production, she generates a meta-narrative propelled by an orchestra of voices carried by one. These voices, while not the same as Sade's or Bill Withers's, still carry intellectual and cultural meanings that, even if not significant to dominant social forces and repositories, live at the center of Smith's mission.

Performing wistful listening, then, necessitates that everyday dialogic encounters be listened to and employed to resonate amid conventionally respected sounds. Reminiscent of the voices fading in and out between songs in hip-hop albums like Lauryn Hill's *The Miseducation of Lauryn Hill*, to name just one, Smith brings to the forefront the sounds of community members often muted from aesthetic production.[57] These silences belie a series of narratives that, while untold, live in minor reservoirs.[58] To labor in this listening is to notice how Smith's pre-recorded narration is far from sped up; it is pointedly slow, measured, stretching across words sometimes too low and muttered to be audible but still a voice that resounds across and with others. Unlike the breadth, speed, and clarity of each song blaring on loop throughout the gallery rooms, including "Mothership Connection (Star Child)," "No Ordinary Love," "Inner City Blues (Make Me Wanna Holler)," "Jazz Is All That Jazz," and "Lovely Day," Smith's voice fades in and against time's tempered spatiality.[59] Slowly, like reverberating feedback, the voice loops in and out, turning over ears to say something about sound's ephemeral and permanent measures amid grief's resurrection as constant refrain.

The audience, unable to easily distinguish one voice from another, listens across and between sound and image, feeling and sympathy. Though Smith gives a playlist link for her audience to revisit in their own time, she refuses to share the pre-recorded narration with anyone.[60] "It's meant to be ephemeral," she notes. "Maybe I ran out of time. Maybe I should go back and transcribe it," she says, but for now "it loops at that moment in space."[61] Sampling ephemera and permanence, citation and the silent footnote, she shatters any easy idea of the archive as a designated and stable place to locate answers or sounds as ever-motionless singularities. Instead, we are greeted by sound's choreographic spills, notes caught and chords mis-stepped, and immersed in and bewildered by rotating loops, we circle the rooms just like the intermixing objects overlying fused forms. This is specifically evident in the generational tribute to sound recording from vinyl records to CDs to cassette tapes to Spotify links, including but not limited to the varying voices one quickly catches that eventually escape notation. Placing pressure on listening as enacted permanence across looping recitations, Smith juxtaposes both transient and taped sounds, including the spectator's temporal and spatial accessibilities. Doing so obliges one to listen to how all sound, like music, circulates vibrationally across resonating frequencies and bodies, and how all sound, although listened to in a specific moment of time and place, is ever-changing and dynamical.

Smith's show cuts across fixed temporalities into futures from past remembrance by moving from sound-on-sound looping to interspersed and spliced visual loops. These temporal choreographies are briefed by the sonic, visual, and textual iterations residing in fundamental sequencing that lacks exit. Using popular music, quotidian sounds, familial images, text, and everyday objects as art, Smith remixes these looping sounds, images, and text as a sampling and editing practice that re-records original items into extended, diverse, and new material. For contemporary Latinx theater and performance scholar Patricia Herrera, the loop, expansive and voluminous, is never neutral or without politics. A historical and political device, the loop is "a sonic-temporal strategy" that accentuates cultural expression across social markers. Herrera argues that loops "sound out" the radical accents deployed by Black and

Latinx communities in the late 1960s and 1970s to recut "the temporal logic of history, performance, and race."[62] By understanding the loop to perform outside and beyond given temporal structures, Herrera suggests that one should listen for how the loop ruptures and deforms sonic temporality "into a different flow, one that overturns preestablished hierarchies and allows for circularity."[63] Insightfully, Herrera adds that while the loop may seem to reproduce the same sound and meaning with little differentiation, "the loop is more than repetition: it produces a new compositional logic that disrupts the linearity of the past with indefinite movement." Like these historical hip-hop hooks, Smith's sampled refrains, innovative material, calls and responses, the referent and its signifier are intermingled to such an extent that every advancing repetition salutes the aesthetic into renewed reproduction. In this way, every one of Smith's samples functions as a fragment to an illustrious whole still sounding in becoming, or snippets of existing sounds, voices, and histories oscillate into new orchestrations for listening. Manipulating speech, melody, and rhythm by layering, splicing, looping, reharmonizing, and re-pitching across form, Smith invites the senses to exist along sound's historical backbeats.

As sounds direct movement from and attention to belonging in *(Refrain)*, so does the image as a haptic experience. Visitors are organically led to a doorless viewing room set up with a large projection screen displayed against a foundational wall, set up like an old-school slideshow. One is pulled into scanned photographs as Smith's narrating voice, along with Black popular music, vibrates across the gallery. In front of this screen lies a fluffy purple area rug, a wooden chair, and a black milk crate holding various vinyl records, along with a projector and remote control, all sitting atop a living room cabinet. Installing a living space that invites the museumgoer into everyday life, this art piece dubbed "Untitled (mixed media film)" is composed of sampled materials gathered from personal archives. Given the layout of the room—an empty chair, furry rug, albums in crates, and family photos—the viewer is prompted to touch, play, and listen-with and across as a portal into Smith's childhood. As some museumgoers listen to images while moving to the contagious melodies over the speakers, still others remain stuck by the opportunity to touch in a space hostile to haptic intimacies. On opening day, I noticed Smith walking through the rooms alongside viewers, offering little direction other than to grab objects as a counter-choreographic measure to those institutionally learned rules of aesthetic engagement that encourage whispering, unhurried movement and touchless encounters.

With movement ensuing amid unbridled directions, how do we intimately look, listen, and learn? There is one looping image, in close-up, that peers across the projection. If we stand still long enough, we can catch the repeating detail looped every few seconds. It is a beautiful image of Smith's parents posing for a camera in front of an old-school black stereo-speaker set. Burn stands behind Beverly, his arms around her waist; both are dapperly dressed. Frozen in time like young love-birds, they stare into the lens dutifully and affectionately. But this image is not entirely chosen to showcase their after-wedding outfit; it rather captures a curatorial pattern rotating in eternal return and deployed throughout the show. Reappearing frequently amid other photos of Smith as a baby, her parents as teenagers, to name a few, we begin to feel the parental presence as a haptic imprint, a temporal reminder to sense them as they are in the present now, and never as they were in the past's past. This image circulates as another reminder to viewers that while the artist has shared grief with us, her lost entities are never meant to be fully apprehended outside of these duplicating loops.

Folded into a video of various looping images, through this photograph, we soon notice that the intended protagonist of Smith's show might not be her parents but the family stereo system. Many, if not all, of the rotating photographs shelter this recurrent signifier, and if at first unassuming, we learn that the stereo is where we come home to be turned on or, when turned on, we come home, together, again—not as a site to visit but a sound to be ignited as *ever wonderful* into a practice of place. Unsurprisingly, the artist spent an entire year digging through family albums "to find photos of this stereo system and albums as these objects" because, according to Smith, they "recall the love shared together as a family."[64] A leading actor in the exhibition, the stereo summons the spectator to notice its significance, for in any way one turns on, the stereo system appears to be asking to be reanimated and set in motion again and again.

So, what might the stereo system's reproduction across other artifacts reproduce in listening? As an evocative object, how might it engender multiple resonances across form, content, and social implication? From

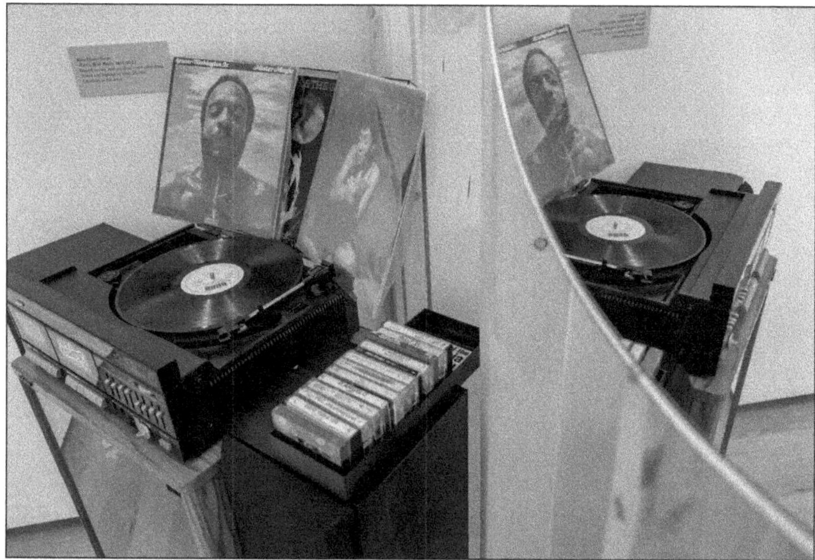

Figure 4.2. *Listening Room*, 2022. Photo by Fred Zwicky. Courtesy of Krannert Art Museum, University of Illinois Urbana-Champaign.

shots of Smith and her older sister Toni as little girls posing next to the stereo to an actual material replica of the stereo live in the exhibition's smaller listening room, this object functions as a phonic sculpture that, while modest in presence, playfully performs the refrain by reiterating, *turn me on, would you come on home?* As an acoustic sculpture it amplifies Smith's deliberate excavation across images and objects whereby to catch sight of any entity is to prepare to wistfully listen. Hardly surprisingly, Smith discloses that her father's stereo now resides in her apartment, and while it is not the original item used in the exhibition, the acoustic sculpture emits cultural sounds and ethereal energies that guide how one leans into listening. Although some of the album covers are original, Smith notes that much of the show is made of copies and scans of things inherited from her parents' deaths.[65] Considering this scanning and looping motif across sound and image, the spectator's eyes are directed to wistfully listen to rotating replicas as the collective ear synesthetically channels embodiment across dimensional terrain. Through it all, the mission retains its reminder: to be turned on is to be stimulated into affinity all over again.

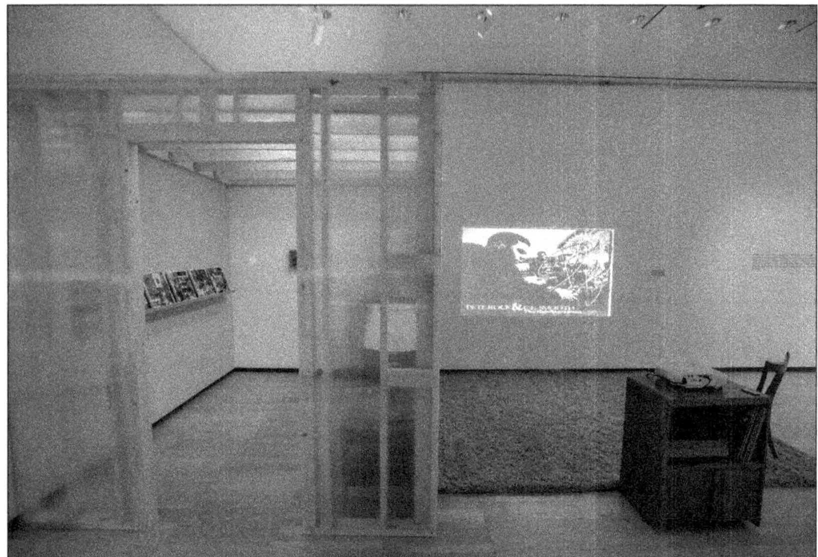

Figure 4.3. *Listening Across Rooms*, 2022. Photograph courtesy of Blair Ebony Smith.

Loop 4: The Object's Haptic Refrain: Sampling in Sonic and Visual Transference

By producing an immersive scene welcoming touch's energy across matter, Smith advances a counterintuitive way of sensorially being with objects. Mitigating what constitutes the politics of aesthetic encounter, this artist advances a haptic visuality throughout *(Refrain)*. In line with Black feminist scholar Tina Campt's idea of how to relisten to images counterintuitively, Smith encourages spectators to escape normative modes of thinking[66] by seeing her childhood, parents, and current life as filled with exquisite significance. For Campt, this process includes engaging with images along an intertwined sensorial scale, including the newfound intimacies within aesthetic objects that may not develop when following traditional viewing scripts. To listen to images, then, is to rearrange the senses to the particularities of sound's vibrational pulls. If sound travels perceptively from the ear, Campt asks us to practice "counterintuitive thinking" by understanding sound as an affectively haptic encounter traveling throughout the entire body, not merely held within the ear. Sound traverses viscerally across overlapping frequencies, making something like the photograph into a haptic object affecting us "through other registers of touch, through other registers of impressions"[67] and often through unseen frequencies. In haptic visualities, the image is best experienced through sensory immersion in the intimacies between things and sounds and the very worlds they animate in co-presence. Campt suggests that by amending how we approach the image, we might comprehend how the photograph is essentially a haptic entity, not merely an ocular experience.

Rendering images this way allows touch to enable memory, an intention, even a longing, or a depiction of someone no longer here within the body's layered skin. If touch travels from and through the skin, it perpetually forms sensorial relations across bodies and bodies of things, here and still hardly seen. That is to say that Campt enlivens the stillness of seeing through hapticality's vitality by disorienting conventional orientations to sight. Seeing extends beyond the ocular to bring to light an enmeshed ensemble of the senses whereby touching a photograph instantiates touch across entities. Like Campt, Smith understands that every image, text, sound, object is sensorially embroiled, and to decipher the enmeshed meaning is to listen wistfully to the layers that compose every artifact, in both material-immaterial regard.

Smith reroutes the dents, details, and patterns of haptic listening across *(Refrain)* by upsetting the strict lines between what remains to be seen and what retains sound, what frames reality and dismembers illusion. This means that as viewers confront the stills through Smith's projection screens, they are simultaneously visually called toward two distinct walls: a yellow wall with black text illuminated by a low-lit standing lamp, and a wall made of blurry plexiglass separating a small mysterious room and the larger screening room. Moving from one listening room to another, the audience member must piece together the show's premise via a potential layout, as every art piece is a deliberate reference to or citation of another entity as words, colors, items, lyrics redouble and resound in surplus and connection. The spectator's job is to think counterintuitively to follow the trails of repeating information, even if slightly disorienting.

For instance, the first wall, covered in Sun Valley yellow, is also an art object called "Landa's Joyful Yellow." Lit by a standing lamp, it contains the lyrical refrain from Roy Ayers's 1979 song "Love Will Bring Us Back Together." With the repeated refrain displayed on the wall, the spectator reads "Turn me on—would you come on home?" seven times, each line lined up to drag downward, leading the eye to alternating album covers sitting on the chair directly in front of the textual wall. To enact counterintuitive listening, however, Smith distorts the viewer's visual relationship to reading, seeing, and hearing. In front of the yellow wall, next to the standing lamp, the wooden chair houses alternating vinyl covers, including Ayers's 1976 *Everybody Loves the Sunshine* LP (covered in the same yellow as the wall) and the 1975 vinyl *African Rhythms,* by Oneness of Juju[68] Using color to elicit sound, and image to elicit social awareness, synesthetic allegiance directs the viewer's sentiments. Smith uses yellow to set up sight and sound as overlapping senses and to fuse and sample across records that rotate on view. Interconnected styles and musical genres mix and mingle to inform family practices of cross-notation between all types of materials superimposed to reproduce the feelings of kinship, political affinity, and belonging. While Ayers's refrain shapes how one engages the yellow wall, Smith disrupts how one further commits to listening as a kind of seeing in color. One might imagine that the prima album cover gracing the wooden chair would be of *Fever* to match the lyrics on the wall, but instead Smith muddies singularity in favor of connection as a conduit for Black study.

Might this all mean that even the whitest of museum walls could be driven into being lit, even bright enough to "get down in the sunshine?"[69] Lyrical play aside, color, text, and image operate intentionally to direct the spectator to look toward the one-sided plexiglass wall and enter a small room. Inside, one finds a painted yellow room and a modified reproduction of Smith's own apartment, where the family's archive is stored, including the stereo system. Within this narrow room, blocked by the plexiglass and fitting at most four people comfortably, reside the three remaining art objects. Through the use of original vinyl covers and liner notes of radio playlists, an old-school stereo system, reproduced family photo albums and original text scanned into collages alongside cassette tapes relabeled from initial scripts, and more dimly lit lamps and side tables, Smith sets another scene for wistful listening. This time, however, the scenario is an enclosed, private enclave, smaller in size but louder in sound. By shrinking sound's waves, motion recoils across objects as spectators eventually begin to grab, stroke, and handle replicas of many replicas and inevitably continue listening counterintuitively.[7]

Cornered and enmeshed, looping sounds vibrate across bodies, affects, objects, and forms; and linked closely together, frequencies oscillate between the spectator's ears across vocal articulations, remixed songs, and looping notes. In displaying replicas of familial artifacts such as labeled cassette tapes, vinyl records and covers, album crates, Virginia lottery tickets, and childhood photos, Smith relentlessly calls back sound's infinite historical time to push forward a kinetic orchestration. While seemingly inanimate, these objects actively resonate across the living, the dead, and their entangled things to such an extent that Smith intentionally clouds meaning to force attention toward the refrain. At times encouraging anxious viewers to pick up, hold, and caress these objects, she extends the deepest love across everything remembered in another's eulogy through haptic and sonic agreement and dissent.[71]

Yet how might one understand the feral movements of objects when handled by someone other than the aggrieved? The moment any object is rigorously contemplated, as Lauren Berlant suggests, it "bobs and weaves, becomes unstable, mysterious, and recalcitrant, seeming more like a fantasy than the palpable object it had seemed to be when the thinker/lover first risked engagement."[72] That is, no object represents singular intention, neutrality, organic evolution interiorly or with other things and entities. To remain intimate with the object's illusory edges, Smith attempts to stabilize objects via repetition-as-new, as an un-expendable method evolving within loops. These strategies are intellectually, creatively, and culturally learned to generate landscapes of remembrance, revitalizing unearthly life through the objects left behind. Put another way, the magical and even mystical capacity of text, image, sound, and their compositions commingle in Smith's sampling aesthetic as careful attention to bobbing and weaving trace alignments across desire and memory. These things, while they are objects that the artist allows the spectator to hold, are often emotionally unavailable, evolving into visual audibilities that one must tune in to as Smith tunes everyone out to tune back in to them personally. In listening for details, asides, traces, tangents, meanders, digressions, references, even sighs as footnotes underneath and beside text, we are left to resample familial sounds to deliberately embrace the sensoriality of things left behind by "those gone too soon."[73]

Be reminded that details across textuality, color, image, and sound operate in ensemble while repetition and reproduction, at times disordered, also play key roles throughout *(Refrain)*. Therefore, it is essential to reshare that Smith's mother's sampled phrase "be ever wonderful" (the opening hook to this chapter) cameos within this narrow room as another aesthetic refrain tuning in to be energetically re-attuned. The art piece "Would You Come On Home?" carries Beverly's three words in handwritten blue ink. It also carries the phrase "Burn's Best of Jazz and Funk" in blue permanent marker, penned by her father. Deliberately repetitive and overlaid, text is scanned from the original objects; and the latter wording is copied from a cassette label. This textual overlap and the possible confusion of text, given each art object's overlapping titles, is intentional and meditative—not meant to cause the viewer overt discomfort but to tenderly disorient one to the arrhythmic temporality of grief. Denying any easy engagement with aesthetics, it leaves us to feel the pangs of loss, not as wounded and toxic attachment but as incorporeal transmutations and transformations lingering within sound. As Smith discloses, to be deliberately bewildered is to be moved into listening historically and spiritually, to follow the ancestors' footprints, the tracks left behind within object to object, word to word, sound between sounds without a definitive flight plan for encounter. If curation, made in collective honor, must abide in fugitive style to think back to ife's contemplations, this exhibition leads the audience to the trails of these textual and textured tracks, not as a non-symphonic symbiosis but as an orchestrated disorientation to perform *being ever wonderful* in grief.

For illustrative purposes, Smith's visual scans often complement the aural/oral samples in a signifying chain of intentional meaning and reservoir. Both these reappearing blue markings (in pen and marker) dwell in the same collage made into a series of six collages, all created to resemble the shape and textures of album covers. Made from "various found materials," "Would You Come On Home?" sits face forward on a slender wooden mantelpiece in this very narrow listening room. Lined up across one exhibition wall also painted in Sun Valley yellow, the six collaged objects are equally assembled to signify glossy and lively album covers. At the bottom of the first collage-as-album, the spectator is drawn to the same blue handwriting again, the uplifting words on a card from a mother to her daughter, all in the same elegant prose and script.

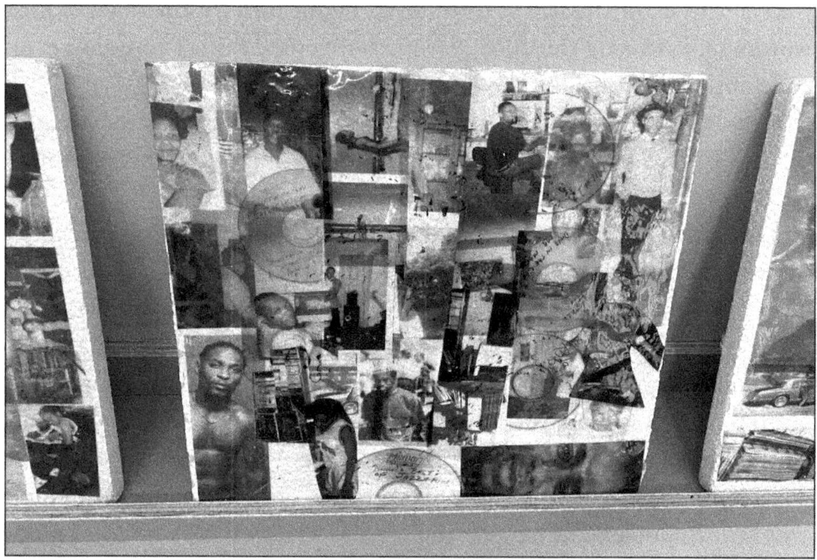

Figure 4.4. *Collage 2 (a series)*, 2022. Photograph courtesy of Blair Ebony Smith.

These six collages are formed from scanned items, or, as Smith specifically notes, "they are a mix of family photos and CD covers, my dad's and mom's CD collections, birthday cards (from my mother and to my mother), my dad's funeral service brochure, and even a letter envelope from my Gran."[74] Of this methodological application, Smith divulges that she "chose to scan and transfer these items to packing tape, and then collage on the vinyl LP size ceiling tile and cassette tape holders."[75] Yet this method is not singular to this artwork; in fact, these scanned images are reproduced from the video projected onto the screen above the fluffy purple rug in the larger listening room.

By thinking of reproductions as bearing their own essences, Smith repeats and replicates into renewed meaning and sentiment across objects and their powerful words and meanings. To sift through these objects is itself a method of sampling that generates the method of display, as Smith further adds that "the artifacts I scanned took the length of a year to re-dig through family archives attuned to any music things that popped up, things that reminded me of my dad and mom's love and joy, things that reminded me of the love they were intentional about giving."[76] In other words, Smith declines to remove desire (in the object's exquisite form) from love's endurance (in the object's little words) by following the affective shifts of copied things and their ever-communicative worlds.

I return to textual references throughout the chapter, as repeated via the objects in the exhibition, to follow Smith's charge. Something about the swirling penmanship, the letters composed by the now dead and placed amid cut-out family photos, symbolically recalls the entity as both mirage and material. There's something cathartic about being with someone's writing, signature, to know they once wrote with and for you, and to be able in unresponsive love to trace over the swirling loops, grooves, and curves of letters as marked entity in presence. Unlike the photograph of a lost loved one staring back in repudiation, penmanship activates a different sense, making one feel as though the word's movements could jump from the pages into ongoing dialogic and kinesthetic encounter. Or the words, so tiny but so large, explode sounds into enlivening worlds.

It likewise recalls Sharon Patricia Holland's idea of the raising of the dead by blurring life and death across Black literature and varied textual objects. Permitting the dead with space for speech and writing is to "raise the dead" and supply them with material embodiment "in order to tell the story of a death-in-life."[77] But it is also, as Holland expresses, and Smith enacts, in critically engaging death that minoritarian subjects are allowed "to speak about the unspoken—to name the places *within* and *without* their cultural milieu where . . . they have slipped between the cracks of language."[78] By refusing to allow her parents to be swallowed by these cracks, Smith enables dialogic jam sessions across words, penmanship, sounds, images, copy, and original text, all reproduced from their very hands. Smith marks their working-class aesthetic practices as fundamental to Blackness, including the archives developed from their respective collections, by repeatedly placing them at the center of intellectual (re)production. On loop and from love, surviving phrases, text's image, and sound's tessellations elicit the feeling of being with loss as life again, being with grief as transformative light into renewed aesthetic manifestation.

With her creation of textual and visual resonance that blurs both mother and father, loss and grief, it becomes clear that Smith not only mixes across genre but smears over the singularity of loved entity. Burn's handwriting reflects this mission as it lies across and between images in that blue marker, alongside Beverly's words. About this blurring of text technique, Smith shares, "The blue markups are scans of mix CDs my father made in the early 2000s. The ink you see is his actual handwriting used to label things." The labeled words "Burn's Best of Jazz and Funk" appear in this collage as a visual detail foreshadowing the next art object on an adjacent wall. As the viewer encounters the six collages on one wall of the tiny listening room, they are led to the symbols and clues leading them to the next art object against another wall. But why confusingly overlay artworks and their titles? Smith suggests that the longevity of found objects is locatable in the overlapping and connecting details of the objects themselves—a type of lost and found interplay that summons the practice of wistful listening by following the tracks between sound and sight without knowing for certain the destination. Wistful listening is a dissonant practice mired in productive disorder, nonlinear affective arrangements that not only loop, but become tenderly remixed into further bewildering logics and shared experiences.

Listening haptically to transfer centuries of intellectual and aesthetic reservoirs and unrelenting grief, the exhibition sets up the spectator with interconnected clues, sharing love as labor as intentional curation. For example, "Burn's Best of Jazz and Funk" is the actual title for the next artwork in the soundhouse—an object one finds after walking intently past the wall collage. Accompanied by a wall tag that describes the materials as "found objects," Smith counter-mines dominant modes of archiving by re-finding loss, or un-losing the lost thing never lost in love. This art object faces the front door of the tiny listening room and includes two music cabinets with mixed CD replicas glued to the sides, two nonfunctioning speakers, a circular mirror at eye level, a lamp, a rug, Virginia lottery tickets, CDs and vinyl records on shelves, a small coffee table, two listening chairs, and a bench. As the viewer approaches these objects, they are led into an even smaller listening corner to find many dynamic objects like original album covers by Anita Baker, Grover Washington Jr., and Kool & the Gang atop the stereo. In building an orchestration of sounds, text, and images blending and blurring into one another, each art piece is a tiny chorus in a larger and longer symphonic score. The question at hand is not whether we can see the dots long enough to connect them but how such seeing turns into listening's haptic portal.

From the yellow wall to childhood photos of her parents and her older sister Toni, to cassette tapes labeled in personal penmanship and the '70s-like lamp shining over vinyl album covers, Smith drops the spectator into a narrow but large Black social scene. These items "represent the durability, endurances of Black sound, text, image, and lyric, permeating across cultures but always taking form in a Black home."[79] That is, Roy Ayers, Earth, Wind & Fire, Anita Baker, and other artists displayed in the exhibition, register the sonic interventions of Black citation—a labor in listening in which Smith shuffles back and forth from private to public in an act of archiving familial artifacts always already in Blackness's province. Smith documents the endurances of a Black family into infinite evidence and reveals that the exhibition "digs deep into personal and familial photographic, oral, and musical memory banks to remember my parents—gone too soon and never forgotten." In Smith's unchanging words: "I will forever mix, layer, and rearrange visual and sonic moments in time to create new memories that treat us and Black people as complex beings who should be remembered."[80]

To summon the "wist"—or is it the "wish"—in listening, *(Refrain)* lands on the remembrance of things—many familial items sheltering and cultivating ethereal breath. Without any hesitation, the Black working class is primed for the museum-going public, parrying the stifling pitches of racialized enclosure, with a staunch commitment to ordinary items as extraordinary artifacts. Enacting Brooks's methodological and theoretical idea of *laboring in listening*—an intentional counteraction to history's effacement of aesthetic work by Black feminist cultural makers—Smith similarly lines out narratives left to un-listening's discursive patterns.[81] Via a careful engagement with notions of the archive, she initiates alternative ways of tracing lines of historical convergence by performing a different type of listening—listening that moves past famous pitches and glimmering figures to write for and with the overlooked and forgotten.[82] Rejecting the allowable scripts for listening, knowing, and storing, Brooks similarly shares that "Black women artists have played crucial roles *as* archives, as the innovators of performances and recordings that stood in *for* and *as* the memory of a people."[83] Interested in the "faded pages" one "might imagine stored in an elderly sister's trunk—as a crucial, culture-making entity," Smith, like Brooks, takes seriously all kinds of warehouses as viable substance, comprehending the making of culture as the remaking of listening through the re-staging of stuff ostensibly "liner" and minor.[84]

How might we understand this commitment to extraordinary arti-facts and their makers as essential in circumventing the archive's ex-tractive tendencies? For Latinx feminist historian Sandy Plácido, the extract (a thing condensed from an illusory whole) counters its own extraction by evolving the essence of archives. Placing a microscopic lens over archival spatiality, Plácido zooms in, for example, on her par-ents' mechanic shop as a haven for the vulnerable, another home away from home, and a prime site of class and aesthetic investigation. To cherish working-class gatherings as *living archives*, she places pressure on three intermingling concerns that also ring across Smith's exhibition: a capacious working-class definition, class as an aesthetic category and operation, and the linguistic value accorded artifacts across place and difference. Participating in what she calls "alternative forms of archiving along the working class as a spectrum," Plácido positions intra-class structure as expansive and mobile, and family objects as "carrying im-mense and varied historical weight."[85] Plácido suggests that one may be surprised by the aesthetic wealth procured across everyday things by dispossessed, working-class communities by shifting how working-class family objects are viewed and engaged. Erasure and racialized disregard occur in how one discursively mobilizes the archive as a place of dead things, a site of closure, and a space for worthy cultural objects. Propos-ing an amendment to the language of conventional archives to include the familial object within epistemological terrain, Plácido regards the capacity of living archives to outlive supposed dead things and their makers. Always alive, these archives include voices, places, glimmers, and stories of the still living often deemed too inconsequential, trivial, and even excessive to be recorded into legitimate documentation. To listen to these entities as archival permissibility is to shift archival atten-tion into sifting as listening, including all the referential asides, details, and quotidian items lost in translation.

Latinx feminist artist-scholar-curator Jillian Hernandez similarly in-tervenes in any absolute and obsolete notions of low and high culture by reframing visual art and the subjects appropriated into archival circula-tion across modes of difference. Hernandez turns the category of aes-thetics on its very head by seeing aesthetics as indivisible from culture.

Understanding aesthetic protocols to be measured by Western judgments and "European stylistic values," she highlights disciplinary blind spots by turning to excess as historical indexicality—one often ironically upheld by the elite to be simultaneously and strategically denied to others.[86] For Hernandez, art history traditions paradoxically devalue their own categorical imperatives across canonical source material, leaving both category and practice open to hypocrisy. Subsequently, she asks that one relearn seeing by shattering the taken-for-granted appraisals of sight. Traveling across Black and Latinx embodiment in art and everyday life, Hernandez draws out this duplicitous rubric by exposing how the art history canon has always awarded and valued white excess, or appropriated excess, or positioned excess as high culture. From Picasso to Dalí and Caravaggio to Velázquez to Oppenheimer and Schiele, and across schools of thought and practice from German expressionism to surrealism, Western art has relied on and valued excess as form, facticity, and viable standards of modernity. To put to bed any easy separation between practice, taste, and style, Hernandez expands the archive beyond its outdated and simulated mandates to land in excess's dynamism across everyday people and newly made aesthetic sites.[87]

Like Brooks, Plácido, Hernandez, Brown, and so many other women-of-color cultural re-makers, Smith returns to the artifact itself to retrace faded outlines and contours imposed by majoritarian standards as the only legitimate practice of aesthetic engagement. Partaking in a tradition of sounding out the ensemblic entanglements of desire and belonging, she lends the audience childhood and parental dreams through the very sounds of objects. Put slightly differently, sampling home is a knotted praxis for Smith, an ongoing tenderness living across unseen loops and evolving into repeatable oscillations that are shared but never entirely given.[88] From sifting through forgotten archives to capturing the meandering details to meditative visual hums, Smith's listening practice, wistful as wishful, repeating in refrain, necessitates deep movements across the senses in her exhibition. While geographically and demographically rooted, her sound-work is always "moving across several places—of arriving while leaving."[89] Both the departure and arrival oblige "being ever wonderful" and "coming on home." Such directives gently invite the question: What might it spiritually, politically, and ideologically imply *to be ever wonderful by coming on home to turn things on when the heart keeps calling?*

Loop 5: Grief as Curation: Everything Bends Back Through

Everything Smith offers in curation is both a continuation and a reconfiguration of introjected sentiment, such that every sound emits inherited feelings through overlapping objects. Smith's objects are projected mirages lingering between love and desire, and offering imitations of things no longer stored by original owners, like the stereo system across photographs. Desiring to give love to what no longer materially exists, love sits within and across loss's objects—not only as a mere nostalgic thing but as historically capacious and culturally loaded signifying relationalities. Thinking through these shifting relations between love and desire as framed by the logics of attachment, Berlant advises one not to misapprehend the revolving internal and external effects of affects. Instead, Berlant sees objects as items and scenarios that one regenerates and transforms into one's everyday life-worlds by rejecting the objectivity of any object. They suggest that "what seems objective and autonomous in them is partly" one's own self-created desires, thus the thing itself is mere illusion, or at least for Berlant, "a shaky anchor."[90] How one engages any object, according to Berlant, is what offers "shape to the drama with which they allow" one to re-engage the self. On the contrary, "love is the embracing dream in which desire is reciprocated: rather than being isolating, love provides an image of an expanded self."[91] But what is love in self across another? How does Smith access love's other across self and object? How does love itself reveal the paradoxical reality of any relation? If love is found within looping objects, and loops themselves are waves of recursive sentiment, as in the case of Smith's items, where does attachment begin and ultimately end? And, if love can be simultaneously sincere and ever synthetic, communal, and selfishly singular, graspable, and secretive, as Berlant testifies, how are love's and desire's knotted movements sustained? For Berlant, "desire will lead to love, which will make a world for desire's endurance."[92]

Smith's unobjective but decodable objects shelter respiration as desire's perseverance, always in tandem, in loop, evolving as care. What I mean to suggest—thinking creatively with Berlant's *Desire/Love*—is that Smith projects desires, memories, and unfulfilled love onto these artifacts, but these items already carry both inherited emotions and unrelenting desire. That is, at least in Smith's case, love's relation, while not audibly relational, glints via the unearthly messages passing through unseen portals in often very hostile and tangible repositories. Always loving and desiring in loop, Smith listens intently to catch the shimmer amid finitude's attempt to deaden vibrancy, to permanently shatter all illusion. Moving literally from curation's etymological directive to care, she travels across text, image, sound, and mirage, all in a haptic syncopation that funnels love through reproduction across the dead and their very living things in spaces known to instigate fetish desire while killing off love.

Smith reminds one of the conjoined portals of longing and love whereby every object shared is also every sound reinforcing the other's arrival and subsequent departure by matching the musicality of sorrow via image and text. But these arrivals and departures flow in cyclical motion, for, as Smith explains further, "looping through sampling is about new ways of being open to messages, the messages of those apparently gone."[93] There is no space for non-listening under these conditions, for "music is both ephemeral and everlasting" and one must listen to "the hands always on deck" reiterating histories and "sifting and shifting" sounds. "Everything loops back through," according to Smith, so much so that the idea of something being gone is itself the only tenet of non-listening.[94] Therefore, listening and sifting across objects enables this cultural worker to uncover the hidden notations muted from archives.

Sifting across artifacts is listening-across and listening-within loss and grief—another level of union that matches the aesthetic and political practices of sampling, collaging, digging, blurring, re-collecting, and looping. If Smith's object of love is also her greatest loss, then one must attune the senses through this resonance's very orchestrations. Through repetition and its renewed reiterations with and across form, this artist enlivens the stationary item of love to its inherited essences.[95] By caring for objects and enlightening them with robust sentiments, senses, and historical demarcation, Smith holds the spectator's hand through elaborate and confusing wall tags, repeating details and titles, looping sounds (audible and inaudible), colored visual markers within visual signs, and listening rooms as haptic movements. She drops us all into grief's contours, unfolding in the refrain of a refrain, by carefully extending affection across objects and senses.

The longer I sifted through Smith's visual and sonic loops, the more I understood *(Refrain)* to encourage shared embodiment as listening and listening as repeated and fugitive movement. The referential, while guiding and at times bewildering, instantiates a series of motions that, like a loop, returns the aesthetic as synesthetically linked across and within bodies. If the senses shuffle across immaterial audiotopias, repetition is made accountable to all the sites one cannot see but can certainly engage ethereally. This means that any fixed idea of affinity is distorted into mixed metaphors for practice as place, leaving the spectator's body to viscerally drift into the sound's objects while winnowing through the unsettled stillness across images. Swerving, looping sounds and photographs compel families back together, back to being ever wonderful, in a time and place prompting listening as range whereby the spectator is never meant to listen outside of any loop.

Caught within multiple loops, spectators receive no direct exit (or entry) plan for how to encounter objects bearing the eternal refrains of grief. But this grief, however agonizing, is not meant to stand still in sentiment; it is meant to transport with objects into a transformative experience across and within listening planes. If grief forms life's evolutionary patterns through the senses, like a refrain on repeat, one is unable to escape any loop; rather, they pull one into melody, or that phrase that hooks one into a song so tightly that returning to it feels like one never left the chorus. Or, as Smith shared with me repeatedly, "there is no song or sampling without the refrain; the refrain is always the call, so you have to sit with it; this is listening; this is response."[96] This listening is coached by textual, visual, sonic iterations and always driven by new visioning of intellectual labor informed by grief's transmutations. A non-chronological, ever-present sentiment, it extends across energies and bodies, or grief as a chain of signifiers links sorrow across histories, never quite exclusively owned by one but always in recursion communally.[97] For this artist, grief is listening-with and listening-within, sensorially stimulating the dispersal and dissipation of all sound as a unifying instrument.

Mobilizing grief as curation is painful, yes, but it also induces creative action led by purpose, cultural meaning, inherited insights, and precision—a thoughtful attention to sounds that stem from following marks with an attention to not only details, but the whole from which they come. An intimate project in longing, loss, love, and wistful listening, Smith enacts what fahima ife dubs in her lyrical essay "Grief Aesthetics" as "founds things in the beginning, finds things by way of subduction." ife continues: "when our black ship comes in, we join up in common study. Love one another in common insofar as we continue in our independent study. A distant time signature, time apart."[98] Like ife, Smith's time signature is co-studied and co-arranged with Beverly, Burn, Black musical history, and the voices of Black feminist intellectual labor resisting sonic erasure and visual de-eulogization. We might understand Blair Ebony Smith as an acoustic echo with an archivist pitch building with and from a series of embodied sound archives.[99] No reverberation is left behind to be uncataloged by the often-immobilizing tendencies of loss and grief.

And yet, questions remain. What does it politically and socially mean to lend familial intimacy to museums, sites participating in practices that have historically mishandled minor objects and subjects? Why share one's grief as an object of and format for analysis for a site mired in colonizing assessment? One might conclude that, compelled by unrelenting sorrow and held by principles to move in feral and counterintuitive ways, Smith impels the museum to rehouse these aesthetic objects against elitist tendencies. Even as such sites wear blinders toward cultural and aesthetic extraction, Smith as artist, archivist, and curator rents this space, but not necessarily the colonial practice of display. It is true that often any museum is just another morgue or cemetery like the conventional archive that perpetuates grief by relying on the commodification of those always encumbered by ongoing loss.[100]

Like any archive, museums are carriers of corpses and mounting dust, and offer strict and often tacit directions for how to properly operate in place and in the world. Cultural studies scholar Tony Bennett reminds us that the museum is not merely a space of education, but a site promoting a series of regulatory manners and performances for being and behaving in the world. Like most institutions, as Bennett argues, museums survive by enforcing rules and codes for cultural comportment through ritualized and repetitive mandates.[101] These rituals not only tame us into respectable cultural etiquette but teach us how to internalize such desire to govern our proper subjectivity. They also present and animate the artifacts that they deem worthy of engagement, contemplation, and circulation—a process encumbered by bias and speculation. Smith, like her fellow group show colleagues, performs a commendable role as artist, archivist, designer, and curator, with close friends and loved ones on deck to help materialize the immersive experience. Her commitment to listening, outside these governing mandates, smears the wistful across the whitest of walls in which homemade items perform a class act aesthetic in the refrain's refrain.

That is to say that Smith intermixes the bodies of objects with present embodiment by performing a reverse extraction through a collection of objects carrying the muted essences of family into citational recovery. One may notice, to return to Julietta Singh again, how the body, in this case, is forever "both archive and archivist," for "in a crucial sense it gathers its own materials."[102] What is found has infinitely survived through an "archive of penetration" or cellular canals, "a history, in other words, of foreign bodily matter left inside us."[103] But as cells morph, so does a body, a body that was never, according to Singh, singularly one's own, not only to know, but to operate. Contrary to conventional historical accounts that refuse the body as an archive, the body is indeed "an infinite collection of bodying,"[104] one that is constitutive of and constituted by legacies of Black girls, Black life, Black endurance amid oceans of Black death. Smith's body as an archive is a collection of things, feelings, significations left behind to be reformulated—no energy lost in the lost and never found boxes that perpetuate disappearing legacies. In finding objects, Smith finds grief, herself, and all the memories that persist in futural import. Or, as she openly shares in this chapter's epigraph, when she's not leaning into grief, she's off, becoming an entity never quite recognizable or found.

To follow Smith's long journey in refrain is to activate grief-work. Every clue, detail, message advanced in curatorial style imparts listening as a portal. The matter at hand is not how to receive the messages but whether one is willing to wistfully listen across them. Smith performs a counter-hegemonic curatorial practice within a conventional space, not as a wounded appendage or violent upriser, but through an ethics of love, explicit attention, and care. Against the deafening rhetoric of convention, aesthetic scenes are re-executed, not in subjection but in redemptive listening; and the audience, ready or not, witnesses Smith return home to re-arrive in kinship as a minoritarian aesthetic practice. This interplay between spatial politics, sonic time, infrastructural reorientation, and the renewed texture of objects accentuates subjects often denied archival legitimacy. In grief and intellectual tenacity, Smith divulges that she is often moved to "fuck around with objects as archive" by "doing as she is in the moment she is in."[105] A fundamental tenet throughout her sampling practice, that, like ife, takes a cue from blood lineage, inherited ancestors, and Black study creatives, is the idea that messing around with objects is to also "fuck around with knowledge production" in the present.[106] It also involves uplifting the very things deemed essential to circulation and currency.[107]

But messing around is not without rehearsal; it happens via an investment in principle through the present activation of lessons. It happens by listening to messages that arrive through portals that exceed the discursive parameters of nostalgia to encourage our responsibility to one another, here and there, now, and always. By highlighting a musical repertoire motivated by her parents, Smith vivifies loss by tending to the grief of things, attending to the sonic things of grief. All these things function across a series of deliberate repetitions whereby the spectator is invited into Smith's deepest love—an inherited enterprise against death as finitude. *(Refrain)* elevates the dead by elevating their artifacts, making home something one does rather than a place (an institution!) one knows in stable attention.

Loop 6: Lights as Lessons (Refrain from the Refrain in Refrain's Return)

How might one re-ground Smith's curatorial choices by returning to repeated signifiers across imbricating familiar archives as interlacing study sessions? Could all this repetition just be the gloomy geometry of grief? I mean, without repetition, how does loss remember one recalling the other in the very act of feeling the recalls of loss?

Like Ayers's refrain, Beverly's "be ever wonderful" appears in a referential loop, not like Ted Taylor's 1959 emotional "Be Ever Wonderful," where the soul-blues singer pines in a gospel-driven falsetto for an unrequited other, but as an expression treasuring self-expression as love, as intrinsic to all relations.[108] Rather than solely relying on another for subject signification amid the world's wretched demands, Earth, Wind & Fire encourage the authentication of the self against the commands to change oneself for the world's normalizing purposes. The song's lyrics and musicality blur the beautifully complicated lines between individuation and communal affection, between a mother's love and the longing desires of a daughter. Between the impermanence of existence and its eternal permanence in repetition, like many other songs and lyrics across the show, words and rhythms keep showing up, recurring as a reminder to trace the inevitable flow as meaning between shimmers. Or to ask again, in the spirit of Smith's stubborn loops, why begin with the phrase "be ever wonderful" as a parallel refrain to Ayers's refrain "Turn me on—would you come on home?" It could all seem a conflation of sound, song, and parental love and loss, but it could also be that the portal receives and retrieves messages, and these messages, crossing wires, must be open to overlap and titillation to return to one another across forms, affections, and ethereal channels. How else do gateways themselves present listening in ensemble?

Throughout most of our conversations about *(Refrain)*, Smith and I were directed by many ancestors, but her mother as a dominant enduring spirit still had study lessons to offer and required extant listening. These avenues to and from Beverly were material and ethereal—a sampling entity reappearing across objects and spaces not yet animated (or seen) by the living. Turning back in time as if it were only yesterday, Smith reveals, "My mother always dreamt of working with Black women, of giving back. She always brings me back to Black girlhood studies."[109] Bringing her back (although she is never quite gone), while a celebration of collective formation, is also a reminder of formlessness, or that, according to living protocol, matter's matter in unknown motion because "she's always here," shares Smith.[110] But she is also always here as Smith's introjected dreams and love's multidirectional desires across abiding forces just like a light that never goes out.

In inquiring about her mother's lessons, Smith unburies any notion of their overlaps and essentiality. For this cultural worker, these study sessions were mighty, lengthy, and clear, and always pulling from Black feminist literature, Black music, and lived experiences. Having stored these lessons to memory, Smith evolves as a living archive, carrying and permeating entities and ideas throughout her body and spaces.

There were many lessons, but there are four that remain entangled for her as tenets of artmaking and curation in minor compositions. The first one she religiously attunes to is the idea "Don't ever forget it," which means remember that, regardless of socially imposed suffering, you are loved. Now a sound recording made by lovenloops by the same title, this lesson is held tightly to her chest as a reminder to be ever wonderful in her shared cultivations even as the world promotes violence, erasure, and separation. The second lesson, and one Smith hears as a constant warning, is "the time you waste is all your own." But this lesson is not about wasting work time but rather about listening to how the spirit calls one forward in purpose, not the world's commercial construction of labor.

The third lesson, so much a part of this exhibition's premise, is a gentle reminder to "never forget that you have a home and can make home." Understanding this as a call to recreate from where one lands, Smith cultivates place as practice while cherishing acts of remembrance. Lastly, and appropriate to repetition as resurfacing in infinite remix, is "to shine your light for the world to see." This latter lesson appears on many of Beverly's cards and notes seen throughout Smith's family archive. Including, not to be too literal, through the dimly lit lamps staged across the exhibition, counterposing the museum's blaring fluorescent overhead lights. When asked why she rejects the institution's light, Smith reveals, "*That* light is not my light; the overhead light is not where we shine." As Smith reminds me often, light, like sound, loops, so we must be infinitely cautious with the elements and materials accessing the portal's entry. Every detail is a reminder of our inherited responsibility to each other across endless omniversal planes and intergenerational dimensions.[111]

All these study sessions are linked to the one lesson Smith reminded me of during our time together—a lesson requiring immediate repetition: "I don't answer for or to these places. I am also not trying to contribute to colonial practices that erase or appropriate Black people." Who do you answer to then, I asked? "To listening. I answer to and by listening to new ways of being open to messages."[112] Following musical citations as wistful listening, as resolute precision to reassemble how we think, write, display, move, remember, and inevitably counterintuitively sound to re-record, Smith invites creation and curation informed by

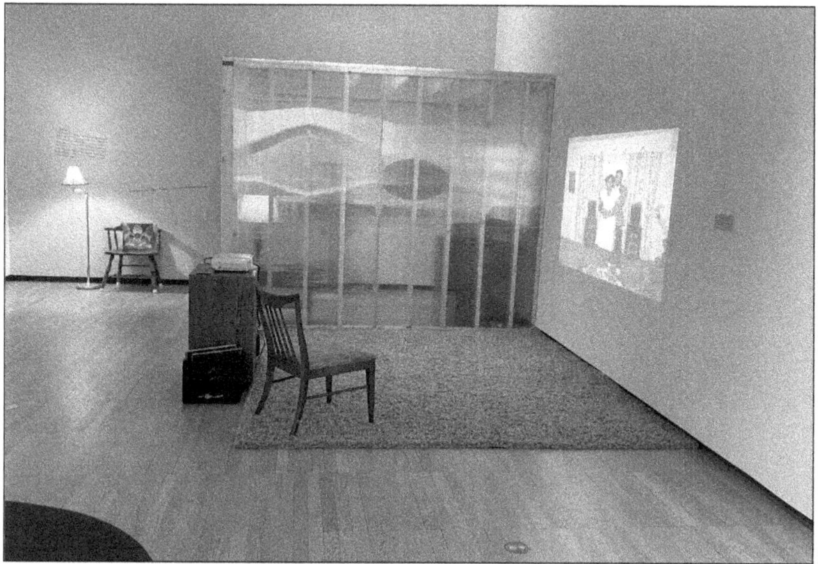

Figure 4.5. View of the exhibition, 2022. Photo courtesy of Blair Ebony Smith.

loss's vibrancy. In listening in this way, everything becomes a sound-house, a vibrational entryway into another doorway to yet another tectonic entrance—the sonic dispatch so abundant that composition forms in refrain as compilation hovers ever so wonderfully. Or maybe over time grief becomes third-eye clarity—a gentle and looping light that settles mourning's ambush, and in radiating, everything gets turned on to come on home, again.

An Afterword

(Entrances)

I hear that grief is where love arrives to rest. That it settles best when shared. Like everything we hear, there are modicums of truth to all the particles of desire. How is it that unrequited affection eventually evolves into a harmonic ambition? Amid consecutive and continuous personal and social loss, answers materialize in negation: I wanted what I could not have alone. There's no solitary kingdom in grief; every municipality is a pathway toward a route crossing another line to land within a series of allied vessels. Like splintered nomads, we set out to find our loss among the treasure and rubble of others. And there, like a stop sign beckoning pause, we hold one another, as if to say, *I hear your sorrow like I hear my heartbreak; together, as one, we emerge in sustaining shimmer.*

And yet, *Tears for Tears* began from internal distress, and every other emotion we harbor in grief's journey, often alone, outside all locations of felt love. In bargaining exhaustion, I requested universal favors: one last word with the dead, one final embrace, one tiny gesture as a sign of closure, one moment of justice that could put social inequalities to bed. All these requests, I hear, are frequent and communal, even if we feel the imminent requisition in singular suffering. What is not always plurally enacted, however, is sharing: sharing out our broken pieces for another's deep-seated lamentations in this everyday life paved in grief for minor subjects. So, the offering of *a tear for a tear*, as this book attempts to do, requires intentionally carrying and releasing one another through interwoven sorrows motivated by the traversing of the rules of responsibility through dynamic immaterial pathways.

Through deathless sounds, flames for flames, spectral choreographies, moving stills, and weeping landscapes, I have tried to honor our collective losses through the touching grief-work of Eva Margarita, Erica Gressman, Pedro Lopez, and Blair Ebony Smith. And they have, in turn, dignified the process by reminding me that to move across the social, political, and psychical constructions of grief is to lay out the stakes of simultaneously embracing the living and the dead by remobilizing personal and mass loss as collective work. Seen as material labor with immaterial force,[1] grief is most profoundly experienced in accompaniment, meditation, effusion, multidimensional mobility across temporal and spatial ensemble. After years of following these brave cultural workers addressing the most harrowing of injustices, a new request materialized: might we join energies to collectively perform and write "the dead" back into existence? Might the journey authorize a communal embrace, together-as-one, in infinite encounter?

Devoted to immaterial grounding and material presence, the longing to touch and despair of no longer touching, the apprehension of death and impenetrability of finitude, we have, together, communally pushed forward, driven and rerouted by grief. Via textured transitions, looping summons, rhizomatic halts, smoky inhales, visual glitches, and sonic samples, we travel in ephemeral permanency to experience accompaniment as historical transmission. From the parental dead summoned via the consumption of ashes, to a light for a light that illuminates our entangled complacency and dissent, to bending before objects in humility and gratitude, to wistfully listening to objects, we course spectral worlds in reverse extraction. Here, aesthetic sites turn sounds into refrain, resolving the silence of dead things through grief's repetitive keys.

From fire to ash and water to salt and air to sound, grief's psychological, visceral, and affective disorientations are enacted by enfolding the very elements contained within us. Though agonizing, we must deliberately turn on those muted remembrances across all types of stabled instabilities and elemental forms. In want of liberation for all sites under siege and to undo what we may become as we watch terror recycle us into gazing simulations, *a tear for a tear* is more than a turn of phrase; it is an activated portal for sharing sorrow, where endless sparks cast light upon transformation's commons.

ACKNOWLEDGMENTS

This project was made possible by the loving and rigorous support of incredible humans and spirit forces across dimensions. For all the care, through all the intimate listening, I am eternally grateful and infinitely indebted to their kindness. I feel fortunate to be able to think, read, write, and dream with others, seeing study as always accountable to and in development and growth with others. In a book about grief-acts that carry the potential to reshape social life, I am thankful for the cultural workers who helped make this text possible. Eva Margarita, Erica Gressman, Pedro Lopez, and Blair Ebony Smith—and the specters living across their brilliant archives—helped move a tiny idea about sorrow into a conjoined constellation of possibility. I have been honored and privileged to hold their grief and deepest desires for a better world. In return, they have equally held our shared sentiments, and by consequence, the writing across these pages.

I'd also like to extend gratitude to the following colleagues, friends, and studiers who held this project with curiosity, intellectual tenacity, and care. Thank you to Shane Vogel, Ruth Nicole Brown, and Laura Harris for feedback across every stage and page of this project and for encouraging me to meet writing where sentiment lands. Thank you to Masi Asare and Sam Dash for listening to ideas and offering feedback. A major thanks to Adrian Jonas Smith, Joshua Chambers-Letson, and Ruth Nicole Brown for phone travels in brainstorming, pontificating, and spiritual awakening. Thank you to all the studiers at Illinois who helped move this work along: Brenda Gisela Garcia, Mark Ebbay, Tai Gómez, Paulina Valencia Camacho, Laura Coby, and Melody Contreras. A special thank-you to Fred Moten, Vijay Iyer, Long Bui, Kevin Hamilton, Jaime Seymour, Christy Acevedo, Valleri Robinson, Jennifer Monson, Siobhan B. Somerville, Anderson, Trish Loughran, Monica Huerta, Dusty Childers, Lutz Abisla, Cy & Y at *Women & Performance*, and Daniel Hughes Vernola. Vernola's beautiful artwork graces the cover of this book. Thank you to Jillian Hernandez and Uri McMillan for offering generous feedback on earlier versions of the manuscript. Huge gratitude is extended to the journal *Meridians* for the special issue created by editors Kimberly Juanita Brown and Jyoti Puri. Thanks to Ginetta E. B. Candelario and Paula Jane Giddings for the opportunity to share these ideas and honor working artists. Thanks to the band Tears for Fears for their inspirational name.

I am thankful to Cynthia Oliver and the Mellon Foundation for their financial support of these ideas and work under the Minor Aesthetics Lab. To the department of Theatre and the College of FAA at Illinois, thank you for providing time, resources, and space to complete this project. I am thankful to Kendra Shaffer and Greg Anderson for their speedy work on financial resources. A heartfelt thank-you to the NYU Press team for all their diligent work on this project, particularly Furqan Sayeed, the three external readers, series editors, and Eric Zinner, staunch advocate and generous editor. An extended thank-you to Cathy Hannabach and the Ideas on Fire team for their copyediting and indexing work. Thank you also to Jess Kadish-Hernández for her exemplary editing support and generosity of spirit in the final stage of this project.

To my families, thank you for the time to meet time where time meets love. To the incomparable Alberto Brandariz Nuñez and beautiful Gali Lolita, it is with the humblest of embraces that I extend eternal gratitude and affection in your directions. To those no longer here in recognizable form, I commit to honor your loss as my own until our returned encounter: Ryan C., Eli, Eric, Mego, José, *abuelita*, Joe, Michael, Edna, *papi*, Randy. And, to all the names never known, carelessly and violently lost to capitalist-colonial-genocidal logics, it is in how we grieve those we could never know that we mourn, in loving regards, those we intimately knew.

NOTES

1. DEATHLESS FIRE

1 During our ongoing correspondences and interviews about this piece and other work related to grief, Eva Margarita shared that her two names honor her ancestors; she carries the names of her maternal and paternal grandmothers and chooses to be referred to by both names. For more information on *Light of Ours* and other work by the artist, please visit her website: www.evamargaritaperforms.com.

2 Eva Margarita in conversation with the author, 2021.

3 Ibid.

4 Sharpe, *In the Wake*, 15.

5 In using the phrase "scene of subjection" (4) within this context, I am thinking of Saidiya V. Hartman's *Scenes of Subjection: Terror, Slavery, and Self-Making in Nineteenth-Century America*. Important to the conceptual and ideological markers of this performance is Hartman's critical attention to slavery as not only an apparatus of forced labor but an inhuman enterprise formed and informed by systemic violence. In this way, the quotidian life of the enslaved was marred by perpetual suffering and brutal pain employed to dominate and subjugate the oppressed into centuries of fear and trauma.

6 Canham, "Black Death and Mourning as Pandemic," 296–97.

7 Ibid., 299.

8 Many of these candles were donated by Eddie Gamboa, her friend from Chicago, some of which were left over from a vigil held in honor and memory of lives lost in the 2019 Walmart shooting that occurred in El Paso, Texas.

9 This conversation occurred over Zoom with Eva Margarita on August 12, 2022, from 11 a.m. to 1 p.m. CDT; we revisited her performances by discussing histories of subjugation and dispossession and her critical attention to everyday grief as ritual. Eva Margarita emphasized the importance of understanding the severity and specificity of US Black death and the violent systems that uphold such brutality.

10 Ibid.

11 Moten, "Black Mo'nin'," 61.

12 Sharpe, *In the Wake*, 21; Muñoz, *The Sense of Brown*, 3; Alvarado, "Ghostly Givings," 246; Nash, "Slow Loss," 2; Butler, *Precarious Life*, 29.

13 Muñoz, *The Sense of Brown*, xxxi and 138.

14 Sharpe, *In the Wake*, 13.

15 Ibid., 10.

16 Ibid.

17 Ibid., 20–21.

18 Gordon, *Ghostly Matters*, 7.

19 For a deeper description of Eva Margarita's body of work, including these referenced performances, please visit her website: www.evamargaritaperforms.com.

20 Holland, *Raising the Dead*, 3–4.

21 Eva Margarita in conversation with the author, 2020–2021.

22 Eva Margarita in conversation with the author, 2021. See a further description of this performance at www.evamargaritaperforms.com/performance-works.

23 Eva Margarita in conversation with the author, 2021.

24 Ibid.

25 Ibid.

26 Ibid.

27 The reanimation of space in *Conjuring Stains* occurs in Coogan's Bluff in Harlem—a site her father frequented while he was living in New York. Eva Margarita's *Conjuring Stains* takes place in the same space some thirty years later. For her, this space importantly solidifies how sites speak across centuries and how bodies share space, and make place, as relational affinity and renewed practices of kinship.

28 Sharpe, *In the Wake*, 11.

29 Gillespie and Lopez, *Vulnerable Witness*, 11.

30 Ibid.

31 Eva Margarita in conversation with the author, 2021.

32 Ibid.

33 In thinking retrospectively about how Eva Margarita considers the anticolonial gathering, I would be remiss if I did not briefly mention Sarah Jane Cervenak's *Black Gathering: Art, Ecology, Ungiven Life*. The author offers a beautiful way to reimagine the potential of the term *gathering* via how Black artists and writers engender unique and alternative venues for coming together outside of dominant forms of management, extraction, and regulation. For Cervenak, the word *gathering* can be a simultaneous doing-together and being-together in both acts and states of "deregulated togetherness" (1). Cervenak carefully states one of the interventions of her project in this way: "Most directly, the artists and writers surveyed in this book advance another ecological and architectural imagination into some undisclosed coordinates where the release of earth from its fraudulent ownership is coterminous with the release of flesh. Such forms of release, the inherent fugitivity of *gathering* as a term, flourish in the recesses of property's afterlife, theorized by innovative assemblages of language, found objects, paint; Black gathering potentiates exits out of the extractive view and into realms that are nobody's business" (11).

34 Nash, "Slow Loss," 2.

35 Ibid., 3.

36 Berlant, *Cruel Optimism*, 38.

37 It is in the spirit of admiration that I engage Nash's beautiful work. I want to extend my deepest gratitude to Nash for placing my work along these debates and making the practice of citation one of both political, social, and aesthetic plenitude, one of an enduring feminist praxis.

38 Nash, "Slow Loss," 3.

39 Ruiz, *Ricanness*, 50.

40 Nash, "Slow Loss," 3.

41 Holland, *Raising the Dead*, 3–4.

42 Nash, "Slow Loss," 2.

43 Muñoz, *The Sense of Brown*, xxxi.

44 Eva Margarita in conversation with the author, 2021.

45 Ibid.

46 Cacho, *Social Death*, 147–148.

47 Eva Margarita in conversation with the author, 2021–2022.

48 Canham, "Black Death and Mourning as Pandemic," 303.

49 See Masur, "Race, Policing, and Reform."

50 Sharpe, *In the Wake*, 130–31.

51 Eva Margarita's work is in communion and conversation with the series of Black Lives Matter vigils that graced the US landscape in response to ongoing state violence against Black life. To learn more about the religious implications of candles and the etymological formations, see Wright, "Why Do Catholics Light Candles?"

52 Eva Margarita in conversation with the author, 2022.

53 Moten, "Black Mo'nin'," 62.

54 Eva Margarita conveys that she usually wears headdresses in all her performances to protect her crown, but also to protect her hair from going up in flames.

55 Eva Margarita in conversation with the author, 2021. I would like to pause here, in honor of the artist's challenging and brave work, to reiterate that this chapter attempts to enact the affective form of Eva Margarita's performance. I hope to encircle the reader through ongoing ritual and repetition in which reproducible repetitions are at the fore of writing performatively with aesthetics.

56 Eva Margarita in conversation with the author, 2021.

57 Ibid.

58 Ibid.

59 Vargas, "Ruminations on 'Lo Sucio' as a Latino Queer Analytic."

60 In my 2022 interview with the artist, Eva Margarita shares the following: "I am always fascinated by how we are all stained by history."

61 The use of Brownness here establishes a direct connection to José Esteban Muñoz's construction of it. See Muñoz's *The Sense of Brown*.

62 This conversation occurred in a 2022 interview when we discussed her performances some time after their initial production.

63 Ibid.

64 Ibid.

65 Ibid.

66 Sharpe, *In the Wake*, 21.

67 The spiritual and gospel song "This Little Light of Mine" has come to symbolize calls for freedom across American history. Records show that it first appeared as a poem and song recited in churches and penitentiaries in the early twentieth century. It was also a staple freedom song during the Civil Rights Movement, and has been more recently sung in counterpose to fascist and white supremacist uprisings. While there are longstanding debates about the song's creator, the spiritual has historically transformed across time, space, and social movement. For more on the details of this song's ongoing transmutations, see Deggans, "'This Little Light of Mine' Shines On, a Timeless Tool of Resistance," and Sabatella, "This Little Light of Mine: About the Song."

68 Eva Margarita in conversation with the author, 2021–2022.

69 Muñoz, *The Sense of Brown*, 146.

70 Here, Muñoz is thinking with Jean-Luc Nancy's contemplations of sharing the incalculable posed in *The Truth of Democracy* to read for how Ana Mendieta's body of work participates in a sharing out of the socially incalculable. He reads this to contemplate his own theory of brownness by restaging Nancy's idea that the real labor of existence is not merely about use and profitability but rather "about a certain sharing (out) of that thing that is without value precisely because it is invaluable." See Muñoz, *The Sense of Brown*, 147; and Nancy, *The Truth of Democracy*, 17.

71 Nancy, *The Truth of Democracy*, 17.

72 Muñoz, *The Sense of Brown*, 147–49; Nancy, *The Truth of Democracy*, 17.

73 Muñoz, *The Sense of Brown*, 149.

74 Ibid.

75 Muñoz, *Disidentifications*, 5.

76 Ferreira da Silva, "On Difference Without Separability," 57–65.

77 Gough, "Burning Bodies: Transformation and Fire," 9.

78 Bachelard, *The Psychoanalysis of Fire*, 7.

79 Sørensen and Bille, "Flames of Transformation," 253. Here, the authors are thinking with Bachelard's meditations on fire in *The Psychoanalysis of Fire*. See page 16 of Bachelard's book for a direct citation of this work.

80 Alvarado, "Ghostly Givings," 246.

81 Ibid., 243.

82 Ibid.

83 Ibid., 247.

84 Ruiz, *Left Turns in Brown Study*, 6.

85 See also Chambers-Letson, *After the Party*, xvi, to further trace the lines of affinity within minoritarian performance across entangled existences.

86 Sharpe, *In the Wake*, 21.

87 Bowles, "Reinscribing the Spectacle of Death," 3–18.

88 Ibid., 4.

89 Ibid., 9.

90 Chambers-Letson, *After the Party*, xvii.

91 Butler, *Precarious Life*, 20.

92 Ibid.

93 Ibid.

94 Ibid.

95 Ibid., 23 and 41.

96 Ibid., 22.

97 Ibid., 42.

98 Ibid., 49.

99 Canham, "Black Death and Mourning as Pandemic," 299.

100 Butler, *Precarious Life*, 49.

101 A title like *Precarious Life* might easily read *Precarious Death* depending on how we understand the human as made comprehensibly possible in how meaning is offered to death within various temporalities of existence.

102 Ruiz and Vourloumis, *Formless Formation*, 8–22.

103 Butler, *Precarious Life*, 30.

104 Ibid.

105 Ibid.

106 Margolles, *What Else Could We Talk About?* (2009). This is an installation consisting of a repeating performance carried out by one to three people mopping the floors of the exhibition space with a mix of water obtained from humidifying fabrics that previously absorbed fluids and of leftovers of crime scenes in different cities of northern Mexico. It was in the Mexican Pavilion at the Venice Biennale, Venice, Italy.

107 Ramos, "The Viscosity of Grief," 299.

108 Ibid.

109 Chambers-Letson, *After the Party*, 5. Chambers-Letson offers narratives of minoritarian subjects who "mobilize performance in both the realm of the aesthetic and the everyday to sustain the fugitive flight and revolutionary fight to produce freedom and More Life in the face of subordination, exploitation, annihilation, and negation."

110 For more information on this event and the participants involved, please visit thebrowntheatrecollective.com, mateohurtadothings.tumblr.com, evamargarita-performs.com, bredioni.com, and thetanknyc.org.

111 For a robust analysis of how Wari' members honor their dead through funerary cannibalism as an act of ongoing love, integrity, and compassion, see Conklin, *Consuming Grief*, xv–xvi.

112 Eva Margarita in conversation with the author, 2021.

113 Ibid.

114 Ibid.

115 Ibid.

116 Eva Margarita in conversation with the author, 2022.

117 In my 2022 interview with the artist, she notes that some of the twelve tamales made with ashes were saved and eaten over the next few days, but that there were still some tamales in the freezer for a later possible gathering.

118 In this claim, I am thinking of Julietta Singh's work where she distills the meaning of matter against material odds. I reproduce the matter here: "Matter is not stable and cannot be mastered, despite the narrative fictions that enable us to imagine and engage it as such. It is not inert in time; it evolves, shifts, mutates, surprises. What is true of matter is true of those forms of matter called humans, who come to resist the narratives of mastery that shaped their subjectivities in surprising and excessive ways." See Singh, *Unthinking Mastery*, 18.

119 Eva Margarita in conversation with the author, 2022.

120 Ibid.

121 In an interview with the author, Eva Margarita describes her research process for engaging endo-cannibalism. During our correspondences, she shares that "endo-cannibalistic approaches vary from culture to culture and are often done as funerary rites of passage. To consume the flesh of the other is to commit to their history and its reinvention through sharing." Eva Margarita also discloses that she turns to the critical work of scholar Julietta Singh, who describes the practice of endo-cannibalism by thinking as Lévi-Strauss does: "It is rarely ever about consuming the whole body, but rather a discrete symbolic act of incorporation. A small act of taking the body of another's into yours. Taking in the flesh of another is a way of claiming it as a part of you." See Singh, *No Archive Will Restore You*, 34.

122 Spillers, "Mama's Baby, Papa's Maybe," 67; quoted in Chambers-Letson, *After the Party*, 11.

123 Musser, *Sensational Flesh*, 20.

124 Conklin argues that it is out of the deepest compassion for the deceased that one eats the dead, according to Wari' views. See Conklin, *Consuming Grief*, xix.

125 Eva Margarita in conversation with the author, 2022.

126 Ibid.

127 Ibid.

128 Ibid.

129 Taylor-Garcia, *The Existence of the Mixed Race Damnés*, 83.

130 Ibid.

131 Ibid.

132 I was struck by the idea of material transformation through resurrection: "Those who had 'lived united on earth through the bond of the communion of saints' could also expect to be 'united in universal resurrection' resting together in consecrated ground, explained the *Boletín del Clero del Obispado de León*, a local church magazine, in 1888." See Martorell Linares, "The Cruellest of All Forms of Coercion," 664.

133 In the same article mentioned above, I was drawn to how Martorell Linares contemplates burial rights and punitive measures for the denial of such rites. He

shares that "the denial of ecclesiastical burial was a punishment that was integrated into the penal sanctions of canon law, one of extreme seriousness because it impeded eternal salvation. It was an exemplary punishment that sought to 'draw the attention of the faithful, strike fear in the indifferent, and perhaps correct the sinners and irreligious and cause them to halt on the road to perdition.'" See Martorell Linares, 664.

134 Sharpe, *In the Wake*, 16.

135 Derrida, *The Work of Mourning*, 10.

136 Gillespie and Lopez, *Vulnerable Witness*, 9.

137 Ibid., 10.

138 Ibid.

139 Del Rosario, "A Journey into Grief," 22–23.

140 Ibid., 4.

141 In "A Journey into Grief," Inge V. del Rosario beautifully and vulnerably recounts the loss of her grandmother and the funerary rites and rituals that leave her struggling to bear grief's grip. Feeling overwhelming guilt and suffering for not being able to say her farewells prior to her death, del Rosario harbors unspoken words of lingering shame and desire. She notes that shortly after the funeral, she lost her voice. For all the words she could not muster and share in life, she remains voiceless after death. I share this story because there is an unfounded tale among my family that those still living, and not at peace with the lost subject, will wear an injury in memory of the dead that resembles the dead in some capacity. The injury is the after-death wound that will appear (somewhat never resolved) in time's chamber. Her grandmother returns to her later through a song that eases the pain of grief somehow. Here, del Rosario can hear and sing along—no longer just voiceless to her death but attuned to the melody. When I read this article, I wondered if the love that one feels in grief has no other option but to literally inflict pain to recall the love object. Where else will grief live, how else will it perform affectively, when closure is foreclosed? See del Rosario, 19–28.

142 Gordon, *Ghostly Matters*, 201.

143 Ibid.

144 In our 2022 interview, Eva Margarita notes that each sibling received an urn of his ashes to do as they chose with them.

145 Eva Margarita in conversation with the author, 2022.

146 Ibid.

147 Ibid.

148 Ibid.

149 Ibid.

150 Ibid.

2. INTO THE STILL OF IT

1 For video and image documentation of this performance and all other work by Erica Gressman, please see the artist's website at www.ericagressman.com.

2 For more information on this series, please see Experimental Sound Studio's *The Quarantine Concerts* series: https://ess.org, March 21, 2020. According to the organization, *The Quarantine Concerts* are a "collaborative endeavor among a growing number of organizations and organizers meant to provide artists experimenting across genres a space to share their work and continue to earn a living during this time when most live performance opportunities have been canceled due to COVID-19."

3 See The Metropolitan Museum of Art, *Alexander McQueen's Voss*, https://blog.metmuseum.org; and Joel-Peter Witkin, *Sanitarium*, www.icp.org.

4 See Alexander McQueen, "Women's Spring/Summer 2001 Runway Show," March 21, 2012, www.youtube.com/watch?v=qynzgm9i4LI.

5 In a diary that Olley kept while modeling for McQueen's *Voss* show, she describes a feeling of sheer terror about her fat figure being cast as the centerpiece of a fashion show in direct contrast to the other models. See Olley, "Diary Entries by Michelle Olley," and Allwood, "If You Like McQueen's Asylum."

6 Witkin shares that the inspiration for much of his work came from early experiences attending carnival freak shows where he took photographs for his brother, who was painting with freaks as his subjects. See Coke, *Joel-Peter Witkin: Forty Photographs*, for more on his photography's freakish subject matter.

7 Erica Gressman in conversation with the author, May 26, 2021.

8 Ibid.

9 Guerrilla Girls, *Do Women Have to Be Naked to Get into the Met. Museum?* (1989), www.guerrillagirls.com.

10 Erica Gressman in conversation with the author, May 26, 2021.

11 Shawn Michelle Smith, *Photographic Returns*, 4.

12 Please turn to the artist's website for more of their aesthetic and political trajectory. These words are taken from their own biographical sketch: www.ericagressman.com.

13 From Gressman, www.ericagressman.com.

14 This concept of an aesthetic-life-world underpins the political and ideological work of Ruiz and Vourloumis in *Formless Formation: Vignettes for the End of this World*, where the authors state that "the aesthetic-life-world (the inherent entanglement of aesthetics and politics) manifests otherworldly social compositions. For it is not incidental that life's momentum often mirrors art and art's momentum parallels life. These are the very stages of the everyday as the everyday is always staged." See Ruiz and Vourloumis, *Formless Formation*, 8.

15 As this book is being written, reports of global COVID-19 death counts are exceeding 5.5 million. Attempts to analyze unreported deaths estimate that the number of deaths could actually be as high as sixteen million deaths. Still, the death toll continues to rise, and new viral strains continue to travel across the globe. It bears noting that the Johns Hopkins Coronavirus Resource Center has stopped collecting data as of March 10, 2023. Please refer to https://coronavirus.jhu.edu/map.html. See Smil and Brooks, "COVID: Excess Mortalities Two Years Later."

16 Many scholars across disciplines have noted the shifts in the use of the term *human* over the course of the pandemic and collectively pondered how ideas of being, life, and subjectivity change under pandemic regimes. For example, Barker et al., "Catastrophe, Care, and All That Remains," quote Neferti X. M. Tadiar, who states that "we live in a time when every day brings ample evidence of the disposability of human life. This is a casual use of the word 'human' because the very disposability of this life, its condition as destined waste, would seem to put into question the designation of this life as human, our inherited term for the defining conditions of ideal, valued, and invaluable existence" (31).

17 See Erica Gressman's website, www.ericagressman.com, for a description of her *COVID-19/What to Watch in 2020*.

18 Shawn Michelle Smith, *Photographic Returns*, 5.

19 Berlant, "The Commons: Infrastructures for Troubling Times," 1.

20 Ibid.

21 Ghosh, "The Costs of Living: Reflections on Global Health Crises," 66.

22 Ibid.

23 Ibid., 67.

24 Ibid.

25 Hartman, "Venus in Two Acts," 11.

26 I ask this question as I think with Saidiya Hartman's "Venus in Two Acts," a piece in which the author challenges us to reexamine what we know by how we recreate knowing, especially when we must narrate impossible stories for those given scant archival attention. In a piece about the pervasive presence of Venus in Atlantic slavery archives, Hartman struggles with how to write this "emblematic figure of the enslaved woman in the Atlantic world" into re-existence, asking how one writes against the unknown, the very brutality and aggression of archives themselves. In writing against the archive's violence, Hartman employs critical fabulation as a method and writerly form and repeats again and again that one cannot ask who Venus is "because it would be impossible to answer such a question" and yet wonderfully offers us a barely known (but overly known) story of Venus in two acts. While Gressman specifically references the reclining Venus by Witkin and McQueen, Hartman's ideas about the impossible narration of Venus recall the possibility of retelling and reshaping historical events by how one transitions the event into translation and reinscribed narrations. See Hartman, "Venus in Two Acts," 2–3.

27 Hartman, "Venus in Two Acts," 3.

28 Ibid., 5.

29 Butler, *What World Is This?*, 5.

30 Ibid.

31 Ibid.

32 Ibid., 101.

33 Ibid., 107.

34 Ibid., 109.

35 Ibid., 108–9.

36 Ruiz and Vourloumis, *Formless Formation*, 40–42.

37 Performance studies scholar Alexandra T. Vazquez smartly notes the following about the detail's potential: "Without reproducing the satisfaction that motivates some projects of recovery—the false belief the work is done when something or someone is made visible or audible—I also mean details as those bits of history that get skipped over or left unattended. Details, are, for many of us, wonderfully disruptive fissures that crack many a foundational premise behind all sorts of narratives." See Vazquez, *Listening in Detail*, 19–20.

38 Doyle, *Hold It Against Me*, 20.

39 In an in-person interview with Erica Gressman on July 24, 2022, the artist shares the following important information about the reproduction of images: "My image of the reclining Venus is first a conversation with Witkin's work, but since McQueen's show is most famous it becomes the main referential object. Witkin's style has remained with me because it portrays the feelings of the government's abandonment of its subjects, institutional sabotage, and decay. His work is powerful in its aesthetic practice and depiction of reality, a version of society focused on those most living on the edges of the world. I am not sure McQueen's fashion show fully honors this tradition although his show was provocative and challenged patriarchal convention in very queer ways. Did he present an honorable illustration of those institutionalized? I'm not certain of that. Every representation is fixed by previous representations already fixed by institutions."

40 Of her decision to appear as she does, Gressman cites the profundity of an image as inspiration. With that apocalyptic gas mask attached to tubes and electrical cords sprawled out dramatically across the sofa, the artist declares her position as an intentionally historical one.

41 Erica Gressman is a member of the band Fetishist, where she helps produce and compose songs and also performs as the band's drummer. See "Musical Projects" at www.ericagressman.com. For more on the band's musical style, see Kendrick, "Chicago Punk Outfit Fetishist Reinvent Themselves on *Austerity Messiah*."

42 In my 2022 conversation with the artist, Gressman elaborates on her body of work's relationship to grief. She makes it clear that she's been sitting with grief prior to her piece *COVID-19*. She states, "I've been thinking with grief for some time now. My piece *Limbs* (2018) is all about loss and the visceral, sonic, visual, and mental and physical ways we process losing those we love often due to politically unjust systems of oppression. This piece extends the feeling." To learn more about the artist, view upcoming events, and view photos and videos of her performances, see www.ericagressman.com.

43 See José Esteban Muñoz in *Disidentifications* and Sara Ahmed in *What's the Use?* for more on queer strategies of subversion, through the praxis of using things improperly and recycling dominating practices into minor orchestrations, in order to survive a hostile and anti-queer world.

44 Ruiz, "Creating La Estación Gallery," 135–47.

45 This controller (Musical Instrument Digital Interface: MIDI), a comprehensive device, enables instruments like drum machines, synthesizers, and computers to interact with one another. Erica Gressman in conversation with the author, May 26, 2021.

46 Erica Gressman in conversation with the author, May 26, 2021.

47 Ibid.

48 Ibid.

49 Ibid.

50 Ibid.

51 Jennifer DeVere Brody, *Punctuation*, 85.

52 Ibid., 87.

53 Brinkema, *The Forms of the Affects*, 76; Cools and Bowler, *Performing Mourning*, 10.

54 Brinkema, *The Forms of the Affects*, 76.

55 Butler and Yancy, "Interview: Mourning Is a Political Act amid the Pandemic and its Disparities," 485.

56 Varshney et al., "Grief in the COVID-19 Times," 70.

57 Higson and Price, "The Application of the Whirlpool of Grief to Support Experiences of Loss in Light of the Covid-19 Pandemic," 19–20.

58 Ibid., 20.

59 See Freeman's book *Time Binds: Queer Temporalities, Queer Histories*, in which she brilliantly theorizes chrononormativity.

60 For more on crip temporalities, turn to the "Crip Temporalities" special issue of the *South Atlantic Quarterly*, vol. 120, no. 2 (April 2021). It features work by editors and thinkers such as Moya Bailey on the "ethics of pace" (285), Mariá Elena Cepeda on "borrowed time" (303), and Jina B. Kim and Sami Schalk on creating "a crip-of-color critique" (325).

61 Kafer, *Feminist, Queer, Crip*; Samuels and Freeman, "Introduction: Crip Temporalities," 251.

62 Samuels and Freeman, "Introduction: Crip Temporalities," 251–252; Koshy, Cacho, Byrd, and Jefferson, *Colonial Racial Capitalism*.

63 Samuels and Freeman, "Introduction: Crip Temporalities," 252.

64 During one of our many conversations, I asked Gressman if she understood *COVID-19* to be following a crip genealogy or crip time study, or if she intended to comment on how pace is reoriented for bodies requiring different accessibilities during crisis. She disclosed that she hadn't intended to deliberately "crip" her new media piece, but as a queer racialized subject performing other being-entities, like this anti-Venus, she's constantly outside "any body known as able while within an estranged body that is always a working body."

65 Erica Gressman in conversation with the author, April 2023.

66 This conversation with Gressman concerning reorientations of the live and liveness and its capability to recall and foresee sensorial experience across viewership, time, and media recalls a moment in Shane Vogel's *Stolen Time: Black Fad Performance and the Calypso Craze*. Vogel underscores the capacious ability of

performance to extend across time, sense, form, and genre without having to reproduce any original event or spectacle. Describing performance across media as "black fad performance," he actuates another kind of liveness. He writes, "liveness can mean not only presence or a fixed space and time (for example, the 'here and now') but can also describe a sensation, a charge carried by some recorded sounds and objects, as in a live wire; the activation of imagination or the fact of necessary chance" (18).

67 Holinger, *The Anatomy of Grief.*

68 Breuer and Freud, *Studies on Hysteria.*

69 Bordere, "Social Justice Conceptualizations in Grief and Loss," 15.

70 Fox and McDermott, "Where Is Leisure When Death Is Present?," 267.

71 Butler and Yancy, "Interview," 485.

72 Barthes, *Camera Lucida*, 15.

73 Schechner, *Restoration of Behavior.*

74 Tapia, *American Pietàs.*

75 Ibid.

76 See Dion Enari and Byron William Rangiwai's 2021 article "Digital Innovation and Funeral Practices: Māori and Samoan Perspectives During the COVID-19 Pandemic" for more on shifting digital borders of grief during the COVID-19 pandemic.

77 See Barthes's book *Camera Lucida* to best consider the role of the punctum across images.

78 Barthes, *Camera Lucida*, 55.

79 Ibid., 57.

80 Ibid., 75.

81 Ibid., 77.

82 Brinkema, *The Forms of the Affects*, 77.

83 Sharpe, *In the Wake*, 10; Freud, "Mourning and Melancholia."

84 Erica Gressman in conversation with the author, May 26, 2021.

85 Ibid.

86 For more on entanglements of Black death and pandemics being only one among the many causes, see Hugo Canham's "Black Death and Mourning as Pandemic" and Sharon E. Moore et al.'s "Six Feet Apart or Six Feet Under: The Impact of COVID-19 on the Black Community."

87 Benjamin, "Theses on the Philosophy of History."

88 Higson and Price, "The Application of the Whirlpool of Grief to Support Experiences of Loss in Light of the Covid-19 Pandemic."

89 Bordere, "Social Justice Conceptualizations in Grief and Loss," 14.

90 Theidon, "A Forecasted Failure: Intersectionality, COVID-19, and the Perfect Storm."

91 Ibid., 529.

92 Ibid.

93 Ibid., 534.

94 Chiu, "Trump Has No Qualms about Calling Coronavirus the 'Chinese Virus.'"

95 Chambers-Letson, "Contracting Justice."

96 While there is consensus about what constitutes a living organism among scientists, some extend the biological conditions for living or non-living organisms. In particular, "a virus that scientists are calling Sputnik was found in a newly discovered strain of so-called mimivirus, which is the world's largest known virus." And "the researchers believe that Sputnik is the first of a yet-to-be-discovered family of viruses that they suspect may plague large viruses that attack ocean plankton." They add that "if mimivirus can both pirate another organism's DNA-copying machinery and fall prey to another virus that does the same to it, then mimivirus is most certainly alive" (Swaminathan, "Viruses: They're Alive, and They Can Infect Each Other"). The details of the virus, such as its temporal, visual, amd spatial characteristics and mutational capacity, may help us draw universal links between worlds and entities, be they alive, almost living, or only living once conjoined. See also Matthews, "Is Anything Ever Absolutely Still?"

97 Swaminathan, "Viruses: They're Alive, and They Can Infect Each Other."

98 Erica Gressman in conversation with the author, May 26, 2021.

99 Ibid.

100 Barthes, *Camera Lucida*, 52.

101 Ruiz and Vourloumis, *Formless Formation*, 44.

102 Ibid.

103 This isn't the first performance that Gressman has organized around a disdain for Trump and his conduits. Many of her works, such as *Limbs* and *Wall of Skin*, reckon with the materiality of minoritarian identity, specifically living under a violent government. The artist has even given a presentation at La Estación Gallery titled "Art Under Trumpism: A Queer Latinx Journey." During this 2018 talk, Gressman led a conversation surrounding art's purpose and urgency under the fascist regime of Trump and how minoritarian aesthetics become both a tool of survival and resistance against white supremacy.

104 Ruiz and Vourloumis, *Formless Formation*, 77.

105 Ibid.

106 Ghosh, "Virus: Tales of Object+," 136.

107 Ibid., 138.

108 Ibid.

109 Ibid.

110 Butler and Yancy, "Interview," 483.

111 Ibid., 484.

112 Ibid., 483.

113 Ibid., 484.

114 Chambers-Letson, "Contracting Justice," 560.

115 Ibid.

116 Ibid., 561.

117 Ibid.

118 See The Felix Gonzalez-Torres Foundation at www.felixgonzalez-torresfoundation.org.

119 Gonzalez-Torres, *"Untitled" (Portrait of Ross in L.A.)* (candies individually wrapped in multicolor cellophane [endless supply], 1991), Art Institute of Chicago, www.artic.edu.

120 Lewis, "Grief Circling," 305.

121 Holinger, *The Anatomy of Grief*, xxvii.

122 Butler and Yancy, "Interview," 483.

123 Holinger, *The Anatomy of Grief*, 29.

124 Lewis, "Grief Circling," 307.

125 In my interview with the artist in 2022, Gressman shares that siren-like sounds are omni-directional; they encircle and hail subjects and landscapes, making it impossible to know exactly the direction of sound. Although we are watching her piece in 2-D, her goal is to use sound to pull us into a 3-D model.

126 Erica Gressman in conversation with the author, May 26, 2021.

127 Ibid.

128 Theidon, "A Forecasted Failure."

129 Bayatrizi, Ghorbani, and Taslimi Tehrani, "Risk, Mourning, Politics," 514.

130 Holinger, *The Anatomy of Grief*.

131 See Fakhruroji, "Texting Condolences on WhatsApp as a Mediatized Mourning Practice," 677–86, for more on how social media technologies allow the emergence of different tendencies in grieving.

132 In *The Death Project: An Anthology for These Times*, Gretchen Eick and Cora Poage curate a collection of essays, poems, and writings of various genres that undertake the tragedy of death, dying, and grieving under "the ravages of COVID-19 across the globe; and the despair that grows suicide" (Eick, "Introduction," 8). The stories assembled span the globe, moving from Australia to Bosnia to the United States to facilitate the intricate workings of grieving, remembering, holding close and delicately letting go. Described as "an intimate conversation about a subject we avoid," the collection emotionally waits-with grief in a scene that throws one into the spasms of immediate and ongoing death.

133 Eick, "Night Quarantine," 78.

134 Ibid., 78.

135 Ibid., 78–79.

136 Ibid., 79.

137 Barthes notes that "it merely makes the emotivity of mourning pass." See *Mourning Diary*, 101.

138 Butler and Yancy, "Interview," 485.

139 An in-person interview with the artist, almost two years after her performance, July 24, 2022.

140 Barthes, *Mourning Diary*, 142.

141 Erica Gressman in conversation with the author, July 24, 2022.

142 Another in-person conversation with Gressman, April 29, 2023, where she shares that the pandemic has left the living shattered, unable to return to what we imagined we were, could be. According to the artist, the grief isn't lifted. We just learn to live with it in simulation.

3. BASINS FOR THE BEREFT

1 Pedro Lopez in ongoing discussion with author, 2020–2024, via text, email, social media, and video. See also the artist's website for further information on this project and other work: www.pedrodaniellopez.com.
2 Pedro Lopez in ongoing discussion with author, 2020–2024. Lopez describes softness as related to intentional human vulnerability that can manifest in many ways. For the artist, these multiple expressions may include deep and intimate reembraces, crying, conjoined silence, and refusal to call on violence as the first and only way to counter colonial domination.
3 Negrón-Muntaner, "Our Fellow Americans," 121; Velez Gonzalez, "Clinton, Rosselló, González and Ferrer Win in Puerto Rico Primaries."
4 Lopez, "Tear Basins."
5 Bonilla and LeBrón, *Aftershocks of Disaster*, 3.
6 Ibid.
7 Ruiz, *Ricanness*, 3–5.
8 Muñoz, *Cruising Utopia*, 81.
9 Singh, *No Archive Will Restore You*, 18.
10 Muñoz, "Ephemera as Evidence," 10.
11 Lopez, *Tear Basin (Vale of Cashmere)*, self-published pamphlet also available on the artist's website: www.pedrodaniellopez.com.
12 These phrases appear in Lopez's *Tear Basin (Vale of Cashmere)* pamphlet with the latter phrase a direct citation from Muñoz's *Cruising Utopia*, 27. Muñoz also states, in accompaniment to said notion, "Utopia is an idealist mode of critique that reminds us that there is something missing, that the present and presence (and its opposite number, absence) is not enough" (100).
13 Lopez, *Tear Basin (Vale of Cashmere)*, pamphlet.
14 Lopez, "Tear Basins," and ongoing correspondence with the author.
15 Nancy DeJesus, "Fountains as a Synthesis of Sculpture, Water, and Land," 16–23.
16 Lopez in ongoing conversation with the author, 2020–2024.
17 Throughout our many-year correspondences, Lopez shared his personal basin archive of images and video, through which I was able to capture a sense of weight and depth and to understand how each basin's size and texture correlate to theme and matter.
18 Lopez in ongoing conversation with the author, 2020–2024.
19 Muñoz, *Disidentifications*.
20 Prospect Park Alliance, "From the Archives: The Vale of Cashmere."
21 Thomas Moore, *Lalla Rookh*. See the section on "The Light of the Haram," 240–270.

22 For more information on how European notions of the exotic were deployed in French musical operas, see Ralph P. Locke's "The Exotic in Nineteenth-Century French Opera," in which he describes a moment of *Lalla Rookh*'s circulation across aesthetic sites. He states, "Somewhat similar in fairy-tale feeling is Félicien David's tuneful and engagingly scored Lalla-Roukh (Opéra-Comique, 1862), based on a book by the Irish poet Thomas Moore about a beautiful Mughal princess from Kashmir who must travel to Samarkand (in what is now Uzbekistan) to marry, against her will, the king of that land. Numerous musical numbers in Lalla-Roukh praise the beautiful surroundings that the anxious heroine and her retinue encounter as they move along their otherwise grim route" (113).

23 Moore, *Lalla Rookh*, 240.

24 For more information on the park, see the online magazine *Atlas Obscura*'s "Vale of Cashmere," www.atlasobscura.com/places/vale-of-cashmere; and Disser, "Inside the Vale of Cashmere, a Bucolic Cruising Spot Threatened by 'Restoration.'"

25 Hartman, "Venus in Two Acts," 11.

26 Singh, *No Archive Will Restore You*, 22.

27 Santiago, "Introduction."

28 Lopez, *Tear Basin (Vale of Cashmere)* pamphlet.

29 Mendieta, *Untitled (Blood Sign #2/Body Tracks)*.

30 Muñoz, *Cruising Utopia*, 27.

31 Lopez, *Tear Basin (Vale of Cashmere)* pamphlet.

32 Ibid.

33 Ibid.

34 Ibid.

35 Ibid.

36 Ibid.

37 Muñoz, *Cruising Utopia*, 49.

38 Lopez in conversation with the author.

39 Rivera-Servera, *Performing Queer Latinidad*, 134.

40 Pollock, *Exceptional Spaces*, 3–4.

41 Muñoz, "Ephemera as Evidence," 10.

42 Ibid., 10–11.

43 Taussig, "Culture of Terror—Space of Death," 468.

44 Derrida, *Specters of Marx*.

45 Gordon, *Ghostly Matters*.

46 Baptist, "Diaspora: Death without a Landscape," 294.

47 Ibid., 305.

48 Ibid., 295.

49 Ibid., 305.

50 Muñoz, *Cruising Utopia*.

51 Taussig, "Culture of Terror—Space of Death," 468; Baptist, "Diaspora," 297; Muñoz, *Cruising Utopia*, 18; Muñoz, "Ephemera as Evidence," 6; Singh, *No Archive Will Restore You*, 29.

52 Lopez in conversation with the author.

53 Ibid.

54 Duany, *The Puerto Rican Nation on the Move*, 4.

55 I am thinking here with a few complementary and contemporary works on the longstanding and multivariate consequences of colonialism. While this list of works merely touches the surface of critical scholarship in Rican anticolonial and decolonial studies, please see the following: Aparicio and Chávez-Silverman, *Tropicalizations*; Maldonado-Torres, *Against War*; Santiago, *Boricuas*; Denis, *War Against All Puerto Ricans*; Zambrana, *Colonial Debts*; LeBrón, *Policing Life and Death*; LeBrón, *Against Muerto Rico*; Negrón-Muntaner, *Boricua Pop*; Flores, *The Diaspora Strikes Back*.

56 Santiago, "Introduction," xiii.

57 Muñoz, *Cruising Utopia*, 81.

58 Ibid., 65.

59 Rodríguez, *Sexual Futures, Queer Gestures, and Other Latina Longings*, 4.

60 García Lorca, *In Search of Duende*, 37.

61 Lopez in conversation with the author.

62 Ibid.

63 Ibid.

64 Ibid.

65 Vourloumis, "Ten Theses on Touch, or, Writing Touch," 233 and 236.

66 Ibid., 237.

67 Muñoz, *Cruising Utopia*, 64.

68 For more information on US colonialism's practices and impacts on the island, see: Marquis and Nordheimer, "U.S. Ready to Remove Vieques Protesters"; La Fountain-Stokes, "Queer Puerto Ricans and the Burden of Violence"; Ferré-Sadurní and Hartocollis, "Maria Strikes, and Puerto Rico Goes Dark"; Robles, Semple, and Pérez-Peña, "Hurricane Irma, One of the Most Powerful in History, Roars Across Caribbean"; Office of Public Affairs, United States Department of Justice, "Former Governor of Puerto Rico Arrested in Bribery Scheme"; Romero et al., "15 Days of Fury: How Puerto Rico's Government Collapsed"; Walsh, "How Puerto Rico Is Grappling With a Debt Crisis."

69 For more information on the history and cultural and spiritual significance of alabaster, please see The Gem Library. "White Alabaster: Meanings, Properties, Facts and More!," https://thegemlibrary.com.

70 Lopez in conversation with the author.

71 Ibid.

72 Ibid.

73 Ibid.

74 Ibid.

75 Ibid.

76 Ibid.

77 Ibid.

78 Ibid.

79 I would be remiss if I did not re-trace another sensual sighting across historical orientation. Christina León, in "Trace Alignment: Object Relations After Ana Mendieta," pulls from Muñoz's ideas on ephemera as evidence and follows artist Ana Mendieta's earthly excavations across Miami and Cuba through *siluetas* and cave paintings (2). León understands Mendieta's markings across stone, sand, dirt, and water as "trace alignments" or traces that produce relational encounters by transcending the past into the domain of the ephemeral; for, as she shares of Mendieta and her work, "the past was her matter and medium, but not her property" (7). Traces reproduce affinities not only between subjects, but within the textured materialities that reshape space, history, and object relations. Interested in what is "hauntologically traceable visually" across elements of the earth, León reminds us that another element such as water "threatens to erode but also unite" (4). It is in this space that elements turn water into invisible ether and earthly cultural bridges remain in outlines over land.

80 Barthes, *Mourning Diary*, 106.

81 Homer, *The Odyssey*, "Book 11," 443.

82 Gibson, "Melancholy Objects," 285.

83 Ibid.

84 Singh, *No Archive Will Restore You*, 23.

85 Singh, *No Archive Will Restore You*, 113; Manning, *For a Pragmatics of the Useless*, 10.

86 Singh, *No Archive Will Restore You*, 97.

87 Derrida, "Archive Fever"; please refer to Singh's reading of Derrida's work on the archive in *No Archive Will Restore You*, 24–25.

88 Derrida, *Archive Fever*, 1.

89 Ibid.

90 Derrida, *Archive Fever*, 1–2.

91 Singh, *No Archive Will Restore You*, 24.

92 Ibid., 25.

93 Ibid.

94 Ibid.

95 Lopez, *Tear Basin (Vale of Cashmere)* pamphlet. Lopez's pamphlet cites the following in the exact same way. Here it is reproduced:

1. The oldest reference to tears was found in Syrian clay tablets near the city of Ugarit, 1400 B.C. The tablets recount the death of Ba'al and his resurrection through the intoxifying tears shed by his sister. The Egyptians believed the Nile flooded and delivered fertile sediments because of Isis's tears. And in ancient Greece it was believed the clay Prometheus used to create man was done with tears, not water. —Ad Vingerhoets *Why Only Humans Weep*

2. In the 1940s physiologists discovered that lysozyme, an enzyme that is a powerful antiseptic found in tears, was also found in abnormally high concentrations in ulcer patients. Excess lysozyme produced in times of emotional upset eats away

at the lining of the stomach, they concluded, and four out of five people afflicted with such ulcers are male.—Tom Lutz *Crying: A Natural and Cultural History of Tears*

3. "The ability to let go of parts of our past, of parts of ourselves, of fantasies, of dreams that are no longer relevant, of pain that has long since served its purpose, is an essential part of our capacity to grieve and to recreate ourselves." —Kay Carmichael *Ceremony of Innocence*

4. Rosalyn Duetshe describes uneven development as the abstract space* capitalism and spatial politics impart vehicles for state domination; including, but not limited to subordination, underdevelopment, surveillance, and manipulation. —*Uneven Development*

   * 'One of the most crying paradoxes of abstract space is that it can be simultaneously the birthplace of contradictions, the milieu in which they are worked out and which they tear up, and finally, the instrument which allows their suppression and substitution of an apparent coherence. All of which confers on space a function previously assumed by ideology." —Henri Lefebvre *The Production of Space*

5. In Sandra Ruiz's seminal work *Ricanness* she presents a poetics of ontology concerning the looping of colonialism that exists for Boriquas, as well as a means to think beyond it. ". . . Ricanness functions as a continual performance of bodily endurance against US colonialism, unfolding via aesthetic interventions in time."

   This basin is dedicated to Borikén. Its past, present, and liberated future.

96 Ruiz, *Ricanness*, 83.

97 Lopez in conversation with the author.

98 Lefebvre, *The Production of Space*, 238.

99 For further information on Lopez's community organizing work, see the Instagram accounts of the following organizations: @comidapalpueblo, "Comida Pal Pueblo," www.instagram.com/comidapalpueblo/; @nyboricuaresistance, "NY Boricua Resistance," www.instagram.com/nyboricuaresistance/.

100 In our conversations, Lopez shares that community work involves listening to multiple voices, not just imposing one on a group of people.

101 Barthes, *Mourning Diary*. He writes: "Not to *manifest* mourning (or at least to be indifferent to it) but to *impose* the *public* right to the loving relation it implies" (55).

102 hooks, "An Aesthetic of Blackness."

103 Ruiz and Vourloumis, *Formless Formation*, 54.

104 Ibid., 65.

105 Pedro Lopez, *Hair Piece* (2012), photographs of varying texture and color of human hair pressed under glass. See www.pedrodaniellopez.com.

106 Hannah Wilke, *Brushstrokes*, www.hannahwilke.com.

107 Lopez, *My Gay Agenda* (2015); Swift, "Gay Revolutionary."

108 Ibid.

109 Lopez in conversation with the author.

110 Sedgwick, *Epistemology of the Closet*.

111 Barthes, *Mourning Diary*, 102.

112 da Silva, "On Difference Without Separability."

113 Lopez in conversation with the author.

114 Frey and Langseth, *Crying: The Mystery of Tears*.

115 Brody, "Biological Role of Emotional Tears Emerges Through Recent Studies."

116 Frey and Langseth, *Crying: The Mystery of Tears*, 6 and 12.

117 Brody, "Biological Role of Emotional Tears Emerges Through Recent Studies."

118 Ibid.

119 Lopez in conversation with the author.

120 Ibid.

121 Ibid.

122 Fisher, *The Topography of Tears*.

123 Ibid., 47.

124 Ibid., 27.

125 Ibid., 30.

126 Ibid., 92–93.

127 Ibid., 44–45.

128 Ibid., 112–13.

129 Ibid., 25.

130 Ibid., 40.

131 Ibid., 66–67.

132 Lauterbach, "On Tears," 11.

133 Ibid.

134 Ruiz, *Ricanness*, 142.

135 Ruiz, *Ricanness*, 160.

136 Muñoz, "Feeling Brown, Feeling Down," 676.

137 Bustamante, *Neapolitan*.

138 Muñoz, "Feeling Brown, Feeling Down," 676.

139 Ibid.

140 Ibid., 684.

141 Muñoz, *The Sense of Brown*, 39.

142 Ibid., 38.

143 Ibid., 39.

144 Ibid.

145 Ibid., xv.

146 Muñoz, *The Sense of Brown*, 149; Williams, *Marxism and Literature*, 128.

147 This information was gleaned from ongoing correspondence with the artist, but also see a discussion of his piece in Ruiz, "A Light for a Light," 33.

148 Lauterbach, "On Tears," 11.

149 Ibid.

150 Lopez in conversation with the author.

151 Cindy Milstein, "Prologue," 4.

152 Ibid., 9.

153 Ibid., 7.

154 Ibid., 6–7.

155 Milstein, "Prologue," 7; Butler, *Precarious Life*, xv.

156 Lopez in conversation with the author.

157 Muñoz, "Feeling Brown, Feeling Down," 684.

158 Ibid., 679.

159 This occurred during several conversations with the artist in late 2023 (after the basin's removal) in which we reflected on notions of ephemerality and permanence across diasporic sites and public places.

160 Lopez in conversation with the author in 2023, shortly after the basin's removal from the Vale of Cashmere.

161 Ibid.

162 Ibid.

163 Muñoz, *Cruising Utopia*, 41.

164 Lopez in conversation with the author.

165 Ibid.

4. IN LOOPS OF WISTFUL LISTENING

1 Smith in conversation with the author from 2022 to 2024, includes ongoing access to a private and familial archival collection.

2 Earth, Wind & Fire, "Be Ever Wonderful," by Maurice White and Larry Dunn, August 1977, track 5 side B, on *All 'n All*, Columbia Records, 1977.

3 Brooks, *Liner Notes for the Revolution*, 8.

4 Ibid., 7.

5 Vazquez, *Listening in Detail*, 19; Vazquez, "Salon Philosophers," 301.

6 For information on the power and legacy of Black girlhood, see Cox, *Shapeshifters*.

7 Woods, "Don't Talk to Me About Racism if You Don't Know Earth, Wind & Fire's Catalog."

8 Ibid.

9 According to Crystal Lynn Webster in "The History of Black Girls and the Field of Black Girlhood Studies," Black girlhood studies is concerned with occupying spaces that were not traditionally designed for Black girls. While a relatively emergent field, the work of Black girls can be traced to the "recorded history of African American childhood in early America."

10 These words were shared by the artist during a conversation in my office on November 21, 2023. They also form the epigraph of this chapter.

11 All this information comes from the exhibition catalog and Smith's own curatorial wall tags along with our ongoing interviews and correspondence. For further information, please see: 2022 School of Art & Design Faculty Exhibition *Black on Black on Black on Black*, Krannert Art Museum, https://kam.illinois.edu/exhibition/black-black-black-black; "Art about Black Experiences Headlines Faculty Exhibition at Krannert Art Museum," Krannert Art Museum, https://kam.illinois.

edu/news-article/art-about-black-experiences-headlines-faculty-exhibition-kran-nert-art-museum; Blair Ebony Smith's website, https://blairebonysmith6.wixsite.com/lovenloops.

12 Ibid.

13 Brown, *Hear Our Truths*, 3–5.

14 Quoted from Smith's previous website, no longer online: www.lovenloops.com/about. Music by lovenloops and SOLHOT is available online: *Don't Ever Forget It (Reissue),* https://failedpoemrecords.bandcamp.com/album/dont-ever-forget-it-reissue; *How I Feel EP*, https://welevitate.bandcamp.com/album/how-i-feel-ep; *We Levitate Presents: Black Girl Genius Week 2016*, https://soundcloud.com/solhot-next-level/sets/we-levitate-presents-black.

15 Brown, *Hear Our Truths*; Smith, *(Refrain)* catalog.

16 Ruiz and Vourloumis, *Formless Formation*, 116–19.

17 Brown, *Hear Our Truths*, 3–5.

18 In a text exchange with Smith, she shares, "I joined SOLHOT in 2014 (for me that means joining the band and doing SOLHOT face to face). In SOLHOT, I brought the music, the sound equipment, the songs, tracks we listened to and made new songs from and I DJed for the band and girls in sessions, making music with girls in SOLHOT." She adds, "Being a homegirl means making whatever needs to be made with the group." Smith also adds, "I have worked on We Levitate projects like *How I Feel EP*, Black Girl Genius Week (BGGW) sounds from 2016–2019 studio session and also *SOLHOT Friends*." See www.solhot.com/music.

19 Smith in conversation with the author.

20 Ibid.

21 Cooper, *Homemade Love*, "Author's Note."

22 Ibid.

23 See Smith's exhibition in the Krannert Art Museum, *Homemade, with Love: More Living Room*, https://kam.illinois.edu/exhibition/homemade-love-more-living-room; also see "Black Girls Create a Space of Their Own in 'Homemade, with Love' Exhibition at KAM," Krannert Art Museum, https://kam.illinois.edu/news-article/black-girls-create-space-their-own-homemade-love-exhibition-kam.

24 Smith in conversation with the author.

25 Smith, "Doing SOLHOT as a Reliable Way of Life."

26 Smith in conversation with the author.

27 For more information on the albums, see *How I Feel EP* and *Don't Ever Forget It*, www.lovenloops.com/how-i-feel-ep-2016; *Homemade, with Love: More Living Room*, www.lovenloops.com/homemade-w-love-more-living-room-20; and *Cherish: A Love Letter to Gwendolyn Brooks* www.lovenloops.com/cherish-2019. See also "Research Conversations: Rikki Byrd with Blair Ebony Smith," Krannert Art Museum, https://kam.illinois.edu/resource/research-conversations-rikki-byrd-blair-ebony-smith. For Yvette Mayorga's work, please see www.yvettemayorga.com.

28 Webster, "The History of Black Girls and the Field of Black Girlhood Studies."

29 Brooks, *Liner Notes for the Revolution*, 4. Brooks also notes that her labor in listening is indebted to Alexandra T. Vazquez's concept of "listening in detail," which includes all the relentless and stubborn information that exists on and off the pages of musical historiography. Thinking with Vazquez, Brooks claims to "pay close attention to the sound produced by the artists themselves (as Alexandra Vazquez does so brilliantly in *Listening in Detail*) but also *listen to listeners listening*—to each other, to distant live performers, to beloved recordings, to nonmusical sounds, to ideas about other sounds composed in the privacy of their own vibrant imagination" (13).

30 Hernandez, *Aesthetics of Excess*, 17.

31 Smith in conversation with author, where she speaks lovingly about her sister Toni and how, together, they keep familial memories alive in their practices of being-together and deliberate actions for living day-to-day, aware and conscious of pressing social realities.

32 ife, *Maroon Choreography*, ix.

33 Harney and Moten, *The Undercommons*.

34 Central to ife's intervention is an amendment to choreography and its documentation. Placing the undercommons theory by Harney and Moten in conversation with curator and performance studies scholar André Lepecki's reconsideration of choreography, ife understands that choreography is not merely a series of diagrams for bodies shifting into motion, but a process much like writing that is molded and organized by dominant bodily discourses.

35 ife, *Maroon Choreography*, xi.

36 Ibid., x.

37 Ibid, xi.

38 Ibid., x.

39 This information may be found in the exhibition catalog. It was also reiterated in ongoing conversations with the artist.

40 For more information on the exhibition, see *Black on Black on Black on Black*, https://kam.illinois.edu/exhibition/black-black-black-black. Other participating artists were Patrick Earl Hammie; Stacey Robinson; BLACKMAU, Robinson's collaboration with Kamau Grantham; and Nekita Thomas. For more information on other participants' work, please see Patrick Earl Hammie, https://patrickearlhammie.com/; Stacey Robinson, https://art.illinois.edu/people/profiles/stacey-robinson/; BLACKMAU, https://buffaloakg.org/person/blackmau; and Nekita Thomas, www.nekitathomas.com.

41 For direct language from the exhibition catalog, see https://kam.illinois.edu/exhibition/black-black-black-black.

42 Ibid.

43 Gorton, "BeatCaffeine's 15 Most Essential Roy Ayers Records."

44 Roy Ayers, "Love Will Bring Us Back Together," by Roy Ayers, 1979, track 1 on *Fever*, Record Plant, 1979.

45 In ongoing correspondence with the artist, we agree to call her parents by their first names and nicknames to reduce any further confusions of the name Smith

throughout the chapter. We also agree over several phone calls that saying their first names and nicknames is a way of bringing their labor and lives to the forefront of critical analysis. This chapter about the daughter's work is also about the labor of family as an ancestral enterprise.

46 It is unsurprising that this funk-disco song has a long history of being sampled across bodies of work, from Mary J. Blige's 1993 hook/riff in "Real Love" (Phat Remix) to The Chimes's 1990 "Heaven" (Summer Breeze Mix) to even Alberto Gambino's 2006 "Tu Dinero." Leight, "Mary J. Blige's 'My Life' Documentary: 8 Things We Learned." For a complete list of songs that sample "Love Will Bring Us Back Together," see www.whosampled.com/Roy-Ayers/Love-Will-Bring-Us-Back-Together/sampled/.

47 Smith in conversation with the author.

48 Ibid.

49 All this info comes from the exhibition catalog and Smith's own curatorial wall tags shared with me over email.

50 Williams, *Marxism and Literature*, 128.

51 Smith in conversation with the author.

52 For more on the pathology of nostalgia, or a psychoanalytic reading of nostalgia's possibilities and hindrances, see Impert and Rubin, "The Mother at the Glen," 691–706.

53 Roy Ayers, "Love Will Bring Us Back Together."

54 Smith shared her entire archive with me electronically after the show had been deinstalled. This allowed me access to images, wall tags, and all other relevant exhibition content.

55 Smith in conversation with the author.

56 This information about family member sounds, details of the exhibition, and extra archival documents was shared over consistent text messages from November 27 to December 10, 2023. We asked questions, responded to each other, and offered feedback through ongoing text messages.

57 Lauryn Hill, *The Miseducation of Lauryn Hill*, Ruffhouse Records, 1998.

58 Brooks, *Liner Notes for the Revolution*, 11.

59 These songs can be found across Smith's personal archive through links shared via personal text messages and located on a Spotify playlist at https://open.spotify.com/playlist/3NAU5L8TadfRJaWMXAeYVR. In particular, see the playlist to listen to the following songs: Parliament, "Mothership Connection (Star Child)," by Bernie Worrell, George Clinton, and William Earl Collins, on *Mothership Connection*, Casablanca Records, 1975; Sade, "No Ordinary Love," by Sade Adu and Stuart Mathewman, on *Love Deluxe*, Epic Records EAS, 1992; Marvin Gaye, "Inner City Blues (Make Me Wanna Holler)," by James Nyx Jr. and Marvin Gaye, on *What's Going On*, Tamia, 1971; Plunky, "Jazz Is All That Jazz," by Al Dokes, James E. Branch, and Jamiah Branch, on *Juju Jazz Poetics*, N.A.M.E. Brand Records, 2022; Snoop Dogg, "Gin and Juice," by Calvin Cordozar Broadus Jr., on *L.A. Originals* (Original Picture Soundtrack), 2020, Universal Music Enterprises; Bill Withers,

"Lovely Day," by Bill Withers and Skip Scarborough, on *Menagerie*, Columbia Legacy, 1977.

60 For the exhibition playlist, see https://open.spotify.com/playlist/3NAU5L8TadfRJaWMXAeYVR.

61 Smith in correspondence with the author through text.

62 Herrera, "A Sonic Treatise of Futurity," 71.

63 Ibid., 72.

64 Smith in conversation with the author, 2023.

65 Ibid.

66 Campt, *Listening to Images*. Also refer to the *Ideas on Fire* podcast, where she talks about counterintuitive listening: "Tina Campt on Listening to Images," *Ideas on Fire*, May 16, 2018, https://ideasonfire.net/63-tina-campt/.

67 Referenced and taken from the *Ideas on Fire* podcast with Campt: https://ideasonfire.net/63-tina-campt/.

68 Roy Ayers, "*Everybody Loves the Sunshine*," Columbia, 1976; Oneness of Juju, *African Rhythms*, Strut Records, 1975. The latter album, as Smith shares, belongs to a "spiritual jazz band her dad followed around Richmond, Virginia."

69 Roy Ayers, "Love Will Bring Us Back Together."

70 I have been sitting with the idea of what a room might or might not be able to do spatially but can effectively enact through writing. I am brought to Vazquez's work again, where, in her preface to *The Florida Room*, she writes, "*The Florida Room* is a method, a spatial imaginary, a vestibule, an addition to the main house of writings about place" (ix). Each section of this book takes on a temporary room, enabling the sound waves as spatial reservoirs to move across location. I am imagining that Smith provides a similar method by compressing sounds across narrow and wide spaces to have the viewer chase sound waves into compositions and remade compilations.

71 I am thinking of Uri McMillan's *Embodied Avatars*, where he discusses the idea of "a sonic of dissent." While McMillan is referencing the long history of the resistance of the object as explicated by Fred Moten's retelling of Aunt Hester's scream in *In the Break*, both attend to how subjects resist objecthood to foreclose infinite negation. McMillan offers sound as embodied knowledge within impossible and troubling performances like that of Heth's. McMillan understands "speaking out of turn" as productive disagreement which has the potential to forge a path toward a renewed imaginary for objecthood's performativity. This recalls Vazquez's "aside" as also holding new meaning through sonic dissent. See McMillan, 58.

72 Berlant, *Desire/Love*, 18.

73 This idea of listening to the "aside" comes from an article by Alexandra T. Vazquez, "Salon Philosophers." The idea of the "beside" comes from Sedgwick, *Touching Feeling*.

74 Smith in conversation with the author.

75 Ibid.

76 Ibid.

77 Holland, *Raising the Dead*, 4.

78 Ibid, 4–5.

79 Smith in conversation with the author.

80 Ibid.

81 Brooks, *Liner Notes for the Revolution*, 8.

82 Ibid., 4–5.

83 Ibid., 4.

84 Ibid.

85 These ideas were presented during "Class Act Aesthetics," an online talk for an event I curated and moderated via La Estación Gallery through the Sue Divan Producing Fund and Minor Aesthetics Lab. The event was held over a Zoom webinar on October 6, 2022 (7–8:30 p.m.). The event asked scholars like Dr. Sandy Plácido, Dr. Jillian Hernandez, and Xavi Luis Burgos to think about class as an aesthetic category by highlighting academics who not only came from the working class but who privilege that angle of research as a political, aesthetic, and ideological one. It is important to note that Blair Ebony Smith, in solidarity with Black and Brown collective formations, was the online DJ for this event. For more information, see https://laestaciongallery.weebly.com/.

86 Hernandez, *Aesthetics of Excess*, 9.

87 Ibid.

88 Thinking with and across performance studies sound theories from "labor in listening" to "listening in detail" to "sonic relationalities" to "hungry listening" to "deep listening" and "against easy listening" to turn to only a few here, Smith's work demonstrates the capacity of active listening to include "spatial practice" across immaterial terrain and singular conceptualization. These various concepts of how to listen vary across scholars. For authors and concepts, see Brooks, *Liner Notes for the Revolution*; Vazquez, *Listening in Detail*; Steinmetz, "In Recognition of Their Desperation"; Robinson, *Hungry Listening*; Oliveros, *Deep Listening*; Kun, "Against Easy Listening," in *Audiotopia*, 29–47.

89 Kun, *Audiotopia*, 288.

90 Berlant, *Desire/Love*, 6.

91 Ibid.

92 Ibid, 7.

93 Smith in conversation with the author.

94 Ibid.

95 Please see *Race and Performance After Repetition*, edited by Soyica Diggs Colbert, Douglas A. Jones Jr., and Shane Vogel, to get a better sense of how to conceptualize beyond conventional ideas of repetition and ritual.

96 Smith in conversation with the author.

97 In an interview with the author, Smith shares that after having lost her father unexpectedly in 2004 and being unable to pause to mourn his death, she began to wonder about the singularity of death and the capacity to mourn individual loss.

In other words, how might one loss evolve into another? Smith goes on to add, "I never got to grieve my father's death because shortly after he was gone, we had to survive as a family and then my mother became ill."

98 ife, "Grief Aesthetics," 94.

99 I am thinking here about how Julietta Singh reimagines the role of any archive. How does collecting and then tracing meaning across objects produce both an archivist and archive that illustrates the interwoven political and aesthetic contours of archiving itself? If the archive is what remains, both residue and vestige, might it also be something that "keeps whispering," as Julietta Singh suggests, to the self, "insisting on its place in [one's] everyday life"? If the self is an entangled ancestral entity always unfolding, then perhaps the archive expands and evolves as the thing itself, as the thing itself as careful precision in listening. Let us recall that for Singh, the archive—disordered, desiring, externally interior—is "a thing made up of infinite, intractable traces" or perhaps the "archive is a stimulus between" the self and the self—the self may serve as the incongruent-congruency of embroilment across embodiment, energy, conscious and unconscious longing. See Singh, *No Archive Will Restore You*, 26.

100 Hartman, "Venus in Two Acts," 2.

101 Bennett, *The Birth of the Museum*.

102 Singh, *No Archive Will Restore You*, 32.

103 Ibid., 31.

104 Ibid.

105 Smith in conversation with the author.

106 Ibid.

107 Ibid.

108 Ted Taylor, "Be Ever Wonderful," *Ted Taylor—Topic*, November 8, 2014, video, 2:33, www.youtube.com/watch?v=kVzo3iQe-jQ.

109 Smith in conversation with the author.

110 Ibid.

111 A conversation conducted in my office with the artist on November 21, 2023, where I asked Smith about the legacies of Black life that are never recorded and if she could remember her mother's teachings that were about life, study, and aesthetic lessons as sessions for living and being together with others.

112 Conversation with Smith in the author's office, November 21, 2023.

AN AFTERWORD

1 Sharpe, *In the Wake*; Muñoz, *Disidentifications*; Muñoz, *The Sense of Brown*; Chambers-Letson, *After the Party*; Viego, *Dead Subjects*; Luciano, *Arranging Grief*; Cheng, *The Melancholy of Race*; Holland, *Raising the Dead*; Hartman, *Lose Your Mother*; Eng and David Kazanjian, *Loss*; McElya, *The Politics of Mourning*; Ricoeur, *Living Up to Death*; Barthes, *Mourning Diary*; Butler, *Precarious Life*; Derrida, *The Work of Mourning*; Sedgwick, *A Dialogue on Love*; Vuong, *Time Is a Mother*; Brinkema, *The Forms of the Affects*; Moten, *In the Break*; Tapia, *American Pietàs*.

BIBLIOGRAPHY

Ahmed, Sara. *What's the Use?: On the Uses of Use*. Durham, NC: Duke University Press, 2019.

Allwood, Emma Hope. "If You Like McQueen's Asylum, You'll Like Joel-Peter Witkin." *Dazed Digital*, August 24, 2015, www.dazeddigital.com.

Alvarado, Leticia. "Ghostly Givings: Nao Bustamante's Melancholic Conjuring of Brownness." *Women & Performance: a journal of feminist theory* 29, no. 3 (2019): 243–255.

Aparicio, Frances R., and Susana Chávez-Silverman. *Tropicalizations: Transcultural Representations of Latinidad*. Hanover, NH: Dartmouth College Press, 1997.

Atlas Obscura. "Vale of Cashmere." Atlas Obscura, October 23, 2019. www.atlasobscura.com.

Bachelard, Gaston. *The Psychoanalysis of Fire*. Translated by Alan C. M. Ross. Boston: Beacon Press, 1964.

Bailey, Moya. "The Ethics of Pace." *South Atlantic Quarterly* 120, no. 2 (2021): 285–299.

Baptist, Karen Wilson. "Diaspora: Death Without a Landscape." *Mortality* 15, no. 4 (2010): 294–307.

Barker, Joanne, Jodi A. Byrd, Alyosha Goldstein, Sandy Grande, Julia Bernal, Reyes DeVore, Jennifer Marley, and Justine Teba. "Catastrophe, Care, and All That Remains." *Social Text* 39, no. 4 (2021): 27–53.

Barthes, Roland. *Camera Lucida: Reflections on Photography*. Translated by Richard Howard. New York: Hill and Wang, 2010.

———. *Mourning Diary*. New York: Hill and Wang. 2009.

Bayatrizi, Zohreh, Hayatri Ghorbani, and Reza Taslimi Tehrani. "Risk, Mourning, Politics: Toward a Transnational Critical Conception of Grief for COVID-19 Deaths in Iran." *Current Sociology* 69, no. 4 (2021): 512–28.

Benjamin, Walter. "Theses on the Philosophy of History." In *Illuminations: Essays and Reflections*, edited by Hannah Arendt. Translated by Harry Zohn. New York: Schocken Books, 1968.

Berlant, Lauren Gail. "The Commons: Infrastructures for Troubling Times." *Environment and Planning: Society and Space* 34, no. 3 (2016): 393–419.

———. *Cruel Optimism*. Durham, NC: Duke University Press, 2011.

———. *Desire/Love*. San Francisco: Punctum Books, 2012.

Bennett, Tony. *The Birth of the Museum: History, Theory, Politics*. London: Routledge, 2013.

Bonilla, Yarimar, and Marisol LeBrón, eds. *Aftershocks of Disaster: Puerto Rico Before and After the Storm*. Chicago: Haymarket Books, 2019.

Bordere, Tashel C. "Social Justice Conceptualizations in Grief and Loss." In *Handbook of Social Justice in Loss and Grief: Exploring Diversity, Equity, and Inclusion*, edited by Darcy L. Harris and Tashel C. Bordere, 9–20. London: Routledge, 2016.

Bowles, Kathy Johnson. "Reinscribing the Spectacle of Death: The Aesthetics of Spontaneous Memorials." *Afterimage* 49, no. 2 (2022).

Breuer, Josef, and Sigmund Freud. *Studies on Hysteria,* edited and translated by James Strachey in collaboration with Anna Freud. New York: Basic Books, 1957.

Brinkema, Eugenie. *The Forms of the Affects*. Durham, NC: Duke University Press, 2014.

Brody, Jane E. "Biological Role of Emotional Tears Emerges Through Recent Studies." *New York Times*, August 31, 1982.

Brody, Jennifer DeVere. *Punctuation: Art, Politics, and Play*. Durham, NC: Duke University Press, 2008.

Brooks, Daphne A. *Liner Notes for the Revolution: The Intellectual Life of Black Feminist Sound*. Cambridge, MA: Harvard University Press, 2021.

Brown, Ruth Nicole. *Cherish: A Love Letter to Gwendolyn Brooks*. Film. Directed by Yvette Mayorga, with a score by lovenloops (Blair Ebony Smith). Chicago, Illinois, June–December 2019.

———. *Hear Our Truths: The Creative Potential of Black Girlhood*. Urbana: University of Illinois Press, 2013.

Bustamante, Nao. *Neapolitan*. 2013, video with text, 3:19. https://vimeo.com/user14069631.

Butler, Judith. *Precarious Life: The Powers of Mourning and Violence*. London: Verso, 2004.

———. *What World Is This? A Pandemic Phenomenology*. New York: Columbia University Press, 2022.

Butler, Judith, and George Yancy. "Interview: Mourning Is a Political Act amid the Pandemic and Its Disparities (Republication)." *Journal of Bioethical Inquiry* 17, no. 4 (2020): 483–87.

Cacho, Lisa Marie. *Social Death: Racialized Rightlessness and the Criminalization of the Unprotected*. New York: New York University Press, 2012.

Campt, Tina M. *Listening to Images*. Durham, NC: Duke University Press, 2017.

Canham, Hugo. "Black Death and Mourning as Pandemic." *Journal of Black Studies* 52, no. 3 (2021): 296–309.

Cepeda, María Elena. "Thrice Unseen, Forever on Borrowed Time: Latina Feminist Reflections on Mental Disability and the Neoliberal Academy." *South Atlantic Quarterly* 120, no. 2 (2021): 301–320.

Cervenak, Sarah Jane. *Black Gathering: Art, Ecology, Ungiven Life*. Durham, NC: Duke University Press, 2021.

Chambers-Letson, Joshua. *After the Party: A Manifesto for Queer of Color Life*. New York: New York University Press, 2018.

———. "Contracting Justice: The Viral Strategy of Felix Gonzalez-Torres." *Criticism* 51, no. 4 (2009): 559–87.

Cheng, Anne Anlin. *The Melancholy of Race: Psychoanalysis, Assimilation, and Hidden Grief*. New York: Oxford University Press, 2001.

Chiu, Allyson. "Trump Has No Qualms About Calling Coronavirus the 'Chinese Virus.' That's a Dangerous Attitude, Experts Say." *Washington Post*, March 20, 2020.

Coke, Van Deren. *Joel-Peter Witkin: Forty Photographs*. San Francisco: San Francisco Museum of Modern Art, 1985. Published in conjunction with an exhibition of the same title at the San Francisco Museum of Modern Art, December 6, 1985, to January 9, 1986.

Colbert, Soyica Diggs, Douglas A. Jones Jr., and Shane Vogel, eds. *Race and Performance After Repetition*. Durham, NC: Duke University Press, 2020.

Conklin, Beth A. *Consuming Grief: Compassionate Cannibalism in an Amazonian Society*. Austin: University of Texas Press, 2001.

Cools, Guy, and Lisa Marie Bowler. *Performing Mourning: Laments in Contemporary Art*. Amsterdam: Valiz, 2021.

Cooper, J. California. *Homemade Love*. New York: St. Martin's Publishing Group, 1986.

Cox, Aimee Meredith. *Shapeshifters: Black Girls and the Choreography of Citizenship*. Durham, NC: Duke University Press, 2015.

da Silva, Denise Ferreira. "On Difference Without Separability." In *Catalogue of the 32nd Bienal de São Paulo, "Incerteza Viva,"* edited by Jochen Volz and Júlia Rebouças, 57–65. São Paulo: Fundação Bienal de São Paulo, 2016.

Deggans, Eric. "'This Little Light of Mine' Shines On, a Timeless Tool of Resistance." *All Things Considered*, August 6, 2018. www.npr.org.

DeJesus, Nancy. "Fountains as a Synthesis of Sculpture, Water, and Land." *Sculpture Review* 56, no. 2 (2007): 16–23.

del Rosario, Inge V. "A Journey into Grief." *Journal of Religion and Health* 43, no. 1 (2004): 19–28.

Denis, Nelson A. *War Against All Puerto Ricans: Revolution and Terror in America's Colony*. New York: Nation Books, 2015.

Derrida, Jacques. "Archive Fever: A Freudian Impression." Translated by Eric Prenowitz. *Diacritics* 25, no. 2 (1995): 9–63.

———. *Specters of Marx: The State of the Debt, the Work of Mourning and the New International*. Translated by Peggy Kamuf. London: Routledge, 2011.

———. *The Work of Mourning*. Translated by Pascale-Anne Brault and Michael Naas. Chicago: University of Chicago Press, 2001.

Disser, Nicole. "Inside the Vale of Cashmere, a Bucolic Cruising Spot Threatened By 'Restoration.'" *Bedford + Bowery*, October 30, 2015. https://bedfordandbowery.com.

Duany, Jorge. *The Puerto Rican Nation on the Move: Identities on the Island and in the United States*. Chapel Hill, NC: University of North Carolina Press, 2003.

Doyle, Jennifer. *Hold It Against Me: Difficulty and Emotion in Contemporary Art*. Durham, NC: Duke University Press, 2013.

Eick, Gretchen. "Introduction." In *The Death Project: An Anthology for These Times*, edited by Gretchen Eick and Cora Poage, 6-8. Wichita, KS: Blue Cedar Press, 2020.

———. "Night Quarantine." In *The Death Project: An Anthology for These Times*, edited by Gretchen Eick and Cora Poage, 78–79. Wichita, KS: Blue Cedar Press, 2020.

Enari, Dion, and Byron William Rangiwai. "Digital Innovation and Funeral Practices: Māori and Samoan Perspectives During the COVID-19 Pandemic." *Alternative: An International Journal of Indigenous Peoples* 17, no. 2 (2021): 346–51.

Eng, David L., and David Kazanjian, eds. *Loss: The Politics of Mourning*. Berkeley: University of California Press, 2002.

Fakhruroji, Moch. "Texting Condolences on WhatsApp as a Mediatized Mourning Practice." *Human Behavior and Emerging Technologies* 3, no. 5 (2021): 677–86.

Ferré-Sadurní, Luis, and Anemona Hartocollis. "Maria Strikes, and Puerto Rico Goes Dark." *New York Times*, September 21, 2017.

Fisher, Rose-Lynn. *The Topography of Tears*. New York: Bellevue Literary Press, 2017.

Flores, Juan. *The Diaspora Strikes Back: Caribeño Tales of Learning and Turning*. New York: Routledge, 2009.

Fox, Karen. M., and Lisa McDermott. "Where Is Leisure When Death Is Present?" *Leisure Sciences* 43, no. 1–2 (2020): 267–72.

Freeman, Elizabeth. *Time Binds: Queer Temporalities, Queer Histories*. Durham, NC: Duke University Press, 2010.

Freud, Sigmund. "Mourning and Melancholia." In *The Standard Edition of the Complete Psychological Works of Sigmund Freud, Volume XIV (1914–1916): On the History of the Psycho-Analytic Movement, Papers of Metapsychology and Other Works*, translated by James Strachey in collaboration with Anna Freud, 243–58. London: Hogarth Press, 1957.

Frey, William H., and Muriel Langseth. *Crying: The Mystery of Tears*. Minneapolis: Winston, 1985.

García Lorca, Federico. "Play and Theory of Duende." In *In Search of Duende*, prose edited and translated by Christopher Maurer, 56–72. New York: New Directions, 1998.

Gem Library. "White Alabaster: Meanings, Properties, Facts and More!" *The Gem Library*. Accessed August 18, 2024. https://thegemlibrary.com.

Ghosh, Bishnupriya. "The Costs of Living: Reflections on Global Health Crises." In *AIDS and the Distribution of Crises*, edited by Jih-Fei Cheng, Alexandra Juhasz, and Nishant Shahani, 60–75. Durham, NC: Duke University Press, 2020.

———. "Virus: Tales of Object+." *O-Zone: A Journal of Object-Oriented Studies*, no. 1 (2014): 136–44.

Gibson, Margaret. "Melancholy Objects." *Mortality* 9, no. 4 (2004): 285–99.

Gillespie, Kathryn, and Patricia J. Lopez, eds. *Vulnerable Witness: The Politics of Grief in the Field*. Oakland: University of California Press, 2019.

Gordon, Avery. *Ghostly Matters: Haunting and the Sociological Imagination*. Minneapolis: University of Minnesota Press, 2008.

Gorton, TJ. 2019. "BeatCaffeine's 15 Most Essential Roy Ayers Records." *Beat Caffeine*, June 20, 2019. https://beatcaffeine.com.

Gough, Richard. "Burning Bodies: Transformation and Fire." *Performance Research* 18, no. 1 (2013): 9–23.

Gressman, Erica. *COVID-19 /What to Watch in 2020*. The Quarantine Concerts, Experimental Sound Studio, Chicago, April 1, 2020.

———. *Dissever. Oscillations Series*, Experimental Sound Studio, Chicago, February 7, 2020.

———. *Full Frontal Biopsy*. Live surgical sound performance. Rumble Arts Center, Chicago, April 12, 2011.

———. *Limbs*. Live performance art/experimental music composition. Krannert Art Museum, Champaign, IL, September 13, 2018.

———. *Monster Wedding*. Theatrical performance. Hyde Park Art Center, Chicago, October 30, 2010.

———. *Tropical Frankenstein*. Performance art collaboration with Mikey McParlane. Digital Arts Demo Space, Chicago, July 9, 2016.

———. *Wall of Skin*. Sound and light interactive performance. Channing-Murray Foundation, Urbana, IL, April 7, 2016.

Hammie, Patrick Earl, Stacey Robinson, Blair Ebony Smith, and Nekita Thomas, co-curators. *Black on Black on Black on Black*. Exhibition, Krannert Art Museum, Champaign, IL. September 24–December 10, 2022. https://kam.illinois.edu.

Harney, Steve, and Fred Moten. *The Undercommons: Fugitive Planning and Black Study*. New York: Minor Compositions, 2013.

Harris, Laura. "'What Happened to the Motley Crew?': James, Oiticica, and the Aesthetic Sociality of Blackness." In *Experiments in Exile: C. L. R. James, Hélio Oiticica, and the Aesthetic Sociality of Blackness*, 17–60. New York: Fordham University Press, 2018.

Hartman, Saidiya. *Lose Your Mother: A Journey Along the Atlantic Slave Route*. New York: Farrar, Straus and Giroux, 2008.

———. *Scenes of Subjection: Terror, Slavery, and Self-Making in Nineteenth-Century America*. New York: Oxford University Press, 1997.

———. "Venus in Two Acts." *Small Axe: A Caribbean Journal of Criticism* 12, no. 2 (2008): 1–14.

Hernandez, Jillian. *Aesthetics of Excess: The Art and Politics of Black and Latina Embodiment*. Durham, NC: Duke University Press, 2020.

Herrera, Patricia. "A Sonic Treatise of Futurity: Universes' *Party People*." In *Race and Performance After Repetition*, edited by Soyica Diggs Colbert, Douglas A. Jones Jr., and Shane Vogel, 71–100. Durham, NC: Duke University Press, 2020.

Higson, H., and K. Price. "The Application of the Whirlpool of Grief to Support Experiences of Loss in Light of the Covid-19 Pandemic." *Clinical Psychology Forum* no. 1 (2020): 19–23.

Holinger, Dorothy P. *The Anatomy of Grief*. New Haven, CT: Yale University Press, 2020.

Holland, Sharon Patricia. *Raising the Dead: Readings of Death and (Black) Subjectivity*. Durham, NC: Duke University Press, 2000.

Homer. *The Odyssey*. Translated by George E. Dimock. Cambridge, MA: Harvard University Press, 2008.

hooks, bell. "An Aesthetic of Blackness: Strange and Oppositional." *Lenox Avenue: A Journal of Interarts Inquiry*, no 1 (1995): 65.

ife, fahima. "Grief Aesthetics." *liquid blackness* 6, no. 1 (2022): 86–95.

———. *Maroon Choreography*. Durham, NC: Duke University Press, 2021.

Impert, Laura, and Margaret Rubin. "The Mother at the Glen: The Relationship Between Mourning and Nostalgia." *Psychoanalytic Dialogues* 21, no. 6 (2011): 691–706.

Kafer, Alison. *Feminist, Queer, Crip*. Bloomington: University of Indiana Press, 2013.

Kendrick, Monica. "Chicago Punk Outfit Fetishist Reinvent Themselves on *Austerity Messiah*." *Chicago Reader*, January 9, 2024. https://chicagoreader.com.

Kim, Jina B., and Sami Schalk. "Reclaiming the Radical Politics of Self-Care: A Crip-of-Color Critique." *South Atlantic Quarterly* 120, no. 2 (2021): 325–42.

Koshy, Susan, Lisa Marie Cacho, Jodi A. Byrd, and Brian Jordan Jefferson, eds. *Colonial Racial Capitalism*. Durham, NC: Duke University Press, 2022.

Kun, Josh. *Audiotopia: Music, Race, and America*. Berkeley: University of California Press, 2005.

La Fountain-Stokes, Lawrence. "Queer Puerto Ricans and the Burden of Violence." *QED: A Journal in GLBTQ Worldmaking* 3, no. 3 (2016): 99–102.

Lauterbach, Ann. "On Tears." In *The Topography of Tears*, by Rose-Lynn Fisher, 11–12. New York: Bellevue Literary Press, 2017.

LeBrón, Marisol. *Against Muerto Rico: Lessons from Verano Boricua / Contra Muerto Rico: Lecciones del Verano Boricua*. Translated by Beatriz Llenín-Figueroa. Cabo Rojo, PR: Editora Educación Emergente, 2021.

———. *Policing Life and Death: Race, Violence, and Resistance in Puerto Rico*. Berkeley: University of California Press, 2019.

Lefebvre, Henri. *The Production of Space*. Translated by Donald Nicholson-Smith. Malden, MA: Blackwell Publishing, 2013.

Leight, Elias. "Mary J. Blige's 'My Life' Documentary: 8 Things We Learned." *Rolling Stone*, June 25, 2021. www.rollingstone.com.

León, Christina A. "Trace Alignment: Object Relations after Ana Mendieta." *Post45*, December 9, 2019. https://post45.org.

Lepecki, André. *Exhausting Dance: Performance and the Politics of Movement*. New York: Routledge, 2006.

Lewis, Sophie. "Grief Circling." In *The Long Year: A 2020 Reader*, edited by Thomas J. Sugrue and Caitlin Zaloom, 305–8. New York: Columbia University Press, 2022.

Locke, Ralph P. "The Exotic in Nineteenth-Century French Opera, Part 1: Locales and Peoples." *19th-Century Music* 45, no. 2 (2021): 93–118.

Lopez, Pedro. *Hair Piece*. Photographs. 2012. www.pedrodaniellopez.com/new-gallery.

———. *My Gay Agenda*. Photographs. 2015. www.pedrodaniellopez.com/objectification-1.

———. "Tear Basins." *Columbia: A Journal of Literature and Art*, no. 57 (2019): 199–201.

———. *Tear Basin (Vale of Cashmere)*. Sculpture, Prospect Park, Brooklyn, NY, July 9, 2022.

———. *Tear Basin (Vale of Cashmere)*. Pamphlet, Prospect Park, Brooklyn, NY, July 9, 2022.

Luciano, Dana. *Arranging Grief: Sacred Time and the Body in Nineteenth-Century America*. New York: New York University Press, 2007.

Maldonado-Torres, Nelson. *Against War: Views from the Underside of Modernity*. Durham, NC: Duke University Press, 2008.

Manning, Erin. *For a Pragmatics of the Useless.* Durham, DC: Duke University Press, 2020.

Margarita, Eva. *Conjuring Stains: (Re)activating an Archive of Blackness in Everyday Life.* Performance. NYU Performance Studies: Graduate Thesis Symposium, New York, June 6, 2020.

———. *Entierro.* Performance. The Vortex Repertory, Austin, TX, November 4–5, 2022, and September 16, 2023.

———. *Light of Ours.* Performance. Private residence, Los Angeles, December 31, 2020–January 1, 2021.

———. *Obituary.* Performance. The Vortex Repertory, Austin, TX, November 13, 2021.

———. *Salt, Fat, Ashes, Heat.* Performance. The Tank, New York, September 23, 2020.

Margolles, Teresa. *What Else Could We Talk About?* Installation, Venice Biennale, Venice, Italy, 2009.

Martorell Linares, Miguel. "'The Cruellest of All Forms of Coercion': The Catholic Church and Conflicts around Death and Burial in Spain during the Restoration (1874–1923)." *European History Quarterly* 47, no. 4 (September 2017): 657–78.

Masur, Kate. "Race, Policing, and Reform." *Washington History* 32, no. 1/2 (2020): 62–64.

Marquis, Christopher, and Jon Nordheimer. "U.S. Ready to Remove Vieques Protesters." *New York Times*, May 4, 2000.

Matthews, Robert. "Is Anything Ever Absolutely Still?" *BBC Science Focus.* Accessed August 19, 2024. www.sciencefocus.com.

McElya, Micki. *The Politics of Mourning: Death and Honor in Arlington National Cemetery.* Cambridge, MA: Harvard University Press, 2019.

McMillan, Uri. *Embodied Avatars: Genealogies of Black Feminist Art and Performance.* New York: New York University Press, 2015.

McQueen, Alexander. "Alexander McQueen | Women's Spring/Summer 2001 | Runway Show." March 21, 2012. Video, 11:12. www.youtube.com/watch?v=qynzgm9i4LI.

Mendieta, Ana. *Untitled (Blood Sign #2/Body Tracks).* 8 mm film transferred to video (Digital Betacam and DVD). Museo Nacional Centro de Arte Reina Sofia, Madrid, Spain, 1974. www.museoreinasofia.es.

Milstein, Cindy. "Prologue: Cracks in the Wall." In *Rebellious Mourning: The Collective Work of Grief,* edited by Cindy Milstein, 1–12. Chico, CA: AK Press, 2017.

Moore, Sharon E., Sharon D. Jones-Eversley, Willie F. Tolliver, Betty L. Wilson, and Christopher A. Jones. "Six Feet Apart or Six Feet Under: The Impact of COVID-19 on the Black Community." *Death Studies* 46, no. 4 (2022): 891–901.

Moore, Thomas. *Lalla Rookh: An Oriental Romance.* New York: Oakley, Mason and Co., 1871.

Moten, Fred. "Black Mo'nin.'" In *Loss: The Politics of Mourning,* edited by David L. Eng and David Kazanjian, 69–76. Berkeley: University of California Press, 2002.

———. *In the Break: The Aesthetics of the Black Radical Tradition.* Minneapolis: University of Minnesota Press, 2003.

Muñoz, José Esteban. *Cruising Utopia: The Then and There of Queer Futurity*. New York: New York University Press, 2009.

———. *Disidentifications: Queers of Color and the Performance of Politics*. Minneapolis: University of Minnesota Press, 1999.

———. "Ephemera as Evidence: Introductory Notes to Queer Acts." *Women & Performance: a journal of feminist theory* 8, no. 2 (1996): 5–16.

———. "Feeling Brown: Ethnicity and Affect in Ricardo Bracho's *The Sweetest Hangover (and Other STDs)*." *Theatre Journal* 52, no. 1 (2000): 67–79.

———. "Feeling Brown, Feeling Down: Latina Affect, the Performativity of Race, and the Depressive Position." *Signs: Journal of Women in Culture and Society* 31, no. 3 (2006): 675–88.

———. *The Sense of Brown: Ethnicity, Affect and Performance*. Edited by Joshua Chambers-Letson and Tavia Nyong'o. Durham, NC: Duke University Press, 2020.

Murphy, Ronan. "VOSS—Remembering Alexander McQueen's S/S 2001 Show." *GATA*, 2021. https://gatamagazine.com.

Musser, Amber Jamilla. *Sensational Flesh: Race, Power, and Masochism*. New York: New York University Press, 2014.

Nancy, Jean-Luc. *The Truth of Democracy*. Translated by Pascale-Anne Brault and Michael Naas. New York: Fordham University Press, 2010.

Nash, Jennifer C. "Slow Loss: Black Feminism and Endurance." *Social Text* 40, no. 2 (2022): 1–20.

Negrón-Muntaner, Frances. *Boricua Pop: Puerto Ricans and the Latinization of American Culture*. New York: New York University Press, 2004.

———. "Our Fellow Americans: Why Calling Puerto Ricans 'Americans' Will Not Save Them." In *Aftershocks of Disaster: Puerto Rico Before and After the Storm*, edited by Yarimar Bonilla and Marisol LeBrón, 113–23. Chicago: Haymarket Books, 2019.

Office of Public Affairs, U.S. Department of Justice. "Former Governor of Puerto Rico Arrested in Bribery Scheme." U.S. Department of Justice, August 4, 2022. www.justice.gov.

Oliveros, Pauline. *Deep Listening: A Composer's Sound Practice*. New York: iUniverse, 2005.

———. *Quantum Listening*. Introduction by IONE. Foreword by Laurie Anderson. London: Silver Press, 2022.

Olley, Michelle. "Diary Entries by Michelle Olley on Appearing in VOSS, Spring/Summer 2001." *The Met*, 2011. https://blog.metmuseum.org.

Pollock, Della, ed. *Exceptional Spaces: Essays in Performance and History*. Chapel Hill: University of North Carolina Press, 1998.

Prospect Park Alliance. "From the Archives: The Vale of Cashmere." Prospect Park Alliance, June 2, 2014. www.prospectpark.org/archives-vale-cashmere/.

Ramos, Iván A. "The Viscosity of Grief: Teresa Margolles at the Scene of the Crime." *Women & Performance: a journal of feminist theory* 25, no. 3 (2015): 298–314.

Ricoeur, Paul. *Living Up to Death*. Translated by David Pellauer. Chicago: University of Chicago Press, 2009.

Rivera-Servera, Ramón H. *Performing Queer Latinidad: Dance, Sexuality, Politics*. Ann Arbor: University of Michigan Press, 2012.

Robinson, Dylan. *Hungry Listening: Resonant Theory for Indigenous Sound Studies*. Minneapolis: University of Minnesota Press, 2020.

Robles, Frances, Kirk Semple, and Richard Pérez-Peña. "Hurricane Irma, One of the Most Powerful in History, Roars Across Caribbean." *New York Times*, September 7, 2017.

Rodríguez, Juana María. *Sexual Futures, Queer Gestures, and Other Latina Longings*. New York: New York University Press, 2014.

Romero, Simon, Frances Robles, Patricia Mazzei, and Jose A. Del Real. "15 Days of Fury: How Puerto Rico's Government Collapsed." *New York Times*, July 27, 2019.

Ruiz, Sandra. "Creating La Estación Gallery." In *Building Sustainable Worlds: Latinx Placemaking in the Midwest*, edited by Theresa Delgadillo, Ramón H. Rivera-Servera, Gerardo L. Caldava, and Claire F. Fox, 135–47. Urbana: University of Illinois Press, 2022.

———. *Left Turns in Brown Study*. Durham, NC: Duke University Press, 2024.

———. "A Light for a Light: Minoritarian Aesthetics and the Politics of Grief-Work," *Meridians: Feminism, Race, Transnationalism* 21, no. 2 (2022): 455–79.

———. *Ricanness: Enduring Time in Anticolonial Performance*. New York: New York University Press, 2019.

Ruiz, Sandra, and Hypatia Vourloumis. *Formless Formation: Vignettes for the End of this World*. New York: Autonomedia Press, 2021.

Sabatella, Matthew. "This Little Light of Mine: About the Song." *Ballad of America*. Accessed August 19, 2024. https://balladofamerica.org.

Samuels, Ellen, and Elizabeth Freeman. "Introduction: Crip Temporalities." *South Atlantic Quarterly* 120, no. 2 (2021): 245–54.

Santiago, Roberto. "Introduction." In *Boricuas: Influential Puerto Rican Writings—an Anthology*, edited by Roberto Santiago, xiii–xxxiii. New York: One World, 1995.

Schechner, Richard. "Restoration of Behavior." *Studies in Visual Communication* 7, no. 3 (1981): 2–45.

Sedgwick, Eve Kosofsky. *A Dialogue on Love*. Boston: Beacon Press, 2000.

———. *Epistemology of the Closet*. Berkeley: University of California Press, 2008.

———. *Touching Feeling: Affect, Pedagogy, Performativity*. Durham, NC: Duke University Press, 2003.

Sharpe, Christina Elizabeth. *In the Wake: On Blackness and Being*. Durham, NC: Duke University Press, 2016.

Singh, Julietta. *No Archive Will Restore You*. Santa Barbara, CA: Punctum Books, 2018.

———. *Unthinking Mastery: Dehumanism and Decolonial Entanglements*. Durham, NC: Duke University Press, 2018.

Smil, Vaclav, and Rodney Brooks. "COVID: Excess Mortalities Two Years Later: The Death Toll Is Increasingly Comparable to That of the 1918–1920 Flu." *IEEE Spectrum* 59, no. 5 (2022): 20–22.

Smith, Blair Ebony. "Doing SOLHOT as a Reliable Way of Life." *The Public i*, January 19, 2017. https://publici.ucimc.org.

———. *Don't Ever Forget It*. Lovenloops, Failed Poem Records, April 2, 2021. https://failedpoemrecords.bandcamp.com/album/dont-ever-forget-it-reissue.

———. *Homemade, with Love: More Living Room*. Exhibition, Krannert Art Museum, Champaign, IL, August 27, 2020–July 3, 2021.

———. *Lovenloops*. Artist website. Accessed October 10, 2024. https://blairebony-smith6.wixsite.com/lovenloops.

———. *(Refrain) Turn Me On—Would You Come On Home?* Exhibition, Krannert Art Museum, Champaign, IL, September 24–December 10, 2022.

Smith, Shawn Michelle. *Photographic Returns: Racial Justice and the Time of Photography*. Durham, NC: Duke University Press, 2020.

SOLHOT We Levitate. *How I Feel EP*. Bandcamp, February 29, 2016. https://welevitate.bandcamp.com/album/how-i-feel-ep.

———. *We Levitate Presents: Black Girl Genius Week 2016*. Soundcloud, 2016. https://soundcloud.com/solhot-next-level/sets/we-levitate-presents-black.

Sørensen, Tim Flohr, and Mikkel Bille. "Flames of Transformation: The Role of Fire in Cremation Practices." *World Archaeology* 40, no. 2 (June 1, 2008): 253–67.

Spillers, Hortense J. "Mama's Baby, Papa's Maybe: An American Grammar Book." *Diacritics* 17, no. 2 (1987): 64–81.

Steinmetz, Julia. "*In Recognition of Their Desperation*: Sonic Relationality and the Work of Deep Listening." *Studies in Gender and Sexuality* 20, no. 2 (2019): 119–32.

Swaminathan, Nikhil. "Viruses: They're Alive, and They Can Infect Each Other." *Scientific American*, August 8, 2008. https://blogs.scientificamerican.com.

Swift, Michael. "Gay Revolutionary." *Gay Community News*, February 15, 1987. Reprinted in *People with a History: Lesbian, Gay, Bisexual, and Trans* History Sourcebook*, Internet History Sourcebooks Project. https://sourcebooks.fordham.edu.

Tapia, Ruby C. *American Pietàs: Visions of Race, Death, and the Maternal*. Minneapolis: University of Minnesota Press, 2011.

Taussig, Michael. "Culture of Terror—Space of Death. Roger Casement's Putumayo Report and the Explanation of Torture." *Comparative Studies in Society and History* 26, no. 3 (1984): 467–97.

Taylor-Garcia, Daphne V. *The Existence of the Mixed Race Damnés: Decolonialism, Class, Gender, Race*. London: Rowman & Littlefield, 2018.

Theidon, Kimberly. "A Forecasted Failure: Intersectionality, COVID-19, and the Perfect Storm." *Journal of Human Rights* 19, no. 5 (2020): 528–36.

Vargas, Deborah R. "Ruminations on *Lo Sucio* as a Latino Queer Analytic." *American Quarterly* 66, no. 3 (2014): 715–26.

Varshney, Prateek, Guru Prasad, Prabha S. Chandra, and Geetha Desai. "Grief in the COVID-19 Times: Are We Looking at Complicated Grief in the Future?" *Indian Journal of Psychological Medicine* 43, no. 1 (2021): 70–73.

Vazquez, Alexandra T. *The Florida Room*. Durham, NC: Duke University Press, 2022.

———. *Listening in Detail: Performances of Cuban Music*. Durham, NC: Duke University Press, 2013.

———. "Salon Philosophers: Ivy Queen and Surprise Guests Take Reggaetón Aside." In *Reggaeton*, edited by Raquel Z. Rivera, Wayne Marshall, and Deborah Pacini Hernandez, 300–311. Durham, NC: Duke University Press, 2009.

Velez Gonzalez, William-Jose. "Clinton, Rosselló, González and Ferrer Win in Puerto Rico Primaries." *Pasquines*, June 6, 2016. https://pasquines.us.

Viego, Antonio. *Dead Subjects: Toward a Politics of Loss in Latino Studies*. Durham, NC: Duke University Press, 2007.

Vogel, Shane. *Stolen Time: Black Fad Performance and the Calypso Craze*. Chicago: University of Chicago Press, 2019.

Vourloumis, Hypatia. "Ten Theses on Touch, or, Writing Touch." *Women & Performance: a journal of feminist theory* 24, no. 2–3 (2014): 232–38.

Vuong, Ocean. *Time Is a Mother*. New York: Penguin, 2022.

Walsh, Mary Williams. "How Puerto Rico Is Grappling with a Debt Crisis." *New York Times*, May 16, 2017.

Webster, Crystal Lynn. "The History of Black Girls and the Field of Black Girlhood Studies: At the Forefront of Academic Scholarship." *Organization of American Historians*. Accessed August 19, 2024. www.oah.org.

Williams, Raymond. *Marxism and Literature*. New York: Oxford University Press, 1978.

Woods, Scott. "Don't Talk to Me About Racism if You Don't Know Earth, Wind & Fire's Catalog." *Level*, April 7, 2021. www.levelman.com.

Wright, Will. "Why Do Catholics Light Candles?" *Catholic Link*. Accessed August 20, 2024. https://catholic-link.org.

Zambrana, Rocío. *Colonial Debts: The Case of Puerto Rico*. Durham, NC: Duke University Press, 2021.

INDEX

Page numbers in *italics* indicate Figures.

Sandra Ruiz is the Sue Divan Associate Professor of Performance Studies in the Department of Theatre at the University of Illinois Urbana-Champaign. Ruiz is the author of *Ricanness: Enduring Time in Anticolonial Performance* and *Left Turns in Brown Study* and creator and producer of the Minor Aesthetics Lab.